Hizmet Means Service

Hizmet Means Service

PERSPECTIVES ON AN ALTERNATIVE
PATH WITHIN ISLAM

Edited by Martin E. Marty

UNIVERSITY OF CALIFORNIA PRESS

University of California Press, one of the most distinguished university presses in the United States, enriches lives around the world by advancing scholarship in the humanities, social sciences, and natural sciences. Its activities are supported by the UC Press Foundation and by philanthropic contributions from individuals and institutions. For more information, visit www.ucpress.edu.

University of California Press
Oakland, California

Library of Congress Cataloging-in-Publication Data
Hizmet means service : perspectives on an alternative path within
Islam / edited by Martin E. Marty.
    p.   cm.
  Includes bibliographical references.
  ISBN 978-0-520-28517-0 (cloth, alk. paper) — ISBN 978-0-520-28518-7
(pbk., alk. paper) — ISBN 978-0-520-96074-9 (electronic)
  1. Gülen Hizmet Movement.   2. Islamic sects—Turkey.
3. Gülen, Fethullah.   I. Marty, Martin E.
BP63.T8H59 2015
297.6'5—dc23   2015010202

Manufactured in the United States of America

24   23   22   21   20   19   18   17   16   15
10   9   8   7   6   5   4   3   2   1

In keeping with a commitment to support environmentally responsible and sustainable printing practices, UC Press has printed this book on Natures Natural, a fiber that contains 30% post-consumer waste and meets the minimum requirements of ANSI/NISO Z39.48-1992 (R 1997) (*Permanence of Paper*).

CONTENTS

ACKNOWLEDGMENTS

As co-director of the Fundamentalism Project sponsored by the American Academy of Arts and Sciences, I and my colleagues grew increasingly interested in individuals and movements that were poised between hard-line religious elements, on the one hand, and militant secularist forces, on the other. We located the work of Fethullah Gülen and the movement that gives its name to this book: *Hizmet Means Service*.

When the Niagara Foundation, with headquarters a mile from where I live, began to make its mark on the Chicago and national scene, I found an advantageous instrument for beginning to satisfy my curiosity, providing information and the company of representatives of the *Hizmet*. The foundation's work also attracted me for its interfaith enterprises. Through several years of interaction, its leadership and I developed confidence in each other, and Niagara asked me to edit this collection of essays, which I was happy to do. First, I thank Hilmi Cinar, who was a virtual co-editor, and his colleagues Yasir Bilgin, Sherif Soydan, Hakan Berberoglu, and Ayse Cinar for their part in helping select scholars and see the project through.

Along the way, the development of this book was greatly enhanced by the addition of Eleanor Peck to the editorial staff. Fortuitously, she was working as an editorial intern in Chicago during the year when Niagara and I needed her kind of expertise, which she willingly and more than capably brought to our efforts. I also thank R. Scott Appleby of the University of Notre Dame at the Kroc Institute for International Peace Studies, my partner in the Fundamentalism Project. His concluding chapter in this book illustrates how fair-minded he is in his appraisals. He and I (and Niagara leaders) alike took pains to ensure that this is a scholarly contribution, not a self-congratulatory promotion by the foundation.

It has also been a pleasure working with the University of California Press, through its editor Eric Schmidt and his colleague Maeve Cornell-Taylor, as well as the fearless copyeditor, Julia Zafferano, all of whom bridged the Berkeley and Chicago bases of operation. I hope that this volume will find a ready readership among people who share concern over religious faiths and who seek the common good in a world where religion is often an agent of conflict, not of education and healing.

Martin E. Marty
Emeritus, The University of Chicago

Introduction

Martin E. Marty

IN 1988, THE AMERICAN ACADEMY of Arts and Sciences chartered a study of religious fundamentalisms around the world and asked me to direct it, with R. Scott Appleby as a full-time associate and eventual co-director. Scholars from numerous nations took part in what became a five-volume work, *The Fundamentalism Project* (University of Chicago Press, 1994– 2004). The authors and editors took pains to define "fundamentalism" and its cognates in an effort to deal fairly with participants in the various movements. Those who inspired the project at the academy were motivated chiefly by their desire to understand phenomena such as the Iranian revolution after 1988 and American Protestant fundamentalism, which was being much noticed in American politics and culture in the 1980s.

Over the next few years, our company of scholars dealt with several dozen movements, but there was no question that Islamic-based expressions attracted the most attention and motivated much of the scholarly inquiry. In time, after the project had been completed, I returned to my career-long focus chiefly on religion in America; Appleby became director of the Kroc Institute for International Peace Studies at the University of Notre Dame, where he formed and led a new school of global studies. Nevertheless, we and the dozens of scholars with whom we had worked could not help but notice that Islamic movements continued to occupy a great deal of attention on the world stage. It also became clear that, in American culture in general and in the media and politics in particular, ideologically motivated public figures often treated Islam as a monolith, whose participants were given to extremism and religious fanaticism. That there were other forms of Islam across the globe was a reality often obscured. When, on occasion, we and our colleagues were challenged to point to forms of Islam that could be called "moderate," "open," or "dialogical," we explored a Turkish-based but international movement often called Hizmet. It is named for its focus on "service" but is also often called a Gülen expression, after the Sufi mystic preacher Fethullah Gülen, known for his interest in interfaith relations. This same interest had drawn me to study Hizmet as a model or exemplar of a promising way of being religious in Islamic contexts.

The present volume collects essays on discrete but sometimes overlapping studies of the main features of what we will here call Hizmet. Some contributors are Muslim, friendly with but also critical of the movement, and others are academics of other or of no particular religious community or commitments. They do not presume that all their readers have been long familiar with these topics, but they move beyond mere introductions into scholarly analysis of Gülen and the manifestations of his movement.

A particular polarity in this volume addresses the terms "secularity" and "religion," both of which are code names for very complex realities. Most of the topics of the following chapters—such as education, politics, and business—are normally treated "secularly" in the world we call "free," which means in this case in cultures or societies where specific religions or religion as such are not established or legally privileged. Yet within that secular order, broadly defined, hundreds of millions of people practice religions and do not want the state to dictate which religion or whether religion shall be legally favored. Millions of people have died, and many still die, when religious forces legitimate or exploit political or military power to serve their ends.

Facing "the secular" in many nations and regions are the voices and forces of religions or religious cultures. Some observers and analysts might cheer or champion the Hizmet movement as an ally on the religious front. Yet they tend to be cautious in their appraisal, because many have seen how the assertive and aggressive religions have often become militant and sometimes even terroristic. In the face of the theory, rhetoric, and practice of such religions, many would simply champion "the secular." Being suspicious, they would therefore withstand the appeal or actions of almost any "open" kind of religious movement, regarding them as irrelevant at best and dangerous at worst. In a world of nuclear arms, terrorist activities, and rivalries ancient and novel, assertive religion, when presented, needs to be justified.

The leaders of the Hizmet movement, aware of the dangers in what we might call "public religion" in Turkey and elsewhere, still see a need to advocate some kinds of religious emphases. They have observed that, in many dimensions of culture, religion does not remain sequestered in private forms, however much some reverent people who practice a religion may wish it to do so.

When we began the Fundamentalism Project as an international, inter-disciplinary, and inter-religious inquiry, we found some academics and other informed citizens who questioned the investment of so much energy, or even any energy at all, in themes that manifest religious phases and faces. The doubts arose because, as some said, "everyone knows that religion has no power in the modern world." Today it would be foolish for anyone to make such an observation. Daily newspapers and hourly reporting in other media focus on and diagnose the place of religion in wars, terrorism, political con-flict, and—it is important to note—in positives like health care, volunteer activities, welfare agencies, peacemaking efforts, and the day-to-day lives of millions.

Gülen and those involved with Hizmet are themselves very much aware of the potential and power of religion(s) for evil and good, but their move-ment has helped provide a fresh and needed perspective and a means for developing positive relations among the religions and for some benign uses of religion as such. It is natural to focus on their understandings of the "sec-ular" and the "religious," as we have coded the central polarity, in the special case of Turkey. Admittedly, those who look on or inquire from a distance (for example, from North America or Western Europe) may find the model of Hizmet exotic, remote, or overheated, but every chapter in this book points to emphases and instances that are analogous to places far from Turkey. As a citizen of such a place, I have participated for decades in inter-faith activities and welcomed the Hizmet movement from the time I began to have occasion to observe and study it. This has been the case with many scholars in many nations. They find Hizmet to be a worthy case study—forbidding or obscure though it may at first glance appear to be—as they become familiar with its ethos, program, and achievements.

Readers might find the organization of the movement puzzling at first. It lacks a central authority, a clear set of "rules of order," or a hierarchy that can enforce policies and standards. So unfamiliar is the set of ideas and practices in the movement that it can arouse suspicion in a time when suspicions about religions abound, or it can produce shrugs among busy and preoccu-pied persons who have other issues on their minds. However, having studied the Gülen movement as a scholar, and as a reporter having observed it in action, I have my confidence in it confirmed. This trust depended on some years of my reading of Gülen movement resources, enjoying Hizmet-hosted events, and—without abandoning scholarly detachment—coming to admire many of its scholars, devotees, and critics. We trust, and here present, twelve informed authors who anticipate the questions readers might have, and who serve as critical guides among phenomena that might at first appear forbidding, confusing, or promising—or, more likely, all three at once. Such readers will find themselves in the orbits of respectful people schooled in and devoted to scholarly hospitality.

I will provide a brief introduction at the beginning of each chapter and then step back, leaving colleague Appleby to write the final chapter in which he provocatively assesses the chapters, full of variety and sometimes in contradiction with each other as they may be. Forcing ideology or uniformity on the scholars who write about this movement could obstruct the efforts of scholars and citizens in general who would move on from here, capable of making their own judgments and acting on them.

ONE

Hizmet among the Most Influential Religious Renewals of Late Ottoman and Modern Turkish History

Carter Vaughn Findley

IN A LANDSCAPE WHERE MANY religious and cultural movements were active, three religious movements emerged to transform late Ottoman and modern Turkish society. The movements emerged in a clear chronological sequence. Each created disruptive changes in Turkish religious culture within the relatively short time span of a few decades. Each of them also has an ongoing history. It is important not to overlook that point: the recent history of the oldest of the three movements includes many forms of activity—such as expansion into electronic media or business ventures—for which the newest of the three is better known. Singly and collectively, these movements tell us a great deal about how Islamic religious movements have changed in their forms of self-expression and organization during the past two centuries. This is probably the most important lesson to learn from comparing the three of them. Historians with a comparative awareness of early U.S. history will be tempted to liken these movements to the Great Awakenings of that period. The comparison is not misleading, yet it is also not very helpful to those who have not studied early U.S. religious history.

Full appreciation of Fethullah Gülen requires contemplating the Hizmet movement in the historical perspective from which it emerged and in a global frame of comparison. Carter Vaughn Findley, professor of History at Ohio State University, first examines Hizmet as the latest of the three most influential Ottoman and Turkish religious renewals since 1800. Over two centuries, the evolution from the movements of Mevlana Halid and Said Nursi to that of Fethullah Gülen vastly expanded the repertory of options for organization and action. In the past few decades, the expansion of horizons from local to national to global created the added potential for teachings of Gülen to inspire the world of the twenty-first century as profoundly as the world of the twentieth century was inspired by those of Gandhi.

In Islamic terms, the movements respond to the pious expectation that every age will have its *mujaddid*, or "renewer." In an environment where many religious movements coexisted, it is not hard to see that these three movements were the "renewals" of their respective times. It may be harder to understand how they achieved the impact that they did. For a historian, this is an interesting question to contemplate.

The three movements are those launched by Mevlana Halid, Said Nursi, and Fethullah Gülen. Together, they carry Islamic religious culture of the late Ottoman and Turkish lands from the last great movement launched within the historical forms of the mystical orders into a new age that left the old forms behind to seek new modes of organization and action. Ultimately, this search produced results of significance not only for Muslims but for people of all the religions and all the world.

MEVLANA HALID AND THE HALIDIYE MOVEMENT

Mevlana Halid, known in Arabic as Shaykh Khalid, lived from 1776 to 1827, but the critical years for launching his movement were from 1811 to 1827, a period of less than two decades. Born a Kurd near Shahrazur in Ottoman Iraq, he studied there and in Sulaymaniyya. Among Kurds, the Islamic mystical brotherhoods (*tarikat*), whose followers are referred to synonymously by the terms *sufi* and *dervish*, were the only institutions that bridged tribal divisions. Early on, Halid was initiated into the Kadiri order, then the dominant order in Kurdistan, and perhaps other orders. But then he did something exceptional: he went to study in India, where he was also initiated into the Naqshbandi (in Turkish, Nakşibendi) order in its reformist, *mujaddidi* form, founded by the Imam Rabbani, Ahmad Sirhindi (d. 1624), a religious reformer recognized as the *mujaddid* of the second Islamic millennium. Halid's Indian teacher not only trained him to teach religious sciences such as Qur'an commentary (*tafsir*) and prophetic traditions (*hadith*) but also appointed him as his deputy (*khalifa*) to spread the *mujaddidi* form of the Naqshbandi Sufi movement in Kurdistan. Halid's experiences in India thus prepared him to reinvigorate the religious brotherhoods of the late Ottoman Empire and to do so in a way that emphasized strict Shariʿa observance, a requirement that some other orders neglected but that Sirhindi demanded.

Only sixteen years passed between Halid's return to Iraq (1811) and his death (1827), but this relatively brief span of time sufficed for him to produce the greatest Islamic renewal of the last Ottoman century. The appeal of his new religious message attracted many followers but disrupted the status quo for the local amirs and Kadiri shaykhs. Their opposition forced Halid to relocate to Baghdad and later to Damascus. However, his expertise in the religious sciences also impressed the strict religious scholars, who disapproved of mystics neglectful of the Shari'a. Halid's impact as both scholar and mystic won him acclaim, even from people who were not his followers, as the *mujaddid* of his century. For Halid, not only the organizational form of the Sufi brotherhood but also traditional techniques of oral teaching and manuscript production still proved effective in propagating his movement; the fact that he expressed himself in Arabic also facilitated the spread of his message among learned Muslims far and wide. He used these traditional techniques innovatively, reportedly sending out seventy *khalifas* who spread his teachings to Istanbul, where earlier waves of *mujaddidi* influence had prepared a receptive audience, and as far beyond as Chechnya and Java. He found many followers among merchants and landowners. Many of his followers were Kurds, and the patterns of Kurdish labor migration to Istanbul helped to broaden the base of his following there.

The Halidiye movement owed its success to many factors. Its founder was both a charismatic ascetic and a man of learning. Strict Shari'a observance helped win support from the ulema. At a time when Christian missionaries were already upsetting intercommunal relations, even in Kurdistan, and nationalism threatened the empire in Greece and Serbia, demands for strict Shari'a observance encouraged Muslims and positioned the movement as a force for Ottoman reintegration. The Naqshbandi principle of "solitude within society" (*halvet der encümen*) enjoined social and political engagement. In the late Ottoman Empire and modern Turkey, no religious movement has gained great influence without running into trouble with the authorities, and that was already true for Mevlana Halid. However, he overcame the suspicions of the Ottoman sultan of his time, Mahmud II (1808–39), by ordering his followers to pray for the state. Neither otherworldly like some other Sufi movements nor anti-Ottoman like the Wahhabis of Arabia, the Halidiye thus became a force for Ottoman revitalization and reintegration. The two later movements discussed below are not direct outgrowths of the Halidiye movement, but they emerged out of zones where it was the most dynamic, recent renewal movement. In that sense, both the Nur and the Gülen movements are at least indirectly indebted to the religious reinvigoration that Halid inspired.

A central element of the Halidiye movement's appeal was its spiritual discipline. Like other Naqshbandis, Mevlana Halid's followers performed their distinctive religious rites (*dhikr* in Arabic, *zikir* in Turkish) silently. To this, Halid added the practice of *rabıta,* the disciple's meditative concentration on the mental image of his shaykh. Halid insisted that his followers concentrate on his image alone. This maintained the centralization of the order, at least until some later *khalifas* permitted their disciples to concentrate on their image, instead. Performing their *dhikr* not only silently but often alone or in small groups meant that the Halidis did not actually need dervish lodges (*tekkes*), although they might use them as meeting places. Eventually, the Halidis had more *tekkes* in Istanbul than any other order but—paradoxically—were better able to live without them after the *tekkes* were ordered closed in 1925. All considered, it is not surprising that the Halidiye achieved sometimes great influence under the empire. Naqshbandis benefited especially from the attack on the heterodox Bektaşis after the Janissaries were abolished in 1826.[1]

Factors like these enabled the Halidiye movement to figure for a century as the most important Islamic revival movement in the Ottoman cultural space. So much of the literature on the Halidis is in Arabic, and so much of the evidence about their history comes from the Arab provinces of the empire as well as from other Ottoman regions and lands outside the empire, that the significance of the movement is impossible to grasp without looking beyond the boundaries of today's Turkey. After the collapse of the empire and the founding of the Turkish republic, the Halidiye movement faced new competition. But its growth and adaptation continued. Strict Shari'a observance, the silent *dhikr* which requires no meeting hall, and the principle of social and political engagement all helped the Halidis endure. During the 1920s and 1930s, the harshest phase of republican laicism, some Naqshbandis in the east took up arms against the Turkish republic. At the same time, others applied for jobs in the new Directorate of Religious Affairs, thus colonizing from within the laicist republic's own agency for controlling religion. New forms of religious organization and cultural production emerged in the twentieth century, and these are most visible in the case of the new religious movements of that century. However, the Naqshbandis also branched out into new ventures in a similar range of ways, from mosque congregations to business ventures and print and electronic media. It is not surprising that the Turkish republic's first openly religious prime minister, Turgut Özal (prime minister, 1983–89, and president, 1989–93), was a Naqshbandi. Recep

Tayyip Erdoğan (prime minister, 2003–14) also comes from a Naqshbandi background. The Justice and Development Party (in Turkish, *Adalet ve Kalkınma*, or AKP), which Erdoğan heads, won three successive general elections in 2002, 2007, and 2011 prior to his becoming Turkey's first directly elected president in 2014.

SAID NURSI AND THE NUR MOVEMENT

The man who next created disruptive change in Turkish religious life, Said Nursi, lived a long life, from 1877 to 1960. Once again, this disruption occurred in a relatively short time span, in this case between 1925 and 1944, when Nursi wrote most of the vast number of treatises known collectively as the *Risale-i Nur,* for which he wished to be remembered. He, too, is sometimes mistakenly referred to as a Naqshbandi. However, the evidence indicates that he had read widely in the literature of both Sufism and formal religious studies but was neither the follower of an existing Sufi movement nor the creator of a new one. By 1925, when the Sufi brotherhoods were closed, not only laicists but also many religious people (in Turkey and in other Muslim countries) felt that the Sufi brotherhoods had outlived their usefulness and that it was time to move on. For practicing Muslims in Turkey, there was an even greater problem: how to find a place for themselves in a new political system that still recognized Muslim holidays and tacitly assumed that being a Muslim was a major marker of national identity, yet the policies and attitudes of the ruling elite equated all religion with the lowest forms of superstition. Under the circumstances, what people of faith needed was truly not a new brotherhood but a new kind of leader who could guide them toward spiritual fulfillment in the face of a regime that did not respect that quest. Just at the moment when the early republic's top-down policies of laicism and populism were at their most aggressive, Nursi emerged to reassert God's sovereignty. Not surprisingly, the official reception he got was by far the most hostile of any faced by religious leaders under discussion here.

Nursi's life story is a fascinating one, combining human quirks and eccentricities with austere asceticism and inspired vision. Early on, he made an impression, both as a nonconformist and as an intellectual and spiritual prodigy, whence the epithet *Bediüzzaman,* "the wonder of the age." Living through a profound personal crisis just as the empire collapsed and the

National Struggle occurred, he came to believe that Ahmad Sirhindi, who had earlier inspired Mevlana Halid, was transmitting to him a message to "unify your *kıble*"—essentially, to face in only one direction to pray. To Nursi, this meant that his only source of inspiration must be the Qur'an. Spending much of his life in internal exile in western Turkey, far from his native region, he began writing religious treatises, which ultimately constituted the *Risale-i Nur*. People joined the movement by gathering to study the treatises, thus becoming *talebe-i Nur,* "students of light." Nursi insisted that, in this case, the renewer (*mujaddid*) was not himself but his writings.

For purposes of brief discussion, two aspects of Nursi's writings appear particularly significant. First, despite one prominent scholar's opinion that the *Risale-i Nur* lacks overall cohesion, and although the treatises do move back and forth in the sense of connecting modern issues with Qur'anic interpretation, other scholars have found the collection to be unified. In a recent study, Serdar Poyraz has demonstrated conclusively that a clear organization governs the entire *Risale*.[2] Starting with "The Words" (*Sözler*) as the foundations, texts grouped under specific titles, such as "The Flashes" (*Lem'alar*) and "The Rays" (*Şualar*), as well as all the other texts of the *Risale*, have programmatic relationships to "The Words" and to one another. The mere fact that "The Words," "The Letters" (*Mektubat*), and "The Flashes" each contain thirty-three parts, which add up to ninety-nine, the number of the "most beautiful names" of God (*esma-yı hüsna*), demonstrates that the ten volumes of the *Risale* have a carefully planned structure.

The other especially significant aspect of the *Risale* pertains to its purposes and goals. Trials and investigations by the government attempted to determine whether Nursi was trying to found a new mystical order or undermine the republic. Talking past those charges, he demanded that European philosophers be brought to examine his works. They—or, at any rate, the European materialists from whom Turkish laicists had taken their inspiration—were Nursi's target. Could European philosophers answer his refutation of them? For Nursi, there were three ways to acquire Islamic knowledge: the Qur'an, the Prophet, and "the Grand Book of the Universe," a phrase from the mystical tradition. Within the universe, just as God "makes the sun and the moon attend to [their] duties," the manifestations of His omnipotence also include "a magical emanation of true planning, administering, regulating, purifying and assigning duties."[3] Nursi wrote to prove that the Master of the Universe is the Master of Modernity.

In addition to arguing that materialist science could not undermine religious truth, Nursi's movement embodied a new phase in the transformation of religious forms of organization and action. Nursi went far beyond merely abandoning the old organizational model of the religious brotherhood (*tarikat*). He founded a text-based movement. During his lifetime, moreover, his movement accomplished the entire transition in the production of Islamic knowledge from oral to textual transmission and from manuscript to printed texts. Unwilling to abandon the script of the Qur'an, Nursi insisted until the early 1940s that his writings be reproduced only in the Arabic script. After 1928, this made it illegal to print them in Turkey. Copying manuscripts became increasingly the occupation of his followers; correcting manuscripts took up more and more of his time. Manuscript reproduction became a major force in perpetuating literacy in the Arabic script in Turkey, among women as well as men. If his followers' claims that they produced 600,000 manuscripts are even remotely true, then one of the largest manuscript production projects in the history of the world occurred in the twentieth century. Finally, the argument that Latin-script texts would make his teachings more accessible to the young convinced him to allow some of his writings to be typed in Latin letters in the early 1940s; some texts were also reproduced photographically then. A 1956 court decision that the treatises did not violate the law finally led to the printing in Latin letters of the entire *Risale*. Increasing the number of readers into the hundreds of thousands, this started the process of moving the treatises into the mainstream of Turkish media.

FETHULLAH GÜLEN AND THE GÜLEN MOVEMENT

The death of a charismatic founder inevitably creates a crisis in the history of a religious movement. In contrast to the lack of a direct connection between the rise of the Halidiye and the Nur movements, a connection does exist between the Nur movement and Turkey's third major religious revival. The Nur movement divided into several branches after Nursi's death in 1960. Gradually, it became apparent that a young religious leader who was also a student of Nursi's writings was going to become a new leader of exceptional impact. This was Fethullah Gülen (b. 1938). In the evolution of new forms of organization and action, beyond the Sufi brotherhood model that had worked for Mevlana Halid, the movement that Gülen inspired takes us again toward new horizons.

Known for his austere lifestyle, inspirational preaching, and profound knowledge of the Qur'an, the *Risale-i Nur,* and other subjects, Gülen has also written a great deal. Yet his movement is no longer text-based in the way that Nursi's was. Known to his followers as Hocaefendi (roughly "teacher-master"), Gülen has defined yet another new model of leadership. Gülen is more interested in action than in writing. Increasingly, *hizmet* (service) is becoming the key term in the way its followers talk about the movement. As in the case of the Halidiye and the Nur movements before it, the Gülen movement's success reflects how well it corresponds to the challenges and opportunities of its times.

Like Halid and Nursi, Gülen made history in a relatively short time span. His movement expanded from local to national to global within twenty years after 1983. The new conditions created inside Turkey by Özal's decade of national leadership (1983–93) and then the wider changes created by the Soviet collapse and the new era of globalization provided opportunities for the movement to grow. Gülen and his followers have responded to these opportunities in inspired ways. Still localized around Izmir in the 1970s, the movement started with Gülen's mosque congregation, the local Qur'an school, the Nur movement's reading groups (*dershane*), summer camps for male university students, and apartments (*ışık evleri*) that supporters made available to provide housing and a motivational environment for same-sex groups of university students.

After 1983, changes in the law on private foundations (*vakıf*) led many supporters to create new foundations, and the movement's decentralization and lack of hierarchy facilitated a proliferation of initiatives, particularly in three fields: media, business, and education. In media, Gülen supporters bought the newspaper *Zaman* (Time) and made it into a large-circulation newspaper. They founded many print publications and expanded into electronic media with Samanyolu (Milky Way) TV and Burç (Tower or Zodiacal Constellation) FM radio. Out of these efforts, the Turkish Journalists and Writers Foundation (Türkiye Gazeteciler ve Yazarlar Vakfı, or GYV) also emerged to communicate between the movement and the outside world.

In the same period, leaders of Turkey's major religious movements encouraged economic growth by persuading conservative families, who distrusted banks and used to keep money in gold, to put their wealth to economically productive uses. This kind of inspiration, coming from Gülen and other religious leaders, is largely responsible for the phenomenon of the "Anatolian tigers" (*Anadolu kaplanları*), the businesses and industries that have grown up mostly outside the geographical sites and sociocultural strata that had dominated industry and commerce in the earlier decades of the Turkish republic. This is the same propertied segment of provincial society that responded to Halid's movement over a century earlier and then more recently to the Nur and the Gülen movements. In some cases, older businesses, like the Ülker chocolate and biscuit firm, identified with the Gülen movement, and many new firms, associations, and foundations also emerged in association with it.

What is most remarkable since the 1980s is both the speed and scale of the "take-off" in this sector of the Turkish economy as well as the growth in its members' philanthropy. Among the new associations and foundations associated with the Gülen movement were the Turkish Teachers Foundation (Türkiye Öğretmenler Vakfı) and the Akyazılı Foundation for Secondary and Higher Education, which owned hundreds of dormitories for university students by the 1990s. "The Light" (*Işık*) Insurance Company was set up by movement supporters in 1995, as was the Asia Finance (*Asya Finans*) bank, which aimed to expand investment in the Central Asian republics. The movement also had its own business council, the Association for Solidarity in Business Life (İş Hayatı Dayanışma Derneği, or İŞHAD). Much of the expansion of Turkish enterprise into the Central Asian republics has been the work of movement supporters.

After 1983, it became possible to found private educational institutions. This quickly became the Gülen movement's best-known endeavor. In addition to vast numbers of secondary schools, Gülen supporters founded Istanbul's Fatih University in 1995, followed by universities in the capitals of all the Central Asian Turkic republics except Uzbekistan. By the early 2000s, Gülen supporters claimed over 1,000 schools in more than a hundred countries. The students of those schools are mostly male, but they include students of different religions and ethnicities, and there are also schools for girls.

The Hizmet movement schools in Kyrgyzstan provide a good illustration of what Gülen supporters have accomplished in general and in Central Asia in particular. Identified with the Sebat Foundation since their beginning in 1992, these schools have grown to the point that they are found in every province. As of 2011, the schools in Kyrgyzstan were educating nearly 8,500 students, selected out of more than 50,000 applicants each year. Many of the students received partial or, in some cases, full remission of school fees. The facilities were new and well-equipped with laboratories, computers, and smart blackboards. Pride among the graduates led many of those who succeeded in business to give back by building gymnasiums or other additional facilities for their schools. Naming schools for national culture heroes added to the pride and consolidated links with the local society, as in the case of the Çıngız Aytmatov Boys High School in Bishkek, named after the great Kyrgyz novelist.

Gülen movement schools have been criticized for educating more boys than girls. As of 2011, this was certainly true in Kyrgyzstan. However, the Silk Road International School in Bishkek was a Hizmet school with a mixed student body, and most Kyrgyz provinces had at least one girls' school. The Issıkgöl Girls' High School, located in a former Soviet vacation colony with its own beach on Kyrgyzstan's warm-water lake, was an impressive institution with an exceptional student body, which was also ethnically and religiously diverse. The demand for more girls' schools was certainly strong. For example, the director of the boys' high school in another province had to drive to Issıkgöl to visit his daughter, who was a boarding student there; then he had to drive back home and answer questions about when a girls' high school would be opened in his province. Parents—even if neither one had a high school education—often wanted their daughters as well as their sons to attend the schools. A visiting scholar was certain to be asked to talk to the students and was bound to be impressed by their neat dress, respectful behavior, and mental sharpness. On any given day, the visitor might also be impressed with the contrast between the young people seen inside the school and those outside on the street. Inside, one saw mostly boys busily studying in white shirts and blue blazers, and outside were more girls going about in tight jeans and high heels. It seemed there was more than one way to be modern in Kyrgyzstan, and more for Hizmet movement supporters to do to contribute to this project. A visit to the Süleyman Demirel University in Almatı (Kazakstan) offered impressionistic evidence to me that the proportion of female students is higher in the universities founded by Gülen supporters.

By 2007, the Gülen movement claimed over six million members all around the world, and it was making itself known for its efforts to promote tolerance and interfaith dialogue everywhere. Working with members of the movement suggests that its greatest contribution may be in character formation and education. Both of these, and character formation especially, are traditional preoccupations of the Islamic mystical movements, which were the historical precursors of the Nursi and the Gülen movements. To any thoughtful observer of the Turkish scene in recent decades, the need for improved education is equally salient. Gülen has specifically articulated the goal of training a "Golden Generation" (*altın nesil*). The downside of this approach has been to perpetuate the historical elitist bias of Turkish education. However, in countries where the state of the public schools is problematic, as in parts of post-Soviet Central Asia, visiting Hizmet schools and encountering their students makes it easy to understand why demand for the schools is so strong. Against the backdrop of Turkish educational history, what is new about Hizmet's educational role is not so much its goal as the vastly enlarged possibilities created by the collapsing of old boundaries between peoples and religions in a world where the global and the local are present everywhere simultaneously.

Even so, as in the cases of Halid and Nursi before him, Gülen's eminence as a religious leader made him a target of official attack and even indictment in Turkey. As a result, he has lived in North America since 1999. Absent from Turkey, he is present everywhere, thanks to the activity of his followers and the globalization of the electronic media. This engagement with global modernity provides the basis on which to appreciate the full measure of the Gülen movement's significance.

CONCLUSION

During the past two centuries, three great renewals have transformed Ottoman and Turkish religious culture. A leader exceptional for his piety, learning, and vision launched each movement, achieving great impact within just a few decades. At some point, each leader ran into trouble with government authorities suspicious of change that challenged state control. These renewal movements won many followers largely because they responded particularly well to the challenges and opportunities that Muslims encountered at the time, whether it was in the 1820s, the 1920s, or the 1980s. In terms of their social organizations and their means for propagating their beliefs, the movements differ notably—yet their differences fit together, end to end, tracing a significant learning curve in religious history. For Halid, the model of the mystical brotherhood (*tarikat*) still worked as an organizational model. In his time, oral transmission and manuscript production still sufficed to convey the movement's ideas and beliefs. In compensation, the fact that his movement originated in the Ottoman Arab lands and that he propagated his message in Arabic facilitated its spread to the wider Muslim world, something much harder to achieve for religious leaders who express themselves in Turkish.

A century younger, Nursi inhabited a world where not only laicists but also many religious Muslims thought it was time to leave the accumulated trappings of the mystical brotherhoods behind. Nursi offered his followers a religious shield against materialism, and he gave it to them in the form of a prodigious body of writings. Those writings became the basis of a text-based movement, which believers could join by studying and reproducing his works. Partly in reaction to the secularization of Ottoman print culture after 1908, Turkish-speaking Muslims now needed print media of their own. As noted, in his lifetime Nursi and his followers lived the entire transition from orality to textuality and from manuscript to print, and they did this with the huge amount of writing that he produced. Unlike Halid, who operated in the larger space of the late Ottoman Empire and whose writings in Arabic were understandable to learned Muslims everywhere, Nursi lived most of his life in the narrower space of the Turkish republic. As a Kurd dedicated to Turkish-Kurdish brotherhood within Islam, he wrote almost entirely in Turkish, aside from a few works in Arabic. As a result, the fact that he produced one of the twentieth century's most important bodies of writing about Islam remained practically unknown outside Turkey for decades, even to experts on Islam.

Turkey's third great renewal movement, the one inspired by Gülen, grew out of the Nur movement and also propagated its message originally in Turkish. However, the fact that the Gülen movement emerged more or less simultaneously with the rise of instantaneous electronic communications has enabled it to spread its message around the world with a speed and efficiency that Nursi could scarcely have imagined. The Gülen movement has explored many new frontiers of social organization and cultural production. It has created print and electronic media. It has set up foundations, businesses, and, especially, schools. It has set the example of how a Muslim religious movement can take advantage of contemporary means of networking to offer a constructive and productive engagement of Islam with global modernity.

Ultimately, the Gülen movement may prove as significant for the world of the twenty-first century as the Gandhi movement proved for the world of the twentieth century. In both cases, a movement launched within a particular faith has addressed its message of peace and fellowship to people of all faiths and has spread globally by emulation, without formal organization. Shaped by the struggle against imperialism and racism in British-ruled South Africa and India, the inspiration of the Gandhi movement spread to all the world, inspiring the civil rights movement in the United States and the anti-nuclear, environmental, and human rights movements of Europe. Having spread around the world even more quickly and already become a part of the fabric of global modernity, the Gülen movement may contribute equally to the future of humankind.

NOTES

1. The Janissaries were the historical infantry corps of the Ottoman Empire, and the Bektaşi order was a Sufi movement closely identified with them.
2. Serdar Poyraz, "Science versus Religion: The Influence of European Materialism on Turkish Thought, 1860–1960" (Ph.D. diss., Ohio State University, 2010), chap. 6.
3. Şerif Mardin, *Religion and Social Change in Modern Turkey: The Case of Bediüzzaman Said Nursi* (Albany: SUNY Press, 1989), 194.

SUGGESTIONS FOR FURTHER READING

Abu-Manneh, Butrus. *Studies on Islam in the Ottoman Empire in the 19th Century.* Istanbul, Isis, 2001.
Algar, Hamid. "Devotional Practices of the Khalidi Naqshbandis of Ottoman Turkey." In *The Dervish Lodge: Architecture, Art, and Sufism in Ottoman Turkey*, edited by Raymond Lifchezj, 209–27. Berkeley: University of California Press, 1992.
Findley, Carter Vaughn. *Turkey, Islam, Nationalism, and Modernity: A History, 1789–2007.* New Haven, Conn.: Yale University Press, 2010.
Harrington, James C. *Wrestling with Free Speech, Religious Freedom, and Democracy in Turkey: The Political Trials and Times of Fethullah Gülen.* Lanham, Md.: University Press of America, 2011.
Hermansen, Marcia. "The Cultivation of Memory in the Gülen Community." Online at http://en.fgulen.com/content/views/2444/53/.
Mardin, Şerif. *Religion and Social Change in Modern Turkey: The Case of Bediüzzaman Said Nursi.* Albany: SUNY Press, 1989.
Poyraz, Serdar. "Science versus Religion: The Influence of European Materialism on Turkish Thought, 1860–1960." Ph.D. diss., Ohio State University, 2010.
Turner, Colin, and Hasan Horkuç. *Said Nursi.* New York: Palgrave Macmillan, 2009.
Vahide, Şükran. *Islam in Modern Turkey: An Intellectual Biography of Bediüzzaman Said Nursi.* Albany: SUNY Press, 2005.
Yavuz, M. Hakan. *Islamic Political Identity in Turkey.* New York: Oxford University Press, 2003.

TWO

Who Is Fethullah Gülen?

AN OVERVIEW OF HIS LIFE

Marcia Hermansen

THE DATE OF FETHULLAH GÜLEN'S birth is disputed. An often-cited account states that he was born on April 27, 1941, in Erzurum's Pasinler (Hasankale) County in the village of Korucuk, a hamlet of some fifty or sixty houses. Informally, I was told that November 11, 1938, is the actual date of his birth, and this date has been confirmed in certain other accounts, as well.[1] The discrepancy is explained by one source, citing Gülen's younger brother, Sibgetullah, who explained what happened when their father went to Erzurum to register Fethullah's birth. He asserted that the official at the registry refused to enter the name "Fethullah," apparently because he felt it was too religious, so his father returned without registering the birth. Three years later, on April 27, 1942, when Sibgetullah was born, their father registered both boys as being born on the same date. Some years later, in order to be eligible for his first posting at the Uçşerefeli mosque, Fethullah had to present himself as being a year older, and therefore he had the registry papers amended to April 27, 1941.[2]

One of the best sources for details of Gülen's early life is the book *Küçük Dünyam* (My Little World), which was drawn from interviews conducted in the 1980s and compiled by one of his close associates, Latif Erdoğan.[3] The idea of the "little world" or "small universe" may be a humble and homey reference to Gülen's moral and spiritual formation. For many associates of

Fethullah Gülen is globally recognized as a contemporary Islamic religious leader and inspiration to an influential social movement. For all his reputation and accomplishments, one cannot assume that his biography is familiar to most readers in the West. Marcia Hermansen, professor of Islamic Studies at Loyola University Chicago, here introduces the life of Gülen as a figure who has been at the center of the Hizmet movement for decades.

Hizmet, the expression now also refers to the small room where Gülen resided during much of his time in the dormitory at Bornova, Izmir, in the 1980s and early 1990s. There Gülen slept, contemplated, and studied books in his library of religious classics.

Gülen was raised in a religious family in the small Turkish village of Korucuk. His ancestors came from Ahlat, a small town in Bitlis Province situated in the mountains near Lake Van in eastern Turkey. Bitlis occupies a special place in the history of Islam in Anatolia: descendants of the Prophet were said to have settled there and established early exchanges between Turkish tribes and Islamic practices. Some believe that this mountainous area protected the traditions of Islamic spirituality that began to flourish there.

Gülen's father, Ramiz Efendi (1905–74), was the preacher at the local mosque. He taught young Fethullah the Arabic language and instilled in him devotion to the Prophet Muhammad and his family and companions. Gülen's mother, Rafia Hanim (1913–93), was also an early inspiration and his first teacher of the Qur'an. He comments that, in retrospect, he could not imagine how this extraordinary woman could prepare daily meals for fifteen to twenty people, do all the housework herself, and still find the time to teach the Qur'an. The influence of parents and the need to respect them is an important part of Gülen's formation and teachings. In fact, according to Gülen, parents rank second only to God in meriting devotion and affection. In the small collection of mementos displayed in the city of Izmir (as part of a spontaneous museum, prepared in his honor by affiliates, on the fifth floor of the dormitory of the Yamanlar School), the copy of the prayer book known as the *Jawshan* that belonged to Gülen's mother is displayed along with his father's personal copy of the Qur'an.

In Gülen's own words:

> My first teacher was my mother. At that time, our village had no elementary school. Later one opened. I began praying when I was 4 years old, and have never missed a prayer since. One of my teachers was extremely hostile to religion and could not accept this activity. Another teacher, Belma, liked me very much and would say: "One day a young lieutenant will pass over Galata Bridge. It is as if I were watching him now."
>
> I ran all of the errands for my family, helped my mother with the housework, and herded our cows and sheep. In my free time, I would read a book or memorize the Qur'an. When my father was an imam at Alvar village, I learned how to read the Qur'an with the correct pronunciation and rhythm from Haci Sidki Efendi of Hasankale, our district. I did not have a place to stay in Hasankale, so I had to walk back and forth on the 7- to 8-kilometer road.[4]

Gülen was the third of eleven brothers and sisters, three of whom died in childhood. They were a closely knit family to whom he was very attached. A story is told that, when Gülen left home, his brother Mesih was so aggrieved that he did not speak for several years, until Gülen returned for a visit. The family home was always open to guests, and scholars were especially welcomed and respected. As a child, Gülen was already drawn to the company of serious and learned elders from whom he could absorb knowledge and gain wisdom. However, the young Gülen had to struggle on various fronts—religious, financial, and physical—to achieve a formal education. In 1949, his father moved from Korucuk to Alvar in order to work as imam of the mosque there. This move interrupted Gülen's primary schooling, and he completed his diploma as an external student in 1958:

> My father had to leave Alvar. After a period of time in Artuzu, he settled in Erzurum. While studying in Erzurum, I could fit all of my belongings in a box I carried in my hand. I continued my education under very difficult conditions. We prepared our food in the same place where we slept. Most of the time we had to bathe in ice-cold water.[5]

Gülen then describes how he stayed in a room that was so tiny he could not stretch out while his roommate was sleeping. Although he was studying for the public entrance exam for high school admission, in 1949 his father enrolled him in a Qur'an school in Hasankale, and he used to walk seven to eight kilometers daily to study there, as mentioned earlier, finishing his memorization of the entire Qur'an in 1951.

In Sufism, Gülen received his early instruction from a teacher in the Qadiri Sufi order, Shaykh Muhammad Lutfi, known affectionately as "Alvarli Efe" (1868–1956). He visited his Sufi lodge (*tekke*) on a regular basis between the ages of ten and sixteen. Some mementos of this relationship, such as the cloak of Alvarli Efe, are also displayed in the Izmir collection.

Of this spiritual guide, Gülen writes:

> Outside of my family, Muhammed Lutfi Efendi had a very great influence on me. Every word coming out of his mouth appeared as inspiration flowing from another realm. We listened attentively whenever he talked, for it was as if we were hearing celestial things that had previously come down to Earth.
>
> I cannot say that I fully understood him, because he passed away when I was not even 16 years old. Despite this, because he was the one who first awakened my consciousness and perceptions, I tried to grasp his points with my mind and natural talents, since my age prevented me from comprehend-

ing him. My intuition, sensitivity, and feelings of today are due to my sensations in his presence.[6]

Scholar Heon Kim makes the point that Gülen's early education exposed him to both the *madrasa* (traditional Islamic) and the *tekke* (Sufi) styles of imparting knowledge, building character, teaching, and learning.[7] A particular aspect of Lutfi's teaching that seems to have influenced Gülen was an emphasis on tolerance and dialogue.[8] In addition, Gülen's father seems to have had connections to both the Qadiri and the Naqshbandi Sufi orders.[9] After Alvarli Efe's death, Gülen studied briefly with a second Qadiri shaykh, Rasim Baba.[10]

In 1952, Gülen began studying basic Islamic sources in Arabic grammar and language in the madrasa of the Kurşunlu mosque in Erzurum under the grandson of Alvarli Efe, Sadi Efendi. At the age of about fourteen, he gave some of his first sermons/lectures during the month of Ramadan in Korucuk and Alvar. As he matured, Gülen studied Islamic law, practical and theoretical, from 1956 to 1958 in Erzurum with a teacher called Osman Bektaş (1914–86).[11]

While studying with Bektaş Gülen was introduced to the works of Said Nursi by one of Nursi's pupils, Muzaffer Arslan, who spent two weeks giving lectures in the area.[12] A few colleagues who joined a local circle formed to study Nursi's works would remain Gülen's friends and associates.

In 1959, Gülen achieved the official rank of government preacher. Due to the Turkish government's control and certification of religion and Islamic discourse, such official recognition was necessary in order to preach or teach. As is common in many Sunni Muslim countries, mosque officials and preachers in Turkey are government employees. In addition to regulating religion, this official status guarantees them a regular salary and pension, and it ensures that only individuals with the proper education and attitudes will hold these positions of public religious authority.

During his career, Gülen was posted to a variety of Turkish towns and cities. As his reputation as a preacher rose, he traveled throughout Turkey, giving religious talks and participating in educational seminars. These trips acquainted him with many areas of Turkey and enhanced his appreciation for the hopes and aspirations of people in various regions and in disparate situations. Gülen is known for his love of his homeland. In his American residence, he is said to keep containers of earth from almost every region of Turkey, as if desiring to remain in contact with his native soil.

In 1959, he was appointed assistant imam at the Uçşerefeli mosque in Edirne. His salary was very low, and he slept in a window-ledge compartment of the mosque for two and a half years, often reading by candlelight. At about this time, Gülen received several overtures of marriage. However, he has remained single, an unusual course for a male Turk of his social standing and generation. It is accepted that the burdens of being a spiritual adviser sometimes demand personal sacrifices of an individual, along with the recognition that it would not be fair to a spouse to join in such an ascetic and committed existence.

In November 1961, Gülen undertook the two-year compulsory military service required of all Turkish males; this took him to the far western Turkish city of Edirne, the second capital of the Ottomans after the city of Bursa. Because of Edirne's proximity to Europe, the culture and attitudes that Gülen encountered there challenged the more conservative traditions of his Anatolian background. Kim suggests that this may have provoked him to adopt a more ascetic lifestyle, and Gülen engaged in spiritual retreats and fasting during this period.[13] It was to be a turbulent time for him personally and in Turkish history as well. His military commander encouraged Gülen to read Western classics along with his usual religious books, so his horizons broadened. He also performed a retreat at the Haci Bayram mosque in Ankara, remaining for several weeks sequestered in a window-ledge compartment there.[14] Such accommodations were already familiar to him since, as mentioned above, Gülen had stayed in a mosque window compartment for over two years during the Edirne period.[15]

During the February 1962 military coup against the Turkish government, most of the troops were confined to the barracks, and Gülen endured a stressful period of uncertainty. By the end of his military service, he had become ill and weak, and he needed to spend some time recuperating in a hospital and later in his family's home is Erzurum. His next post was officially at Iskander, but he often spent time in Edirne and Erzurum as well. During this period, Gülen was frequently invited to give guest sermons and talks. In 1964, after completing the military service, Gülen was again posted to Edirne, this time as chief imam at a smaller mosque. Later, in 1965 and 1966, he preached at the Hızırbey mosque in Kırklareli.[16]

It was in his next official position (1966–71), in the coastal city of Izmir, that Gülen began to develop a substantial following, and his mission assumed its initial form and began to crystallize. He usually gave the Friday sermon at the Kestanepazarı mosque and weekend talks in nearby smaller towns. At first, he was occupied as a tutor and mentor in a Qur'an school attached to the mosque; he was also responsible for tutoring students at a nearby *imamhatip*, or religious school established to train imams. (A number of these pupils, such as Abdullah Aymaz and Ismail Büyükçelebi, became life-long friends and assumed prominent roles in the leadership of the Hizmet movement.) Gülen initially slept on a couch in the director's office, and later his lodging was near the mosque school in a small shed where he could barely stand or stretch out full length.[17] His preaching at this point was generally in the form of moral admonishments, known as *vaaz*, and lectures on piety. Beyond the mosque, his broad interests and extensive reading led him to participate in cultural and intellectual conferences—lecturing, for example, on the poet and Sufi mystic, Rumi. Sometimes, topics of intellectual debate of the time, such as religion and science, were the subjects of his conferences.

It is said by associates who attended these sermons and lectures during Gülen's stay in Izmir that he would prepare well ahead of time through a period of reading and contemplation. Ultimately, he would become extremely tense and focused but also physically drained by the great amount of energy and concentration that he directed to the responsibility of delivering the speech. His colleagues sometimes considered dissuading him from attempting to speak in such a depleted state. However, once he had mounted the pulpit or the podium, a current of energy seemed to enter and animate him, restoring to him the ability to project a larger-than-life presence and force. In such inspired states, captivating and inspiring teachings and messages would issue forth from Gülen.[18] His style of public preaching is a particular and distinctive element of his reputation. His individual lectures are often cited and remembered by his admirers who attended, saw them on video, heard tape recordings of them, or were simply told about them. According to one anecdote related to me, Gülen, while preaching at the Hisar mosque in Izmir on one memorable occasion in the early 1990s, was so affected by a discussion of the war in Azerbaijan that he fainted. His style of preaching may be characterized as highly emotional, and he often weeps during his sermons, talks, and lectures.[19] In Islamic religious circles, such articulations of affect are appreciated and interpreted as demonstrating commitment and sincerity. His rhetoric is moving, dramatic, and anecdotal, and his Turkish language is inflected with Arab and Persian expressions and vocabulary, evoking the Ottoman Islamic heritage. His mastery of oratory is a phenomenon commented on by movement affiliates and highlighted in academic studies on his sermons and discourses.[20] The fact that many of his sermons were later published in book form underscores the value of their intellectual content and pedagogical significance.

The mosque where he often preached in Izmir is known as the Kestane (Chestnut) Bazaar, or Kestanepazarı mosque. It is located in the courtyard of a bazaar consisting of small shops whose revenues sustain the mosque and its expenses as part of a religious endowment (*vakf*). This mosque is frequented by students and teachers from the nearby local university as well as area businessmen. This social combination was to prove an important factor in setting a model for the future success of the Hizmet movement by encouraging cooperation between these disparate professional, social, and age groups. A number of initiatives that became characteristic of the Gülen movement emerged at this time: outreach to new sectors of the public; involvement in practical elements of the educational system; and religious instruction in new settings. Although he formally resigned from his position at the Kestanepazarı mosque in 1971, Gülen remained in residence near the Aegean Coast area, characterizing himself as an "itinerant" preacher until the 1980s.

In his memoir, Gülen speaks of his early postings leading up to Izmir:

> In that second term of my stay in Edirne, I stayed with my superior Suat Yildirim, who was the mufti there. When I met with some pressure during my duty, I asked to be transferred to Kırklareli. I did not stay there long. During my yearly leave, I was transferred to Izmir. I went to Kestanepazarı Qur'an school in Izmir. At Kestanepazarı, I was busy with students. My official duty was not limited to Izmir, for I was expected to travel around in the Aegean part of Turkey. From time to time I would go to coffeehouses to explain things to the men who were killing time there.
>
> Most students at Kestanepazarı were talented. I was not being paid there, because I did not want any payment for what I was doing. At night I would visit the dormitory and cover [with blankets] those who had become uncovered. After 5 years, I had to leave Kestanepazarı for some reasons.[21]

This biographical excerpt mentions one of Gülen's striking initiatives of the Izmir period, the Kahvehanesohbet (Coffeehouse Discourse) that began in 1969. Coffeehouses have been and, in many regions, are still a large part of male social networking and evening entertainment in Turkish society. During the Ottoman period, these were often referred to as Kiraathane, or "reading rooms," and some establishments still use this designation on their signboards. Gülen's remarkable initiative in this case was to leave the safe and familiar environment of the mosque and Qur'an school and go out with a few affiliates to local coffeehouses to try and connect with a new and broader audience. According to his companions on these forays, he was initially greeted with some resistance and disparagement, but in some cases he found receptive listeners, and his circle expanded accordingly.

Gülen's memoir quoted above also mentions the dormitories in Izmir, for it was here that the first Gülen-inspired schools and the first dormitories were built. One of the distinguishing features of the Gülen movement became the new concept of residential mentoring for youth. A story about Gülen that is fondly recounted by associates regards his meeting in the 1970s with a group of businessmen from his congregation who wanted to support some charitable cause. They proposed the idea of building a new mosque. Gülen replied, "Turkey already has so many mosques—what we are going to need now is dormitories for students."

Why dormitories? In the 1970s there was an explosion in education in Turkey and in the Muslim world at large. This created a particular need. Many of the students from smaller towns were coming to larger centers to become the first in their families to receive high school and university training. A great need for affordable housing and board existed. In addition, families were very concerned about the safety and well-being (both physical or moral) of their children, not only after their move to the "big city" but also in the climate of clashes between rightists and leftists that provoked a state of continuous violence. Many parents feared the possibility that their youth might be violently targeted by members of opposing factions. One may also imagine that Gülen's own struggles to achieve learning in a deprived and sometimes hostile environment made him especially aware of the challenges that these young people would face. The exceptional element is that he displayed both vision and activism in choosing to concretely address these problems and by mobilizing others to effect this massive project to solve them.

Another result of establishing dormitories in various Turkish cities was to enable increasing numbers of young women to pursue higher education. Girls from traditionally religious families were often prevented from pursuing university studies by parents who feared exposing their daughters to a secular system and the potentially alienating or corrosive influence in a new environment. The educational system in Turkey is such that admission to university studies is based on competitive exams that not only determine the subjects that one may pursue but also often necessitate relocating to attend universities where openings in specific fields are available. Naturally, the idea of girls leaving home for studies was threatening to traditional families. Alternatively, the new Gülen dormitories were perceived as providing a safe and wholesome environment, both physically and morally. Typical of the debates that were going on in this period is an account related to me by a young Turkish-American lawyer, the first in his family to attend college, who described his parents' discussing sending their sons and daughters to university. The mother insisted that, if the father deprived his daughters of this opportunity, then the sons also should not be further educated. The availability of Gülen dormitories and networks made such choices much easier for families, and a new cohort of females commenced higher education.

These dormitories and schools were more than structures and efficiently run institutions. The spirit that infused them arose from Gülen's call to foster a "Golden Generation" that would restore, heal, and carry forward the best potentials of humanity in harmony with a modern and pluralistic world. At the heart of these environments was the human capital, dorm mentors, known as "belletmen" in Turkish, along with school teachers who would work selflessly with their pupils, seeing them as individuals needing positive role models and dedicated mentoring.

Another Hizmet initiative that was expanded during this period were the summer camps held for the students surrounding Gülen. These camps started in 1968 and rapidly drew increasing numbers of young male attendees. At the same time, despite a relatively low profile, the camps were periodically visited by military detachments and even on occasion by politicians looking for support.

I was invited to observe a Hizmet "camp" in the United States during the Christmas holidays of 2005 in the Chicago area. My pre-existing impression of camps was of tents pitched in a forest. This camp, however, was held in a summer resort hotel for which a very appealing rate could be negotiated during the winter season, especially at a time when most American families were at home with relatives.

The activities of this camp consisted of reading and discussing religious writings, including Gülen's book on the Prophet Muhammad, *Infinite Light*.[22] No dramatic religious practices took place, just a simple round of communal ritual prayers and devotions.[23] Evening lectures were presented by visiting senior teachers (*abiler*) and a few outside guests. Almost all sessions were conducted in Turkish. It was a family atmosphere with special classes and activities for children and young people.

It did not occur to me to ask—why call it a "camp"? It was only later that I learned about the first camps and their place in the memory of the Gülen movement from one of the first members of Gülen's circle in Turkey, a man who was an early affiliate from the days of the Kestanepazarı mosque in Izmir, Ismail Büyükçelebi.[24]

After his evening discourse (*sohbet*) in Chicago, I was granted an interview, conducted in Turkish. The following account of the first camp, held in 1968, is based on my notes:

> At the first camp in 1968, there were about 50 students from local high schools and colleges in attendance. They lived in tents in an open field at Kaynaklar village near Izmir. It was in the open air, and there was a row of pine trees on one side of the field. There was a one-room house that had been used as a barn and needed to be cleaned up. For cooking, we made a hearth out of stones.
>
> All the [male] students were used to dorm life and had never cooked. They learned by experience, taking turns and having Hocaefendi [i.e., Gülen] comment on the meals as they were progressing.
>
> The water came from a well and there was no electricity, only the light of oil lamps.
>
> The only place to do laundry was in a stream located about 30 minutes away.
>
> The second year of the camp, there were 120 students, and in the third year, 275.
>
> In the 1970s, Hocaefendi moved to the city of Enderem and so did the camps for four years. During this period, in fact, after the 1971 coup, there was more pressure on the movement from the state authorities. Gülen himself was jailed for holding the camps because they were viewed as being potentially subversive.
>
> When camps were held, soldiers would routinely come and check for clandestine activities.[25]

When the students were alerted that such a raid was imminent, they would hide their religious books. In order to give the impression that fewer attendees were at the camp, they would put one bedroll on top of another. They recited litanies of protection such as the prayer (*du'a*) of those who were at the early Islamic battle of Badr. One time, Gülen had a dream about the Prophet's uncle, Hamza. The campers later learned that, at that very moment, the jeep full of soldiers who were coming to investigate had an accident on the road, thereby delaying the raid.[26]

Once in the late 1960s, the future leader of the Refah Party, Necmettin Erbakan, came to the camps to attempt to rally support for his party. This type of political solicitation, however, was not of interest to Gülen's students.[27]

In the spring of 1971, shortly after moving to a nearby town called Guzelyali, Gülen was arrested and spent seven months in prison after a military coup.[28] The charge was that he was engaged in activities—such as founding dormitories and holding camps—that could be construed as sustaining opposition to the secular government.

Upon his release from prison in 1972, Gülen was posted to Enderem, a coastal town some one hundred miles from Izmir, and, in 1974, to Manisa, even closer to Izmir. In 1975, he initiated a series of conferences on topics of current public interest, such as "Science and the Holy Qur'an," "Darwinism," and "the Golden Generation." These conferences took him to the cities of Ankara, Corum, Malatya, Diyarbakir, Konya, Antalya, and Aydin.

The theme of religion's compatibility with science is a significant one for contemporary Muslims and an especially relevant one for modern Turkey. Republican Turkey under Mustafa Kemal Atatürk and his successors had embraced a project of positivism and were confident that modernity and scientific progress would form the core of a successful Turkish state. Many Muslim thinkers in Turkey, responding to the Ottoman "Young Turks" and to the challenges of the late nineteenth and early twentieth centuries, also had articulated the understanding that Islam was pro-science and "modernist." In embracing this theme, Gülen follows, for example, Said Nursi but is more specific in his engagement with scientific theories such as evolution and with particular Western thinkers such as Darwin.

In 1976, Gülen returned to Izmir and was appointed to the mosque in Bornova, near the local Ege (Aegean) University. There he became aware of the plight of talented students who lacked the means to gain university admission without some remedial tutoring. In response, he encouraged the establishment of free tutoring centers to provide this service.[29] Bornova had been the site of the first Hizmet dormitory, memorable as a place where university faculty and students worked alongside workers to construct the building, inspiring local businessmen to contribute further material resources toward this good work.

In Izmir, the presence of so many students in his congregation led Gülen to convene special sessions on Friday evenings where there would be a discourse followed by open question-and-answer sessions. Many of the questions dealt with the challenges of being a Muslim in the modern world. In later years, the students' comments were collected and published in the four-volume series *Questions Raised by the Modern Age* that became a best seller in Turkey and has been translated into several other languages. In 1977, Gülen traveled to Germany and presented lectures and sermons there, finding audiences among the Turkish guest workers who had come to meet the need for labor.

In addition to traveling and meeting with a wider public at that time, Gülen began to have his ideas published in the popular press. In 1979, with the help of qualified associates, he inaugurated the first publishing project of the movement on a regular basis, a monthly journal called *Sızıntı* that still comes out regularly.[30] This project was initially undertaken by Irfan Yilmaz, a biology professor. The purpose of the magazine was to demonstrate the harmony of science and religion. Each issue featured a column by Gülen, and usually a striking image or photograph would be chosen, for which Gülen would write a thought-provoking caption. These images were later collected into two volumes entitled *Truth through Colors*. A close study of their epigraphs reveals that the seeds of Gülen's future projects had already been sown, even at this early period in the growth of his following. Gülen combined his visionary ability with a penchant to use natural symbols in a sort of poetic embrace of the surrounding natural world combined with a strong urgency that human life should fulfill a higher purpose. For example, the series opens with the image of a mighty waterfall, accompanied by the caption that reads, in the English version, "Those who belittled you, considering you just a drop, never thought that one day you would grow into such a waterfall."[31]

In Gülen's other writings, the waterfall, as in many spiritual traditions, stands for the power of water, patient and gentle yet ultimately strong:

> Stagnant waters become mossy; inactive limbs are subject to over-calcification. By contrast, waterfalls are always clean. Those who always keep their brains active and souls purified will one day see that they have germinated numerous "seeds of beauty" in themselves and all their efforts have come to fruition. Only ploughed land can be sown; only gardens trimmed and trees pruned yield the best fruit.[32]

Other repeated images in this series include "ruins" and the "ethnographic museum"—representing the idea that one's life work, and that of entire peoples, will be later regarded from the standpoint of history. The idea of purposefulness and even of urgency to make a positive contribution is one that is repeatedly emphasized in Gülen's sermons and epitomized by such symbols.

The Hizmet ventures into the print media have expanded to numerous journals geared to diverse interests, the most successful of which, the newspaper *Zaman*, now has Turkey's largest circulation. These media efforts have grown into radio programming and a major television station, Samanyolu (Milky Way) TV, in 1994.

THE HIZMET MOVEMENT, 1980–94

In Turkey, 1980 was a critical year because of the military coup that took place there. On the one hand, street violence was curtailed. On the other, Gülen was perceived by some in the military as being allied with forces on the right. His home was raided on September, and he was put under pressure to maintain a low public profile. He took a permanent leave of absence from his position as a preacher and did not speak publicly again until June 1986, when he inaugurated the Camlica mosque in Istanbul.

The period from 1980 to 1994 was nonetheless a fruitful one for Gülen and the Hizmet movement. During this time, he usually lived on the top floor of dormitories established in either Izmir or a suburb of Istanbul, or in an educational institute (Firat Egitim Merkezi, or FEM, which could be translated as the Euphrates Center for Education) located in Altunizade.[33] These aeries of Gülen came to be known as the "fifth floor," the top level of the building where Gülen held sessions for the new generation of young students, often graduates of the movement schools, who were inspired by his message and by the treatment and mentoring they had received from committed teachers there. In some of his writings, the balcony or terrace, or even his small room on the fifth floor, is memorialized by Gülen as a place where he received inspiration for future projects that needed to be undertaken. This time seemed to be a seminal or incubation period for the remarkable initiatives that were to follow. Gülen's reflections from this period are among the more mystical of his writings, describing the spiritual and visionary states that he experienced.[34]

In his study of Sufi elements in Gülen's life and thought, Heon Kim notes how the political environment in Turkey of the 1980s allowed a relative tolerance of Islam. Gülen's ties to prominent politicians, in particular to Turgut Özal, who was prime minister and president between 1983 and 1993, gave him and his affiliates some official protection.[35] Still, in 1986 he was detained and questioned by the authorities, then released. When Gülen made the pilgrimage to Mecca later that year, he was offered the opportunity to stay in the Muslim holy cities and thereby avoid problems in his homeland. He preferred to return, however, and quietly made his way home unofficially across the Syrian border.

The 1990s marked the opening of two major new horizons for Gülen and the Hizmet movement: expansion beyond the borders of Turkey, and dialogue beyond the frontiers of Islam.

Gülen by this time had become well known on the national Turkish stage because of the expanding network of dormitories and schools, his growing following, and its more visible media presence. He was interviewed by important journalists in the mainstream press, where his views were sought and disseminated. He met with politicians up to the level of prime ministers and heads of opposition parties. Scholars of politics characterize this relationship as mutually beneficial. Major Turkish politicians such as Özal, Bülent Evecit, and Tansu Ciller, by meeting with Gülen, established their religion-friendly credentials and thereby garnered broader public support. At the same time, these associations confirmed Gülen's support for the Turkish republic and the democratic electoral process, thereby avoiding suppression of the Hizmet movement and facilitating its expansion. However, both the Turkish political system and Turkey's civil organizations remained vulnerable to interference by the military.

It was also in the 1990s that Gülen initiated meetings with Turkish interreligious partners such as Patriarch Vartholemeos of the Fener Patriarchate of the Greek Orthodox Church in Turkey and David Aseo, the chief rabbi of Turkey's Jewish community. This dialogue initiative ultimately spread to such a high level that Gülen eventually traveled to meet Pope John Paul II in Rome in 1998.[36]

In 1989, the Berlin wall came down, symbolically bringing the Cold War to a close. In 1994, the Soviet Union offered its Central Asian satellite countries autonomy, and they became the "ex-Soviet" or "former Soviet" republics. Among these five countries, all had historically Muslim backgrounds. Four of them—Uzbekistan, Turkmenistan, Kazakhstan, and Kyrgyzstan— shared both history and language with the Turks. Tajikistan, where the majority language is Tajik, a dialect of Persian, has a significant minority Turkic population.

The first major international outreach began for Gülen when students and businessmen among his following accepted his suggestion to undertake exploratory visits to these new Central Asian republics. They came back with accounts of a crying need for development—most critically in the educational sphere. Thus, the first international "Turkish" schools were born.

Dialogue has become a watchword in recent years. Political theorists such as Samuel Huntington have drawn a negative map of an impending "clash" of civilizations—based on the diverse histories and religio-ethical visions of competing world blocks—but others, including many from the Muslim world, have proposed the need for a "dialogue" rather than a clash.[37] Among interfaith activists, the new framing of interreligious *dialogue* (as opposed to debate) began with increased ecumenism on the part of Christians, following initiatives by churches such as the 1962 Vatican II Council convened by Pope John XXIII.

Interreligious meetings, debates, and discussions go back many centuries, whether sponsored by rulers or spontaneously emerging through natural human encounters. However, systematic dialogue without a triumphalist objective of conversion or "scoring points" against another faith is generally a modern phenomenon. For Muslims in the Muslim world to take initiatives in this regard had been rare and even extraordinary until very recently.[38] We may thus see Gülen as a Muslim pioneer in interreligious dialogue.

This dialogue actually began not with those from other religious communities but among those within Turkey of various ideological stripes—especially the right versus left—that were set up on Gülen's initiative. In 1994, an organization known as the Journalists and Writers Foundation was established under Gülen's aegis to foster and support this sort of dialogue within Turkish society. The initial promotional meeting was held at Istanbul's Dedeman Hotel. There, Gülen appeared before the media, stating that "there will be no turning back from democracy either in Turkey or in the world." These activities become a platform of the movement program both in Turkey and abroad. Within Turkish society, meetings known as the Abant Platforms were initiated in 1998. Specifically inter-religious dialogue, which began in earnest after 1997, was to become more prominent within the context of the Hizmet movement's global activities.

Gülen also traveled more extensively in the early 1990s. In the fall of 1990, for example, he visited several European countries, beginning with the Netherlands. Cassettes of his lectures and sermons had been widely circulating among Turks residing abroad since the 1970s, and therefore many in these communities knew about Gülen and Hizmet. As he learned more about the conditions of Turkish workers who had settled in Europe, he advised them to "remain in Europe, become citizens, take part in elections, and send their children for higher education."[39] Gülen also visited Germany, Denmark, France, and Italy on this trip. In 1992, he traveled around the United States, visiting many states at the invitation of Turkish students at various educational institutions. In Ohio, he lectured in Columbus and Cleveland. In Texas, he went to Lubbock and Houston, visiting ex-prime minster Özal at the Houston hospital where he was being treated. Gülen finished in Colorado, Nevada, and California, departing for Australia in May 1992.[40]

Meanwhile, the political climate in Turkey was in flux. The tensions between religious and militantly secular factions in society still persisted. Opponents targeted Gülen as a public figure associated with an Islamic religious movement. On the basis of certain comments taken out of context or even inserted into his sermons and public interviews, charges were brought that his projects ultimately aimed at dismantling the secular state. Cassette recordings of some past sermons were broadcast on television that suggested he had the goal of an eventual Islamic state.[41] After percolating throughout the 1990s, the anti-Gülen campaign crested in 1999.

Gülen described the context of the initial charges against him in the following way:

> A newspaper columnist instigated action against me. It was one of my last sermons in Bornova. I talked about ash-Shariʿa al-Fitriya. God has two collections of laws: one, issuing from His Attribute of Speech, is the principles of religion, also called the Shariʿa. However, in the narrow sense they mean the political laws of Islam. The other, issuing from His Attributes of Will and Power, is the principles to govern the universe and life, "the natures of law" that are the subject-matter of sciences. In Islamic terminology, this is called Shariʿa al-Fitriya. Respecting these two collections of laws will make us prosperous in this world and the next, while opposing them will lead us to ruin. The Muslim world remained behind the West because it opposed Shariʿa al-Fitriya.
>
> I explained this matter to the congregation. I encouraged them to undertake scientific research and advancement. However, the next day a columnist wrote about this and claimed I had made propaganda for the Shariʿa, meaning the political laws of Islam.
>
> This matter was investigated officially by the public prosecutor's office. Later, this office understood its mistake and referred the case to the head office of the religious affairs department. This office said that no action was needed. But I guess, just as today some people are allergic to the word shariʿa, the martial law commander in Izmir was bothered by that word. He put me under surveillance. That situation was very difficult. Of course some people supported me, but it was very hard to make the military regime listen.[42]

These court cases persisted in various sessions and jurisdictions, based on excerpts taken out of context from old sermons and lectures, but nothing concrete ever emerged. Finally, after six years, a court in Ankara acquitted Gülen.[43] Even this judgment was appealed, and only in 2008 was the acquittal upheld.[44]

TOWARD A NEW MILLENNIUM

In 1997, a military crackdown know as the "soft coup" occurred in Turkey when the Kemalist military-bureaucratic establishment overthrew the democratically elected coalition government, which was led by the pro-Islamic Refah Party under the leadership of Erbakan.

Gülen had been in the United States at this time having heart surgery and consultation at the Mayo Clinic. He did not return to Turkey after 1999 but instead took up residence in Pennsylvania in a lodge located in a quiet rural environment. Meanwhile, many of the seeds sown in Turkey and internationally during the 1990s began to flower. Under senior leaders who had participated in the early cohorts of Gülen's students, projects such as schools continued to expand in Turkey and in diverse parts of the globe, and new initiatives in religious dialogue and cultural exchange were taking place. The network of Hizmet schools also continued to flourish, and, by the new millennium, additional dialogue centers had been established in major European cities, in the United States, and worldwide.

Hizmet's attention to religious tolerance and interfaith dialogue took on increased urgency after the September 11, 2001, terrorist attacks on the World Trade Center in New York and the Pentagon. By that time, the Hizmet movement had become established in many countries, either through the "Turkish" schools or by means of the activities of cultural dialogue associations. In the United States alone, such centers and institutions had been quietly growing since 1997. The role of moderate Islamic organizations ready to dialogue and contribute in global contexts and plural societies found increased receptivity and even urgency, both in the West and in the Muslim world.

In recent years, as the Hizmet movement continues to grow and expand its global influence, Gülen has become increasingly well known outside of Turkey. Inside Turkey, with the victories of the Justice and Development Party (AKP) under Recep Tayyip Erdoğan in the 2002 and subsequent elections, Islamic movements were initially seen as political allies, and the expectation was that Hizmet would continue to achieve prominence in public life. However, beginning in 2013, an increasing rift became apparent between the leadership of Erdoğan's party and a number of groups and lobbies within the country, most notably the followers of Gülen, who were accused of infiltrating various institutions such as the police force and the judiciary. It remains to be seen what the local and global implications of this political struggle for the Hizmet movement will be.

A DAY IN THE LIFE OF GÜLEN

In Pennsylvania, Gülen lives near the Pocono Mountains in a building that is reminiscent of a country house or hunting lodge; it is called the Golden Generation Worship and Retreat Center.[45] It is modestly but tastefully decorated, and Gülen is known for his aesthetic sense and particularity about order and cleanliness. Even in his autobiographical statement about his school days, Gülen noted that:

> I was very careful about my dress. My clothes were very clean and a little expensive for that time. Sometimes I would be hungry for days, but I never wore pants that were not pressed or shoes that were not polished. When I could not find an iron, I would put my pants under the bed so that they would look pressed.[46]

Gülen does not live in isolation. A number of his students as well as a Turkish physician and his family reside in small cabins scattered around the property that hosts those fortunate enough to have the favor of personal interviews. The upper floor of the main building contains a prayer room with a balcony available for women visitors to join in the prayers and attend lectures.

Gülen's own training was in a madrasa setting, and his writings reflect the Ottoman Turkish intellectual tradition. For most of the generation of businessmen and activists following Gülen in the 1970s and 1980s, this knowledge seemed to lie in a remote past. Today, however, we see a revival of this classical learning tradition at the core of the Gülen movement through the education of a special group of students selected by senior mentors. These students, generally Turkish graduate students in theology with a good command of Arabic, study in this intimate residential setting with Gülen himself. This tradition began in the 1970s, was interrupted in 1980, and was reinstituted in 1985.[47] It is estimated that seven or eight students are currently chosen each year to join this program.[48]

One scholar connects this style of teaching with early Islamic learning by a group of the Prophet's companions known as the Ahl al-Suffa:

> Gülen has been consistently providing personal tutelage over the last two decades to hundreds of theology graduate students. Students gain admission to Gülen's informal school by passing a rigorous exam in Islamic sciences and Arabic. Thereafter extensive study and an ascetic lifestyle await them. Students can remain as long as they wish, some for even as long as ten years. Gülen has been known to have had up to 40 students at times, although given his ill-health this number has dropped to 15 in recent years. In their lifestyle, daily programme and efforts post "graduation" these students resemble the first *Suffa* Companions.[49]

According to one interviewee who has passed through this system, first-year students simply listen to instruction and may achieve results through peer learning. In subsequent years, they are increasingly permitted to participate in the lessons and to ask direct questions. The curriculum includes heavy tomes of Hanafi jurisprudence (*fiqh*) such as a fourteen-volume commentary (*sharh*) on al-Tirmidhi by the contemporary Indian scholar Mubarakpuri,[50] or the twenty-five-volume work *'Umdat al-Qari* of al-Ayni. In addition, at least one work of classical Sufism by an author such as al-Muhasibi or al-Qushayri is covered each year.[51]

Although Gülen avoids traveling and public speaking today, he regularly communicates with his affiliates through broadcast messages and transcripts of his lectures and discourses available on various websites.[52] A specific website, Herkul.org, is a source for ongoing selections from Gülen's discourses (*sohbets*) and other lectures. Excerpts from his talks and sermons, past and present, have been edited and compiled, leading to an extensive and growing body of literature in print as well as to many sources archived in video and audio format. A translation bureau in Istanbul ensures that versions become available in English and other major world languages to meet the growing interest in Gülen's thought.

Gülen personally follows a simple and consistent daily schedule. As described by A. Said Tuncpinar, he begins each day by performing the *tahajjud*, a prayer that pious Muslims undertake between midnight and the compulsory dawn prayer. He follows this with devotions consisting of reciting litanies from the collection of prayers known as *Al-Qulub al-Daria*.[53]

At dawn, he performs the *fajr* prayer, and then he and his students communally recite the *tesbihat,* a selection of pious litanies. He then listens to his students' readings of either the *Risale-e Nur* or selections from his own work on Sufism, *Emerald Hills of the Heart.*

After taking his breakfast, he works with his students, providing an exegesis of passages from basic classical Islamic religious texts, then he rests in his room until the noon prayer. Following the noon prayer and recitation of *tesbihat,* Gülen has lunch and engages in conversation with whomever joins or visits him that day. Then he works on books and articles in his private room.

The afternoon (*'asr*) prayer is again followed by *tesbihat.* At this point, Gülen will give a conversational instruction (*sohbet*) that is attended by students and any guests. On doctor's instructions, he follows this with twenty minutes of treadmill exercise.

Up until the sunset (*maghrib*) prayer, Gülen may perform communal devotions with others. After prayer and dinner followed by tea, he spends time with associates. Following the night (*'isha*) prayer, he retires, though he is known to sleep little.[54]

Thus concludes an overview of Gülen's life up to the present. It is an unlikely voyage from a small Turkish hamlet to training in the classical Islamic tradition, a career in preaching and lecturing, and finally to a visionary spiritual leader whose teachings have inspired a broad and diverse section of the modern Turkish public to embark on altruistic paths of service as well as effective media strategies to garner support and mold opinion on many fronts.

NOTES

1. This date is cited by Rainer Hermann, "Fethullah Gülen—eine muslimische Alternative zur Refah-Partei?" *Orient* 37, no. 4 (1996), and the article "Fethullah Gülen: His Remarkable Achievement," *Fountain Magazine* [a Hizmet publication] 23 (1998), gives the birthdate as April 1938. However, the correspondence of age with events in *Küçük Dunyam* seems to better match the 1941 date.

2. "1941–1959 Hayat Kronolojisi," http://tr.fgulen.com/content/view/3502/5/ (accessed Aug. 24, 2009).

3. *Küçük Dunyam* was serialized in 1992 and published in book form for the first time in 1995. The edition cited in this chapter is Latif Erdoğan, *Küçük Dunyam* (Istanbul: Ufuk Kitap, 2006); translations are either from Gülen websites (anonymous) or, in some cases, my own.

4. Erdoğan, *Küçük Dunyam*, 36–37.

5. Ibid., 40.

6. Ibid., 29.

7. Heon Kim, "The Nature and Role of Sufism in Contemporary Islam: A Case Study of the Life, Thought and Teachings of Fethullah Gülen" (Ph.D. diss. in Religion, Temple University, 2008), 119.

8. Ibid.

9. Zeki Saritoprak and Sidney Griffith, "Fethullah Gülen and 'the People of the Book': A Voice from Turkey for Interfaith Dialogue," *Muslim World* 95, no. 3 (2005): 331.

10. Erdoğan, *Küçük Dunyam*, 43.

11. Details of Bektaş's life may be found in the article by M. Fatih Turan, "Osman Bektaş Hocaefendi'nin Vefat Yıldönümü," *Yeni Ümit* (July 2007): 77. Reproduced with added photographs at http://tr.fgulen.com/content/view/14589 /13/ (accessed Aug. 18, 2009).

12. Erdoğan, *Küçük Dunyam*, 47.

13. Kim, "Nature and Role of Sufism in Contemporary Islam," 124.

14. Faruk Mercan, *Fethullah Gülen* (Istanbul: Doğan Kitap, 2006), 47; Erdoğan, *Küçük Dunyam*, 49.

15. Mercan, *Fethullah Gülen*, 42; Erdoğan, *Küçük Dunyam*, 52.

16. Mercan, *Fethullah Gülen*, 47.

17. Ibid., 49–50.

18. Interview with Barbaros Kocakurt, Yamanlar Dormitory, Izmir, Dec. 18, 2007.

19. Esra G. Özyürek, "'Feeling Tells Better Than Language': Emotional Expression and Gender Hierarchy in the Sermons of Fethullah Gülen Hocaefendi," *New Perspectives on Turkey* 16 (July 1997): 41–51.

20. As discussed in ibid.

21. Summary from Fethullah Gülen, *My Little World,* interviewed by Latif Erdoğan at http://en.fgulen.com/fethullah-gulen-biography/755-edirne-kirklareli-and-finally-izmir (accessed May 17, 2014).

22. Fethullah Gülen, *Sonsuz Nur* [Infinite Light] (Izmir: Nil, 1999). An English version is *The Messenger of God Muhammad: An Analysis of the Prophet's Life* (Somerset, N.J.: The Light, 2005).

23. Primarily from *Al-Jawshan al-Kabir* (Somerset, N.J.: The Light, 2006).

24. Interview with Ismail Büyükçelebi, Chicago, Apr. 16, 2007. He belongs to the early generation of movement intellectuals and activists. He holds a Ph.D. in Islamic jurisprudence (*fiqh*) and has worked for *Zaman* newspaper. A number of his books on Islam have been published by Hizmet presses.

25. At that point, openly practicing Islam in Turkey was considered subversive.

26. This incident is discussed in more detail in Kim, "Nature and Role of Sufism in Contemporary Islam," 164–65. It is also recounted in the section "Berzahi Tablolar" in Fethullah Gülen, *Varlığin Metafizik Boyutu* (Izmir: Nil, 1998), http://tr.fgulen.com/content/view/1347/150/ (accessed Aug. 15, 2009).

27. A further description of the early camp is found in Mercan, *Fethullah Gülen*, 49–52.

28. On this, see Hakan Yavuz, *Islamic Political Identity in Turkey* (New York: Oxford University Press, 2005), 183. Erdoğan, *Küçük Dunyam*, 134–45, provides details on Gülen's prison experiences at this time.

29. Mercan, *Fethullah Gülen*, 66.

30. The English-language version is called *The Fountain Magazine*.

31. Fethullah Gülen, *Truth through Colors* (Izmir: Nil, 1992). In the Turkish version, *Renklerin Diliyle* (Istanbul: Nil, 2004), 5, the caption expresses that "our pain is the wretchedness of the masses." This may evidence a shift in focus from Gülen's original to his translator's understanding of the message of the Hizmet movement.

32. Fethullah Gülen, "Towards the Lost Paradise," original in *Sızıntı* 7 (Mar. 1985).

33. Kim, "Nature and Role of Sufism in Contemporary Islam," 158.

34. Fethullah Gülen, *Işığın Göründüğü Ufuk* [The Horizon of Light] (Istanbul: Nil, 2003), 196–210. This was described by Gülen in *Sızıntı* 19 (Aug. 1997), 223.

35. Kim, "Nature and Role of Sufism in Contemporary Islam," 133. A privatization of education also occurred in 1983. The initial circles of devoted affiliates spread out to additional areas within Turkey and duplicated the earlier successes in founding dormitories, lighthouses, and schools.

36. See Ali Unal and Alphonse Williams, eds., *Advocate of Dialogue: Fethullah Gülen* (Fairfax, N.J.: The Fountain, 2001).

37. In an influential *Foreign Affairs* article and then in a book, *The Clash of Civilizations and the Remaking of World Order* (New York: Simon and Schuster, 1996), political scientist Samuel P. Huntington posed this influential yet controversial theory of impending conflicts. Muslims, in particular, felt that this thesis reinforced the idea of Islam as a threat to the West, and former Iranian president Mohammad Khatami introduced the idea of "Dialogue Among Civilizations," which the United Nations General Assembly adopted as an initiative.

38. Most notably, the Common Word initiative of 2007 in which a broad coalition of Muslim religious leaders invited their Christian counterparts to engage in constructive interfaith dialogue.

39. Mercan, *Fethullah Gülen*, 133–34.

40. Ibid., 142.

41. For more details, see Filiz Baskan, "The Political Economy of Islamic Finance in Turkey: The Role of Fethullah Gülen and Asya Finans," in *The Politics of Islamic Finance,* edited by Clement M. Henry and Rodney Wilson (Edinburgh: Edinburgh University Press, 2004), 236.

42. Nuriye Akman, *Sabah* daily, Jan. 23–30, 1995. Translated excerpts are available at http://en.fgulen.com/fethullah-gulen-biography/758-being-pursued (accessed May 17, 2014).

43. "Gülen Acquitted of Trying to Overthrow Secular Government," *Turkish Daily News,* May 6, 2006.

44. "Court of Appeals Clears Gülen of all Allegations," *Today's Zaman*, June 26, 2008.

45. Kim, "Nature and Role of Sufism in Contemporary Islam," 162.

46. Erdoğan, *Küçük Dunyam*, 44.

47. Ahmet Kurucan, "Introduction," in F. Gülen, *Fasıldan Fasıla* 1 (Izmir: Nil Yayinlari, 1995), xxiii.

48. Interview with Cemal Türk, Istanbul, July 24, 2005.

49. Rifat Atay, "Reviving the Suffa Tradition," in *Muslim World in Transition: Contributions of the Gülen Movement*, edited by Ihsan Yilmaz, 459–72 (London: Leeds University Metropolitan Press, 2007).

50. Interview with Enes Ergene, Istanbul, July 23, 2005.

51. Interview with Cemal Türk. A list of books studied by Gülen and his students is provided in Ibrahim Canan, *Fethullah Gülen'in Sünnet Anlayışı*, (Istanbul: Ufuk Kitap, 2007), 78–83.

52. See, for example, the archive in English at http://en.fgulen.com/ (accessed May 17, 2014) and http://fgulen.com/en/press/news with translations of weekly sermons; see http://fgulen.com/tr/ for the Turkish version. Multiple other languages are also available.

53. This is a summarized collection of prayers and litanies from those compiled by an Ottoman Naqshbandi shaykh, Ziyaettin Gumushanevi (d. 1893) in his *Majmu'at al-Ahzab*. The *Jawshan* is a prayer that is very popular among Hizmet movement affiliates. Gülen alerts to its sacrality and importance, pointing out that it was used by great Muslim saints such as al-Ghazali and Nursi. Gülen, "Cevşen hâlisâne yapılmış bir duadır," *Zaman*, Oct. 26, 2007. Cited in Kim, "Nature and Role of Sufism in Contemporary Islam," 151–52. An English translation by Nursi devotee Shukran Vahide is available online at http://www.rso.wmich.edu/mda /jawsan/index.htm (accessed Aug. 17, 2009). For further details on *Jawshan*, see Lucinda Allen Mosher, "The Marrow of Worship and the Moral Vision: Said Nursi and Supplication," in *Islam at the Crossroads,* edited by M. Abu-Rabi' (Albany: State University of New York Press, 2003), 182.

54. A. Said Tuncpinar, "Hocaefendi'de İsrafa Karşı Tavır," *Herkul*, Mar. 12, 2007, http://tr.fgulen.com/content/view/13364/12/ (accessed Aug. 15, 2009).

THREE

The Institutions and Discourses of Hizmet, and Their Discontents

Jeremy F. Walton

HIZMET, CIVIL SOCIETY, AND THE DILEMMAS OF THE TURKISH PUBLIC SPHERE

AS HE GATHERED HIS THOUGHTS, Cemal Bey,[1] a member of the organizing committee of the Journalists and Writers Foundation (Gazeteciler ve Yazarlar Vakfı; GYV), the flagship Hizmet civil society organization in Turkey, paused to offer me a dried apricot, a delicacy from the southeastern Turkish city of Malatya. He then continued to articulate a subtle contrast between Ottoman and contemporary models of the public sphere [*kamusal alanı*]. In his estimation, the public sphere today has become a space of mere transit [*geçiş*] from home to work, whereas the Ottoman public sphere was a space of dwelling and social plenitude. Drawing on this contrast, Cemal Bey

---

It is difficult, if not impossible, to acquire an instant understanding of Hizmet if those who define it and those who ask questions about it bring only conventional "Western" concepts of societal tolerance and dialogue to the inquiry. This is not because Hizmet's main inspirer, Fethullah Gülen, and his colleagues bring obscure philosophy to bear on its actions. Anything but that. Thousands of people imbued with the philosophy and traditions of Hizmet are happy to point to institutions to which it has given rise and the discourse it fashions and favors. Complications arise simply because such creations are unfamiliar: they embody and articulate ideas rooted in Islam, the Qur'an, and Sufi mysticism. Jeremy Walton, a research fellow in the CETREN Transregional Network at Georg August University of Göttingen, here provides context and definition to the subject. His writing reflects first-hand experiences that, as a scholar, he has enjoyed with Hizmet and with the texts that inform Gülen—and that Gülen, in turn, expounds. As a bonus, Walton also shines light on more current events, since the Erdoğan government has exerted particular pressure on the movement. Tolerance and dialogue, as described here, may be in short supply but are needed more than ever in contemporary Turkey.

then outlined the relationship between institutional organization and philanthropy that subtends the activities of both the GYV and Fethullah Gülen's Hizmet movement in their aspiration to revivify the public sphere.

Cemal Bey's nostalgia for the Ottoman public sphere and his criticism of contemporary publicity offered key insights into the institutional culture and activism of Hizmet. He went on to explain that, from Hizmet's perspective, the institutions of civil society (*sivil toplum*), in particular the pious foundation (*vakıf*), are uniquely suited to the articulation of a public Islam oriented toward charitable good works on both a local and a global scale. As I have argued at length elsewhere, this valorization of civil society as a domain of authentic piety and disinterested philanthropy—what I have described as the "civil society effect"—is deeply characteristic of Muslim civil society organizations in Turkey generally.[2] For Hizmet representatives such as Cemal Bey, the public sphere should be a space that is simultaneously vivacious, a Muslim analogue of Jane Jacobs's urban utopia, and utterly separate from the intrusive effects of the Turkish state and its politics.[3]

In this chapter, I adumbrate and analyze the discursive traditions, moral disciplines, and institutions of Hizmet in Turkey with reference to debates over the public sphere, civil society, and politics on the part of both Hizmet actors and its critics. My presentation, which draws on ethnographic research with Hizmet organizations—especially the GYV—as well as other Turkish Muslim nongovernmental organizations, proceeds in two broad sections. In the first half of the chapter, I examine the relationship between Gülen's moral-theological arguments and the institutional culture of Hizmet, with particular emphasis on the cardinal virtues of *müspet hareket* (positive action), *hizmet* (service), *hoşgörü* (tolerance), and *diyalog* (dialogue). Following this, I summarize, analyze, and adjudicate among debates over the various categories and names that are applied to Hizmet, both by Hizmet actors themselves and by commentators in the Turkish media and public sphere at large.

Before proceeding, however, a cautionary note is necessary. As this volume goes to press, Hizmet is embroiled in an ongoing political dispute in Turkey, one that has pitted it against its erstwhile political allies, the governing Justice and Development Party (Adalet ve Kalkınma Partisi; AKP) and Turkey's powerful president (and former prime minister) Recep Tayyip Erdoğan, in particular. Although the details of this controversy are beyond my purview here,[4] the intense politicization of Hizmet within Turkey gestures directly to the precariousness of Hizmet actors' attempts to distinguish strictly between philanthropy within the sphere of civil society and "politics" within the orbit of the state. In light of this politicization, the institutional cultures and discursive practices of Hizmet defy the classic anthropological description of culture as a distinct, coherent, and self-contained domain of meaning and activity.[5] On the contrary, as anthropologist Talal Asad has vigorously argued, the institutions and discourses of religion in the contemporary world are inseparable from, and conditioned by, the relationship *between* religion and the dynamics of the public sphere and the state.[6] Therefore, in what follows, I explicitly foreground the relationship between Hizmet's moral-theological disciplines and institutional cultures, on the one hand, and broader public, political debates that aim to define, and often to interrogate, these disciplines and cultures, on the other.

MORAL PHILOSOPHY AND INSTITUTIONAL CULTURE

Hizmet institutions, both in Turkey and across the globe, are remarkably diverse—they include a variety of NGOs and charities, private businesses, primary, secondary, and postsecondary schools, publishing houses, and mass media outlets.[7] Gülen's theology constitutes the unifying bond among these disparate sites and institutions. Therefore, an examination of the ethical principles that animate Gülen's theology and moral philosophy is key to comprehending Hizmet's institutional culture.

One noteworthy ethical precept characteristic of Hizmet is that of *müspet hareket,* or positive action. The Ottoman-Turkish theologian Bediüzzaman Said Nursi (1877–1960)—Gülen's principal forebear and source of inspiration—first articulated the concept of *müspet,* which is particularly favored by Turkey's Nur community.[8] Nursi distinguished between positive and negative actions in his final epistle: "Our duty is to act positively; it is not to act negatively. It is only to serve belief in accordance with Divine pleasure; it is not to meddle in God's business. We are charged with responding with patience and thanks to all the difficulties we may encounter in this positive service of belief which results in the preservation of public order and security."[9] Aladdin Basar, a contemporary interpreter of Nursi, illustrates the distinction between positive and negative actions with a practical example: "If you build a house on what was empty ground and then offer it for habitation, that is a positive act. But if you destroy it and make it uninhabitable, it would be negative."[10]

In a panoramic sense, a pious life for members of the Nur community and the Hizmet movement entails the pursuit of positive, altruistic actions, while immorality consists of self-interested, negative actions (*menfi hareketler*). Due to its social orientation—positive actions not only are in keeping with the imperatives of pious worship (*ibadet*) but also provide the fundament for proper relationships among Muslims and humankind at large (*muamele; muamalat*)—the principle of *müspet* is also a means to and form of service, *hizmet*. The principles of *müspet* and *hizmet* necessarily imply each other because they both presuppose and entail the absence of self-interest. In order for an action to qualify as positive, not only its end or object but also its means and the intention with which it is performed must exhibit an absolute lack of self-interest. As Nursi argued, positive action is a means both to living "in accordance with Divine pleasure" and to assuring a harmonious, stable social order in this world—the reciprocal duality of worship (*ibadet*) ands social relationships (*muamele*). As an aspect of one's duty to God as a Muslim, *müspet* is an apical theological-ethical principle for members of Hizmet; in relation to one's duty to other human beings, *müspet* is a comprehensive socio-ethical imperative. *Hizmet*, as service both to God and to other human beings, encompasses both aspects of *müspet*.

Zain Abdullah, an anthropologist who has conducted research among West African Muslim immigrants residing in the New York neighborhood of Harlem, has analyzed the concept of *hizmet* (which, in the Senegalese language of Wolof, is transliterated from the Arabic as *khidma*) among the followers of the Muridiyya Sufi order in an analogous fashion. Although Murids, as followers of Senegalese Cheikh Amadou Bamba are known, have no direct connection to the Hizmet movement, Abdullah's rendering of *khidma* captures the spirit of Gülen's enthusiasts as well: "*Khidma* encompasses the total round of one's activities, both secular and religious, blurring any distinctions between them, since *its focus is to transform all actions into divine service*."[11] Echoes of the principle of *müspet* are strong in this quotation: *hizmet* (*khidma*) demands the integration of all actions in accordance with a comprehensive, altruistic piety oriented toward the fulfillment of divine service in this world. Here, we can also perceive an affinity between *hizmet* and Gülen's reflections on the theological principle of *taqwa* (mindfulness or piety). In his discussion of *taqwa*, Gülen writes: "A servant (of God) must ... ascribe all material and spiritual accomplishments to God; not consider himself or herself as superior to anyone else; not pursue anything other than God and His pleasure."[12]

In the summer of 2010, during a research trip to Turkey, I engaged in an illuminating conversation with several members of the GYV that exemplified the interrelationship between *müspet* and *hizmet*. Over lunch in the foundation offices, I asked my friends to evaluate the recent events surrounding the Turkish ship Mavi Marmara and the Humanitarian Relief Foundation (IHH) flotilla to the Gaza Strip.[13] One of my fellow diners immediately pointed out that, regardless of the motivations of the individual activists on the flotilla or the administration of the IHH, the Mavi Marmara incident had resulted in the opening of the Rafah border crossing between Egypt and Gaza, an undeniable success. Cemal Bey, whom we have already encountered above, responded with an assertion of the principle of *müspet*. Although he agreed that the opening of the border crossing was a positive outcome, he questioned the motivations of the activists. In his view, anyone genuinely devoted to "service" (*hizmet*) would necessarily eschew the self-promotion that characterized the Mavi Marmara activists. In other words, Cemal Bey argued that the ends of an action are not the only criterion of its ethical status—in order to determine this, one must also examine the intentions of the actors. By this standard, the Mavi Marmara event was not clearly an instance of *müspet*; indeed, it might even qualify as an instance of self-interested action, *menfi hareket*. And if an action is self-interested, it also fails the criteria of service, *hizmet*.

As moral-theological principles, *müspet* and *hizmet* draw directly on a discursive tradition of ethical reasoning that extends back to the basic roots of Islam—the Qur'an and the Sunna (the authoritative example of the Prophet Muhammad, as recorded in the *ahadith,* the Prophetic traditions). Gülen interprets these and many other key concepts through the prism of Sufi theology, as exemplified in his influential book, *Emerald Hills of the Heart*. Crucially, however, *müspet* and *hizmet* are also the ground on which Gülen erects a moral philosophy that bridges and synthesizes Islamic and liberal-democratic traditions of reasoning. The key concepts of this synthesis are tolerance (*hoşgörü*) and dialogue (*diyalog*), each of which is rooted in the ethical dispensation of *müspet* and *hizmet*.

Gülen and Hizmet conceptualize dialogue as an ineluctable means to the desired end of societal tolerance. This means/end relationship suffuses Gülen's writings—take, for instance, the following passage: "At a time when we are in great need of tolerance, with the grace of God, every sector of society will stand up for tolerance and dialogue, and the good things that come from this will spread faster than ever hoped for in all directions."[14] As an ethical practice, dialogue demands the displacement of one's own interests and desires in order to comprehend those of another; in this respect, dialogue fits the definition of positive, altruistic action. For Hizmet, dialogue is not merely a political project or gesture toward religious or cultural pluralism—it is an ethical act in its own right that performs a double service, both to one's specific partner in dialogue and toward the ideal of altruism that Gülen's writings incessantly stress.

The ideal of tolerance and practice of dialogue are clear demonstrations of the synthesis between Islamic and liberal-democratic traditions that Gülen and Hizmet forge. Recently, critical political philosophers such as Wendy Brown have interrogated the genealogy and limits of tolerance as a principle of liberal governance.[15] As my analysis of the dense relationship among *müspet, hizmet,* tolerance, and dialogue demonstrates, however, Gülen's concepts of tolerance and dialogue cannot be reduced to a simple appropriation of liberal ideals. Indeed, his writings constantly stress that Islam is by definition a religion of tolerance, and, at least from his perspective, secular modernity rather then religion is the principal antagonist of tolerance in the contemporary world. Nowhere is this argument more explicit than in a chapter of Gülen's book *Toward a Global Civilization of Love and Tolerance,* titled "Islam—A Religion of Tolerance." Gülen draws on Qur'anic verses, the example of the Prophet Muhammad (Sunna), and the works of Sufi theologians such as Rumi, Yunus Emre, Ahmed Yesevi, and Said Nursi in order to establish the essential relationship between Islam and tolerance as an ethical virtue.[16] Although his aim in this chapter is to interrogate and reject the association between Islam and terrorism and, consequently, to render Islam commensurable with contemporary liberalism, all of his sources and precedents stem directly from a well-established Islamic discursive tradition.

Taken together, the assemblage of theological and moral principles of *müspet, hizmet,* tolerance, and dialogue defines the distinctive institutional culture of Hizmet. It is important to keep in mind, however, that Hizmet organizations are not only avatars of Gülen's ethical and theological arguments but also professional office spaces in their own right. The GYV, for example, is housed in a large, modern office building in the neighborhood of Altunizade on the Asian side of Istanbul; in addition to conference salons and rooms equipped with state-of-the-art audio-visual equipment, the foundation headquarters includes the cubicles and individual offices characteristic of any corporate or NGO office setting. Yet within this familiar office environment, the theological and moral sensibilities of Hizmet suffuse interpersonal interactions and the aesthetics of the space. Over the many hours and days that I spent at the GYV, I frequently witnessed the distinctive respect and sincerity (*samimiyet; ikhlas*) that mediates the more hierarchical, vertical relationships within the organization—this sincerity is a reflection of *müspet* and its denigration of self-interest, as well as a key moral end of Sufi theology that Gülen stresses in his writings.[17] A noteworthy detail of the symposium room of the GYV is the ring of divan-style sofas that line the walls; these sofas are both a metaphor and a means for the ethic of sincerity that undergirds Hizmet. Individuals seated on divans can only address one another in an intimate, face-to-face manner, and the conversation among them is necessarily a conversation among spatial equals, as everyone sits at the same low level.

Divan-style sofas, which I encountered at nearly all of the Hizmet institutions I visited, point to a more general facet of the aesthetic culture of Hizmet, which I have analyzed at length elsewhere: Neo-Ottomanism.[18] We have already encountered the premium that Hizmet actors place on the Ottoman era in Cemal Bey's contrast between Ottoman and contemporary models of the public sphere. As his valorization of the Ottoman public sphere suggests, Neo-Ottomanism—the recuperation of Ottoman ideals and practices to address the contemporary age—is not just a matter of aesthetics. Hizmet's image of interreligious pluralism, for instance, draws directly on the Ottoman *millet* (community; nation) system, which organized relations among distinct religious communities during the Ottoman era. More generally, Gülen frequently praises the Ottoman synthesis of piety and tolerance; as he writes, "[B]eing tolerant does not mean foregoing the traditions that come from our religion, or our nation, or our history; tolerance is something that has always existed. The Ottomans were faithful both to their religion and to other values, and, at the same time, they were a great nation that could get along with other world states."[19] Beyond such sweeping historical and political judgments, Neo-Ottomanism is also evident in the quotidian details of the institutional spaces that Hizmet inhabits. In addition to divan-style couches—a distinctive appropriation of Ottoman interior design to contemporary ends—another prominent Neo-Ottoman motif that frequently adorns Hizmet institutions is *ebru sanatı* (marbled watercolor painting). *Ebru* is the preeminent artistic genre in Hizmet spaces, and Hizmet actors eulogize its link with the Ottoman era. Finally, Neo-Ottomanism functions as a comprehensive model of urban space in Istanbul, which idealizes and aspires to reinvigorate the piety and religious pluralism of the Ottoman era.

In nearly all of my discussions with Hizmet activists, the topic of politics has loomed silently, conspicuous due to its relative absence. Hizmet representatives consistently and forcefully deny that they are engaged in "politics" (*siyaset*). From their point of view, philanthropy and piety within the sphere of civil society are incompatible with politics, understood as the domain of the state, military, political parties, and their affiliated actors. This insistence on a firewall between civil society and "politics" is precisely what I have elsewhere identified as the "civil society effect." Although Hizmet undeniably maintains strong relationships with state actors and politicians, both in Turkey and elsewhere—in particular, the bond between Hizmet and the governing AKP was quite strong prior to their recent friction—Hizmet affiliates typically characterize these relationships as a form of lobbying that befits third-sector organizations. And while critical political theorists have argued that discourses of tolerance are deeply political, in that they embody the power of liberal governance, advocates of tolerance such as Hizmet rarely view their own practices as "political." Nevertheless, Hizmet actors cannot ignore the pervasive politicization of Gülen and his enthusiasts in Turkey. At a slightly earlier moment, Hizmet was lumped together with myriad other Turkish Muslim communities and political actors as part of an anti-Kemalist,[20] anti-modernist monolith. More recently, the acrimony between President Erdoğan and Hizmet, which achieved a climax with the December 17, 2013, corruption inquiry, has witnessed the unanticipated politicization of Hizmet in relation to the AKP, the principal heir to Turkey's Islamist political movement. Erdoğan has gone so far as to accuse Hizmet of constituting a "parallel state" (*paralel devlet*) within the Turkish state bureaucracy.

Against this deeply politicized backdrop, public debate over the proper categorization of Hizmet quickly becomes heated. Detractors of Gülen often seek to describe Hizmet enthusiasts in terms that deny them a legitimate role within contemporary Turkish society. Hizmet representatives therefore tread lightly when naming themselves—in doing so, they respond to a broad field of public, political debate over what, exactly, Hizmet is. In this section, I attempt to navigate a course through these troubled political and categorical waters. I devote attention to a variety of categories that frequently apply to Hizmet, including "Sufi brotherhood" (*tarikat*), "community" (*cemaat*), and "movement" (*hareket*), in order to examine the relationship among these categories and the theological and ethical concerns that I

addressed in the previous section. Following this, I discuss Hizmet's understanding of the charitable foundation (*vakıf*) as both a contemporary civil
society institution and a traditional mode of philanthropy within Islam.

Among Turkey's Kemalists, Hizmet is often thought of as a Sufi brotherhood, or *tarikat* (Arabic: *tariqa*), akin to such groups as the Naqshbandi and
Mevlevi Sufi orders. However, despite Gülen's recapitulation of Sufi theological precedents and concepts, the category of *tarikat* is entirely inappropriate to the sociological and institutional forms of Hizmet. Ali Bulaç, a
prominent journalist and Muslim thinker, decisively made this point several
years ago when he classified Hizmet as a characteristically modern, urban
community (*cemaat*).[21] Bulaç argues that the categories of *tarikat* and
cemaat are sociologically and historically incompatible: the first emerged in
a broadly agrarian, preindustrial society, whereas the second is characteristic
of urban modernity and its modes of social organization. As a social and
institutional form, a *tarikat* is defined above all by the hierarchical relationship between a shaykh (*şeyh*) and his followers, whereas a *cemaat* is a relatively horizontal sociological entity defined by a shared object or cause
(in the case of Hizmet, the aim of achieving a superior Islam through
ethical probity and philanthropy). Seen in this light, Gülen is better understood as a moral philosopher and theologian than as a shaykh addressing his
disciples.

Unsurprisingly, Hizmet affiliates do not use the term *tarikat* to refer to
themselves; the category is solely an ideological bludgeon for skeptics and
antagonists of the movement. The political use of *tarikat* rests on a simple
ideological arithmetic: the Turkish state and Turkish society are (or at least
should be) modern; *tarikats* are the quintessence of a non-modern social
order; therefore, qua *tarikat*, Hizmet has no legitimate role in contemporary
Turkish life. An exemplary instance of the political use of *tarikat* (rendered
here as "Islamist brotherhood") can be found in an editorial against the
Turkish constitutional referendum, which passed with some 58 percent of
the vote on September 12, 2010. The author of the editorial fulminates over
the specter of Islamist democracy unseating Kemalist governance in Turkey
and comments on Hizmet in this context, decrying "the level of infiltration
of the Islamist brotherhood, the 'Gulen Community,' into state institutions."[22] The description of Gülen's devotees as an "Islamist brotherhood"
exemplifies Kemalist anxiety: as an anti-modern *tarikat*, Hizmet "infiltrates"
the sacred domains of the Turkish state. This paranoid logic is simple. The
denial of modernity to Gülen and his supporters justifies their unilateral

exclusion from the political process and prospectively categorizes Hizmet as *irtica,* reactionary and divisive. One of the more fascinating aspects of the recent dispute between the AKP and Hizmet is the manner in which Erdoğan has appropriated and inhabited this paranoid discourse to inveigh against Hizmet. As a devout Muslim, Erdoğan does not criticize Hizmet for its piety, but his contention that Gülen's devotees have "infiltrated" the state bureaucracy in order to create a "parallel state" precisely replicates earlier Kemalist panic.

In contrast to the category of *tarikat,* the categories of *cemaat* (community) and *hareket* (movement) are multivalent, irreducible to their political deployments. Furthermore, Hizmet enthusiasts often apply both categories to themselves, a fact that grants each term a reflexive legitimacy that absolutely does not hold for the category of *tarikat.* Again following Ali Bulaç, I argue that the concept of *cemaat* effectively describes the voluntaristic nature of Hizmet (as well as the Nur community and other urban Mulsim groups in contemporary Turkey): religious communities,or *cemaatler,* come into being on the basis of the active initiative of their members, who coalesce initially as strangers living in the relatively anonymous social environment of the contemporary city. The concept of *hareket,* in contrast, underscores the relationship between the ethos of Hizmet and its aims: as a "movement," Hizmet marshals its resources toward the ends of pious philanthropy, interreligious tolerance, and a public vision of Sunni Turkish Islam.

Hizmet actors vigorously debate the virtues and shortcomings of *cemaat* and *hareket* as categories applicable to their activities and identity. In particular, I recall a lively discussion that emerged after my own presentation of a rudimentary version of this essay (in Turkish) at the GYV in the summer of 2010. Throughout my presentation, I consistently referred to Hizmet as a *cemaat* rather than a *hareket,* but I soon discovered that my audience disagreed with this preference. Ekrem Bey, a radio journalist and employee of the foundation, disputed my use of *cemaat* and argued that *hareket* more accurately captures the sociological and political plurality of Hizmet. For him, the category of *cemaat* implied a homogeneity that is impossible for a group of Hizmet's global scope.

Ekrem Bey illustrated this with an anecdote. Once, while traveling with several other Hizmet activists in Kiev, he stayed with a Ukrainian Catholic man who had been trained in one of Hizmet's Turkish Schools [*Türk Okulları*]. On the night of his arrival, the hour for the nighttime prayer [*yatsı namazı*] had passed, and Ekrem Bey was seeking a place to perform his prayer. His Ukrainian Catholic host graciously opened a small chapel in the building where they were staying so he was able to do so. Ekrem Bey then emphasized that it would make no sense to call this Ukrainian Catholic a member of the community [*cemaat*], but, as a product of a Hizmet school, he certainly qualified as part of the movement [*hareket*].

After Ekrem Bey had concluded his point, another member of the audience raised a more fundamental objection. For him, the debate over the relative accuracy of *cemaat* and *hareket* was a red herring; rather than deciding on the most comprehensive name for Hizmet, he advocated a focus on the activity of *hizmet* itself. Unlike *cemaat* or *hareket*, *hizmet* emphasizes process and ethos, rather than belonging and identity, and one can engage in *hizmet* irrespective of one's membership in one group or another.

Even as Gülen's followers continue to debate and adjudicate among the various names that seek to define their identity and activities, Hizmet is also the object of broader public discourse in Turkey. This discourse inevitably exerts pressure on Hizmet activists themselves. In the wake of the December 2013 corruption inquiry, Gülen and Hizmet have been especially prominent topics in the Turkish news and mass media. In general, this mass media discourse refers to Gülen and his devotees as "the *cemaat*." Although this public naming of Hizmet as "the *cemaat*" is not attuned to the conceptual nuances that I have delineated in this chapter, the new hegemony of this term has nevertheless affected the discourse of Hizmet itself. During a recent trip to Istanbul in September 2014, I found that almost all of my interlocutors from GYV and other Hizmet networks had begun to refer to themselves as "the *cemaat*," though they were careful to highlight the imposed character of this name. The recent dominance of *"cemaat"* as a name for Hizmet in Turkey vividly illustrates the dynamic politics of naming that Gülen's followers negotiate. Even as Hizmet seeks to name and to categorize itself, it is also named and categorized within a broader field of political debate.

Conversely, the sociological and institutional forms of the Hizmet are not exhausted by political and conceptual debates over categories such as *tarikat, cemaat,* and *hareket.* The cosmopolitan horizons of Hizmet determine a unique relationship to the concept of the *ummah* (*ümmet*), the universal community of Muslims. From the perspective of Hizmet, the *ummah* is best served and organized through the institutions of civil society and their philanthropic activities. The preeminent civil society institution of Hizmet, the foundation or *vakıf,* embodies a direct link to both an Ottoman dispensation of charity and a longer genealogy of Muslim philanthropy: the religious legitimacy of the *vakıf*

(Arabic *waqf*), or charitable endowment, derives from a *hadith* of the Prophet Muhammad related by a companion of the Prophet, Abu Hurairah.[23] As an institutional form, the *vakıf* also represents a tie to the Ottoman era, during which most activities that today count as social services were carried out by religious foundations. Simultaneously, the *vakıf* is one of the two legal categories of nongovernmental organization in contemporary Turkey—unlike the other category of NGO, the association (*dernek*), foundations can hold property and are thereby able to engage in much more significant charitable projects. In this respect, the *vakıf* is uniquely suited to the aspirations of Hizmet; it constitutes an elaboration of the philanthropic tradition of Islam and partakes in a mode of contemporary nongovernmental institutional legitimacy.

WHAT MIGHT "LIBERAL ISLAM" MEAN?

By way of a conclusion, I would like to offer a few general reflections on the implications of my argument for questions of Islam, liberalism, and secularism broadly. On the whole, I have avoided the topic of secularism in this essay, largely because it remains so fraught and over-determined in Turkey. As I briefly discussed, laicist-secularist discourse in Turkey denigrates Hizmet by identifying it with anti-modern social and religious forms such as the *tarikat*. Hizmet activists have responded to this denunciation by asserting that Hizmet advocates a distinctly modern vision of Islam, fully commensurate with the ostensibly universal imperatives of democratic citizenship. Gülen himself has frequently pursued the opportunities that accrue to occupying a position of "moderate Islam" (*ılımlı İslam*), most notably in his swift denunciation of the attacks of September 11, 2001.[24] The liberal discourse of Hizmet actors articulates a critique of Turkish laicist secularism, which maintains an illiberal, monopolistic relationship to matters of religion in Turkey. More recently, the GYV has countered Erdoğan's and the AKP's belligerence with a similar valorization of liberal principles. In a press conference in early February 2014, held in Istanbul's luxurious Swiss Hotel, GYV representatives responded to Erdoğan's claims that Hizmet constitutes a "parallel state" and that the December 2013 corruption inquiry amounted to a coup attempt by reasserting their commitment to "*demokrasi, hukuk, ve insan hakları*" (democracy, law and human rights).[25]

On the whole, Hizmet's public statements and self-characterization hew closely to the methods and anatomy of the liberal public sphere, à la Jürgen

Habermas's classic analysis. Setting aside this liberal Hizmet discourse for a moment, however, we might productively ask: Do the characteristic discourses and institutions of Hizmet elucidate what we might mean by the phrase "liberal Islam"? A full reckoning of this question demands a more thorough treatment than I can offer here.[26] Nevertheless, the distinctive institutional culture of Hizmet indisputably articulates a practice and ideal of liberal religion that extends beyond political posturing. The appeals that Hizmet spokespeople make to liberal principles in relation to religion should not be understood as "mere ideology"—to do so would be to dismiss them in the same manner as their critics in Turkey do. Rather, as I have endeavored to show, liberal principles of tolerance and pluralism hinge on the very theological and ethical concepts and practices that underpin Hizmet. In summary, the "liberal Islam" of Hizmet (and I insist on the scare quotes, lest we risk essentializing both liberalism and Islam) emerges along two distinct axes. On the one hand, Hizmet actors advocate a liberal model of religion as a counter-argument to the dismissals of Turkish critics, and, in doing so, they both respond to and embody what I have called, following anthropologist Hussein Agrama, the "questioning power" of liberalism itself.[27] On the other hand, the liberal ideals and practices of Hizmet—tolerance and dialogue—are inseparable from the principles of positive action (*müspet hareket*), service (*hizmet*), piety (*taqwa*), and the entire edifice of Gülen's theology and moral philosophy. Thus, the discourses and institutions of Hizmet achieve form both in relation to a broader political terrain and in reference to specific ethical and discursive disciplines and genealogies. It is this constitutive duality, above all, that serves as a bulwark for Hizmet against the discontents of its critics in Turkey, secularist and Islamist alike.

NOTES

My debt of gratitude to my many readers is incalculable. I offer hearty thanks, in particular, to Hussein Agrama, Adam Becker, John Comaroff, Karin Doolan, Catherine Fennel, Andrew Graan, Timur Hammond, Kimberly Hart, Veronika Hartmann, Angie Heo, Kelda Jamison, John Kelly, Martin Marty, William Mazzarella, Sean Mitchell, Iren Özgür, Noah Salomon, Brian Silverstein, Martin Stokes, Kabir Tambar, Arzu Ünal, Lisa Wedeen, and Angela Zito. My research on Hizmet and the Nur community would have been impossible without the generosity of countless individual; Cemal Uşak and Faris Kaya deserve special mention. Research for this paper benefited from the generous support of the Fulbright-Hayes

Doctoral Fellowship, the American Research Institute in Turkey, the Institute for Turkish Studies, the New York University Religious Studies Program, the Georgetown University Center for Contemporary Arab Studies, and the CETREN Transregional Research Network at Georg August University of Göttingen.

1. "*Bey*" is a common honorific in Turkish, roughly equivalent to the English "mister"; I use it throughout in reference to my interlocutors. (The feminine version is "*Hanım*.")

2. Jeremy F. Walton, "Confessional Pluralism and the Civil Society Effect: Liberal Mediations of Islam and Secularism in Contemporary Turkey," *American Ethnologist* 40, no. 1 (Feb. 2013): 182–200.

3. See Jane Jacobs, *The Life and Death of Great American Cities* (New York: Random House, 1961).

4. A brief sketch of this controversy is as follows: In October 2013, Erdoğan announced his intention to outlaw all non-state, extracurricular test-preparation courses (*dershaneler*), the majority of which are affiliated with Hizmet; on December 17, 2013, Hizmet actors ostensibly retaliated by initiating a corruption inquiry focused on figures in Erdoğan's inner circle, including his son. Although Gülen has adamantly denied active involvement in this confrontation, most notably in a well-publicized interview with the BBC, commentators in the Turkish and international press have unanimously interpreted the corruption inquiry as a power play by Hizmet against the AKP. Erdoğan responded by denouncing Hizmet as a "parallel state" (*paralel devlet*), and, following the AKP's success in local elections in March 2014, publicly vowed to "root out" Gülen's supporters wherever they might be found, in Ankara and Pennsylvania alike. (Since 1999, Gülen has lived in self-imposed exile from Turkey on an estate in the Poconos Mountains of Pennsylvania.)

5. See Clifford Geertz, *The Interpretation of Cultures* (New York: Basic Books, 1973), 91; Philip Bagby, *Culture and History: Prolegomena to the Comparative Study of Civilizations* (Berkeley: University of California Press, 1959), quoted in Martin Marty, *Building Cultures of Trust* (Cambridge, Engl.: Wm. B. Eerdmans, 2010).

6. Talal Asad, *Formations of the Secular: Christianity, Islam, Modernity* (Stanford, Calif.: Stanford University Press, 2003), 183.

7. For a comprehensive portrait of Hizmet globally, see Joshua Hendrick, *Gülen: The Ambiguous Politics of Market Islam in Turkey and the World* (New York: New York University Press, 2013).

8. The Nur community is an overlapping Sunni group in contemporary Turkey that shares many ideals and activities with Hizmet but focuses specifically on Said Nursi and his magnum opus, the *Risale-i Nur*. In addition to Hizmet, I conducted much of my research with Nur institutions and followers of Nursi. Both Gülen himself and Hizmet in general have consistently acknowledged their debt to Nursi and the *Risale-i Nur*. While the two groups are sociologically and politically distinct, the dense institutional and personal ties between them suggest that they are better thought of as partially integrated social and cultural elaborations of a shared theological project.

9. Bediüzzaman Said Nursi, *Emirdağ Lahikası* (İstanbul: Envar Neşriyat, 1996), 241 (my translation).

10. Aladdin Basar, "A Lifelong Principle: Positive Action," http://www.nur .org/ (last modified 2007).

11. Zain Abdullah, *Black Mecca* (New York: Oxford University Press, 2010), 190 (my emphasis). For another anthropological treatment of *khidma*/"service," specifically in relation to the uptake of Sufi devotional practices in the Tahrir Square protests during Egypt's Arab Spring, see Amira Mittermaier, "Bread, Freedom, Social Justice: The Egyptian Uprising and a Sufi Khidma," *Cultural Anthropology* 29, no. 1 (2014): 45–79. I thank Timur Hammond for pointing out this reference to me.

12. M. Fethullah Gülen, *Key Concepts in the Practice of Sufism: Emerald Hills of the Heart* (Rutherford, N.J.: The Light, 2004), 48.

13. In brief, the IHH, an Istanbul-based NGO, coordinated an international coalition of activists determined to run the Israeli naval blockade of the Gaza Strip in order to provide medicine, foodstuffs, and other humanitarian aid to Gaza. Israeli naval forces boarded the flotilla on May 30, 2010, resulting in the deaths of nine Turkish activists and precipitating a major diplomatic crisis between Turkey and Israel. I arrived in Istanbul only a week following the Mavi Marmara event, and I discussed it with many of my friends and research contacts, including those at the GYV.

14. M. Fethullah Gülen, *Toward a Global Civilization of Love and Tolerance* (Rutherford, N.J.: The Light, 2004), 56.

15. Wendy Brown, *Regulating Aversion: Tolerance in the Age of Identity and Empire* (Princeton, N.J.: Princeton University Press, 2008).

16. Gülen, *Toward a Global Civilization of Love and Tolerance*, 58–59.

17. Gülen, *Key Concepts in the Practice of Sufism*, 60.

18. Jeremy F. Walton, "Neo-Ottomanism and the Pious Aesthetics of Publicness: Making Place and Space Virtuous in Istanbul," in *Orienting Istanbul: Cultural Capital of Europe?* edited by Deniz Göktürk, Levent Soysal, and İpek Türeli, 88–103 (New York: Routledge, 2010).

19. Gülen, *Toward a Global Civilization of Love and Tolerance*, 43.

20. Kemalism (*Atatürkçülük*) is the Turkish term for the strict principle of laicist, state-based secularism, known eponymously after Mustafa Kemal Atatürk (1881–1938), the military hero and founder of republican Turkey.

21. Ali Bulaç, *Din-Kent ve Cemaat: Fethullah Gülen Örneği* (İstanbul: Ufuk Kitap, 2007).

22. Ceren Coskun, "Don't Sweeten the Bitter Pill of an Illiberal Democracy," http://www.opendemocracy.net/ceren-coskun/don't-sweeten-bitter-pill-of-illiberal-democracy (accessed Sept. 13, 2014).

23. Murat Çızakçı, *A History of Philanthropic Foundations: The Islamic World From the Seventh Century to the Present* (İstanbul: Boğaziçi University Press, 2000), 6.

24. Gülen's remarks on the attacks that day were unequivocal: "Please let me assure you that Islam does not approve of terrorism in any form. Terrorism cannot

be used to achieve any Islamic goal. No terrorist can be a Muslim, and no real Muslim can be a terrorist." *Toward a Global Civilization of Love and Tolerance,* 261.

25. "Gazeteciler ve Yazarlar Vakfı basın toplantısı düzenledi," http://www.gyv.org.tr/Haberler/Detay/2623/Gazeteciler (accessed Sept. 14, 2014).

26. I treat this question at much greater length in an earlier article. See Jeremy F. Walton, "Is *Hizmet* Liberal? The Moral-Theological, Institutional, and Aesthetic Dimensions of Gülen Organizations in Istanbul," *Sociology of Islam* 1, nos. 3–4 (2014): 145–64.

27. Hussein Agrama, *Questioning Secularism: Islam, Sovereignty, and the Rule of Law in Modern Egypt* (Chicago: Chicago University Press, 2012), 107.

SUGGESTIONS FOR FURTHER READING

Asad, Talal. "The Idea of an Anthropology of Islam." Occasional Paper Series, Center for Contemporary Arab Studies, Georgetown University. Washington, D.C.: Georgetown University Center for Contemporary Arab Studies, 1986.

Hart, Kimberly. *And Then We Work for God: Rural Sunni Islam in Western Turkey.* Stanford, Calif.: Stanford University Press, 2013.

Hunt, Robert, and Yüksel Aslandoğan, eds. *Muslim Citizens of the Globalized World: Contributions of the Gülen Movement.* Somerset, N.J.:: The Light, 2007.

Salomon, Noah, and Jeremy F. Walton. "Religious Criticism, Secular Critique and the 'Critical Study of Religion': Lessons from the Study of Islam." In *The Cambridge Companion to Religious Studies,* edited by Robert Orsi, 403–20. Cambridge, Engl.: Cambridge University Press, 2011.

Sevindi, Nevval. *Contemporary Islamic Conversations: M. Fethullah Gülen on Turkey, Islam and the West.* Albany: SUNY Press, 2008.

Silverstein, Brian. *Islam and Modernity in Turkey.* Hampshire, U.K.: Palgrave MacMillan, 2011.

Tambar, Kabir. *The Reckoning of Pluralism: Political Belonging and the Demands of History in Turkey.* Stanford, Calif.: Stanford University Press, 2014.

Turam, Berna. *Between Islam and the State: The Politics of Engagement.* Stanford, Calif.: Stanford University Press, 2007.

Vahide, Şükran. *Islam in Modern Turkey: An Intellectual Biography of Bediuzzaman Said Nursi.* Albany: SUNY Press, 2005.

White, Jenny. *Muslim Nationalism and the New Turks.* Princeton, N.J.: Princeton University Press, 2013.

Yavuz, Hakan. *Islamic Political Identity in Contemporary Turkey.* New York: Oxford University Press, 2003.

Yavuz, Hakan, and John Esposito, eds. *Turkish Islam and the Secular State: The Gülen Movement.* Syracuse, N.Y.: Syracuse University Press, 2003.

FOUR

The Role of Religion in the Gülen Movement

Zeki Saritoprak

THE CORRUPTION SCANDALS OF 2013 and 2014 in Turkey and the swift and heavy-handed response by then–prime minister Recep Tayyip Erdoğan and the ruling AKP party to them have put an ever-increasing global spotlight on the Hizmet movement or what is colloquially known as the Gülen movement. From its origins in Turkey, this movement has grown large and complex, with followers and sympathizers around the world. In this chapter, I will examine the nature of the movement, placing it within the context of a social civic movement, and then explore the often-overlooked role that Islam plays in it. The importance of religion in the life of Turks remains strong despite attempts to marginalize it, and as such it is a major player in the shape and nature of the Gülen movement.

This chapter will also elaborate on the undefeatable nature of Islam and how it functions to transform the lives of individuals, as is evident in the case of the Gülen movement. I argue that the spiritual and mystical dimensions of Islam—and particularly Sufism—have been engines in the workings of the movement. These spiritual foundations have been among the least discussed aspects of the Gülen movement in academia. I have elsewhere

Of course, the Hizmet movement is, at its heart, religious in character. Fethullah Gülen, its leader, is most devoted to Sufi Islam, and he uses this commitment to study and expound on Sufism, Islam at large, and the world of religions. The question that prompts this chapter by Zeki Saritoprak, who teaches at John Carroll University, a Jesuit-based school in Cleveland, is: How is it religious? He guides readers through features that mark many religions, and he shows how Hizmet addresses each. These include "sacrifice, eschatology, sincerity, living for others, meditation on the sacred texts, and prayer." The non-Muslim public, which tends to hear mostly about the political aspects of the movement, will understand Hizmet better if these specifically religious themes are clear.

explored the spirituality of Fethullah Gülen, the eponymous "founder" of the movement, and discussed whether he could be a Sufi in a classical sense.[1] My contention is that he is not, strictly speaking, a Sufi but that he successfully combines the principles of Sufism with modern life. Because, in practice, he applies all Sufi principles in his life and suggests that his disciples should do the same, I consider this spiritual dimension to be a part of what are called the "nonattached" Sufi traditions—that is, those that are not related to one of the major Sufi orders. According to these traditions, which are essential to the Qur'an as well, this world is transient and temporal, whereas the hereafter is eternal. An important element of such traditions is drawing on spiritual strength in a variety of forms. Gülen himself finds and uses truth wherever possible. For instance, in one of his famous books, *Beyan*, which can be translated as "Clear Speech," he uses the first stanza of Rene Francois Armand Prudhomme's (d. 1907) poem "In This World" for its eloquent explanation of the nature of this worldly life:

In this world all the flow'rs wither,
The sweet songs of the birds are brief;
I dream of summers that will last
Always![2]

He finds great strength in this way. Spirituality and strength seem to be divergent. The movement is full of such combinations, one of which, the bringing together of piety and tolerance, will receive special treatment since the movement's successful promotion of these two seemingly enigmatic forces accounts for a large measure of its success and influence.

HISTORICAL BACKGROUND

Although it is clear that the movement is an Islamic one, based on the Qur'an and the Hadith (sayings of the Prophet), knowledge of the basic outlines of twentieth-century Turkish cultural history is important to fully understand it. The movement emerged within the secular milieu of the modern Turkish republic yet is rooted in the religious and intellectual life of the Ottoman Empire. The last period of the Ottoman state, the period of decline, saw a tremendous upswing of intellectual debates regarding the future of the state, its identity, and its relation to religion. Broadly, we can place the interlocutors into three main camps. First was a group that claimed that Islamism was the remedy for the sickness of the empire. This group advocated for the application of Islamic law and the establishment of a pan-Islamic empire or caliphate. The political Islam movement of the Turkish republic is the inheritor of this approach. A second group advocated for an Ottomanism focused on the revival of the Ottoman state and integration of all Ottoman-affiliated nations. The third and ultimately politically success-ful group claimed that Turkish nationalism was the solution. Turkish nationalists wanted to bring all Turks together under one flag. Amid these heated debates, the catastrophe of World War I erupted. After the defeat of the German and Ottoman alliance, the Ottoman Empire officially came to an end in 1920. On the ashes of the Ottoman state, the Republic of Turkey republic was declared an independent state on October 29, 1923.[3]

The modern republic was established on the principles of Turkish nation-alism, and the leaders of the newly established state attempted to gradually replace Turks' religious and cultural identities with a unified secular Turkish identity. Even great scholars of Islam were praised because they were Turkish, not because they were scholars of Islam. Despite the new republican govern-ment's open hostility toward the vestiges of the Ottoman state and the sul-tanate, the religion of Islam remained enshrined in the Constitution of 1924. Despite this and other actions, such as the opening of the first session of parliament with a recitation from the Qur'an, readings from the sayings of the Prophet, and the inclusion of Islamic scholars in the parliament, the new government's original tolerant approach toward Islam was just a politi-cal tactic. In 1928, the constitutional clause maintaining Islam as the religion of the state was formally removed, and the secular system was enshrined. The new establishment aimed to direct human energy from the idea of eter-nal salvation to the security and comfort of worldly life; physical well-being was more important than spiritual well-being. This new policy was under the influence of materialistic philosophy and the French concept of *laïcité*, a form of secularism somewhat different from that in the United States.

Under this new approach to religion, the secularism of the state was no longer simple neutrality between religion and non-religion; rather, the state itself established religious institutions to control religion. Loyalty to the state became more important than loyalty to God. Any possible religious development out of the state's control was prohibited. Despite this prohibi-tion, it was naturally impossible for the state to control all religious develop-ments, and a dichotomy developed between religiosity by the state and religiosity by the public. Many people would go to the mosques for Friday prayer but afterward ridicule the content of the sermon dictated by the Directorate of Religious Affairs, the highest governmental religious institution. Today, the state still sanctions the Friday sermons, and though local imams have more control over the their content, the state still has the final say in appraising the appropriateness of those sermons.

Despite such official constraints placed on Islam, the religiosity of the people has never been eclipsed in the modern Turkish republic. If people did not want to go to the mosques due to some concern over government policies, they would perform their prayers and other religious obligations privately rather than in congregation. Religion has always been an essential need of any society, and Turkish society is no exception. The powerful role of Islam in the communal and individual life of the Turkish people, generally speaking, is indefatigable. As John Locke (d. 1704) rightly said, "Man's [sic] first care should be of his soul." And again, "nothing belonging to this mortal condition is in any way comparable with eternity."[4]

Since my goal in this chapter is to focus on the role of Islam, particularly its spiritual dimension, in the Gülen movement, I will not delve into the establishment of the movement itself; its history is discussed and elaborated upon in other chapters. Suffice it to say here that the movement can be described as a civic, religious, and social movement named after the founder, Fethullah Gülen—though, evidently due to his humility, he claims no role in its founding. The multidimensional nature of the Gülen movement shows that it was inspired by religious, national, and universal values. In fact, it can be argued that these inspirations are what give it strength.

The movement is most famously dedicated to education but also works on social issues, such as advocacy for democracy and human rights. It also devotes time, effort, and financial resources to disaster relief aid as well as health institutions, both in Turkey and around the world. The movement is highly involved in interfaith dialogue with adherents of other religions, most notably Christianity and Judaism, but members of the movement also participate in dialogues with Hindus, Buddhists, and others. Another dimension of the movement is that, through education, it contributes to peace building in many regions of conflicts, such as the Balkans, Philippines, northern Iraq, and some African countries such as Nigeria. As indicated by scholars of sociology and social movements, "the practical concerns of a movement, and the human problems it is trying to solve[,] have a major impact in motivating people to become engaged not only in a movement but also specifically in the work of culture making."[5]

The exact number of people affiliated with the movement is impossible to identify because it is loosely knitted and has no policy regarding registration or membership, but it is estimated that the movement's supporters number around eight million in Turkey alone. One of the largest and most effective organizations affiliated with the Gülen movement is the Turkish Confederation of Businessmen and Industrialists (TUSKON), which, according to an interview with its president published in 2013, has roughly 46,000 members who, combined, own 120,000 companies.[6] In May 2011, an article in *Le Monde Diplomatique* stated that TUSKON has over 29,000 members and includes representatives from over 100 of the 500 biggest businesses in Turkey.[7] From a practical point of view, the presence of a large number of participants in the movement from the business world is of great importance because the movement is well financed and has significant financial resources at its disposal. As is well known, Islam makes obligatory upon those who have enough wealth to give away at least 2.5 percent of their income, which is known as *zakat*. Throughout Islamic history, Muslims have been using the proceeds from *zakat* for various purposes. It is given, for example, to the poor, the destitute, and those who are unable to pay off their loans or debts. Traditionally, Muslims also use this resource to build mosques and schools. For much of the twentieth century, the understanding of charity among most people in Turkey was to put a small amount of money after their Friday prayer in a charity box. Gülen has done much to change the idea of charity in contemporary Turkish culture. He suggested to his admirers from the business community that they give more and participate in the establishment of dormitories and schools. Hence, not only do they give the obligatory 2.5 percent but some also give between 10 and 20 percent of their wealth for those purposes. It can be argued that the motivation behind this strong support is not worldliness; it is grounded in the Islamic spiritual life that contributes to such a sacrifice.

Although the witchhunt begun by Prime Minister Erdoğan in 2014 has exposed deep divisions within Turkish society, this is not something new. In fact, Gülen has been the subject of constant criticism from government officials dating back to the days of the military dictatorship, whose leadership suspected that one day he might try to usurp their political power. In addition, there have been religious zealots who think Gülen is too flexible about Islam to the extent that he has established good relationships and dialogue with Christians and Jews since the 1990s. His most pointed critics have gone so far as to claim that he is a secret cardinal in the Catholic Church because he had a meeting with Pope John Paul II at the Vatican. Though these critiques continue, Gülen and the movement are always positive and seek dialogue, even with those who criticize them. On one occasion, Gülen spoke of a columnist, Hikmet Çetinkaya, who had been criticizing him in print for many years. Instead of having hatred toward him and cursing him, Gülen prayed that both he and the columnist would be in paradise, hand in hand.

The broad nature of the movement again is influenced by the all-encompassing nature of Islam. The Qur'an strongly emphasizes the importance of giving charity for the sake of God and without expecting anything in return in this worldly life. The reward, instead, is in the afterlife. This aspect of belief in the afterlife is absent in many contemporary social movements. However, giving charity just to help other human beings may still have some religious implications, since human beings are regarded as the most precious creatures of God in the universe. To protect and take care of such an addressee of God is Islamic. In fact, Muslim mystics would argue that it is even more Islamic to give charity just for the sake of God without expectation of reward even in the afterlife.

There is no doubt that ideas of eschatology and life after death play an important role in the movement's actions and perhaps may be counted as the most powerful source of motivation. As the Qur'an says, the consequence of every action, good or bad, will be seen in the afterlife, no matter how small or large (99:7–8). There is great trust in God's decision, and, therefore, one is hopeful about the reward of God, yet there is no guarantee. One of the sayings of the Prophet is considered a very good reference concerning positive deeds in this worldly life: according to a *hadith*, once a person dies, the account that records his or her deeds is closed, with the exception of some groups of people. These groups are those who teach and disseminate knowledge, those who help with raising a child of good character, those who leave a copy of the Qur'an for someone to benefit, those who build a mosque or a house for travelers so that they can rest during their journey, those who open channels for a river or who provide wells and fountains to bring water to the needy, and those who give charity from their own wealth while they are alive and healthy. For these people, their accounts remain open and their good deeds continue to increase even after death. It can be argued that this sense of eschatology and selfless dedication to education has some roots in a certain type of the saying of the Prophet, which inspired both Gülen and his community. In many of his recent talks, Gülen has said something similar to what he told an interviewer in 2012: "If you go to help others, God will help you. Help is both spiritual and material."[8] According to Gülen, this is the way of all prophets. His philosophy can be summed up as: This world is not a place of reward but is *darul hizmet*, the abode of service. The place of reward is the afterlife.

Scholars of social movement theory argue that, for a movement to be effective, it needs to have a shared identity as well as a large number of participants. As the sociologist Christian Smith, in a volume on the role of religion in social movements, rightly puts it, "The larger the numbers of participants, the better, for larger numbers of grassroots activists helps to spread work out, reduce the expected costs of high-risk activism, and boost activists' perceptions of political efficacy."[9] By providing this strength to any movement—and, in our case, to the Gülen movement—religion plays a key role. It seems to me that one thing distinguishing the Gülen movement from many other social movements is that the Gülen movement prefers to be proactive, not reactionary. It also prefers to avoid disruption and considers itself to be pro social order. As a philosophy, the movement avoids any physical confrontation. It speaks out against injustice yet with no violence. Traditionally, sacred sources share a strong criticism of social injustice, or, as Smith puts it, "[R]eligion's very sacred transcendence—with its conservative inclinations—also contains within itself the seeds of radical social criticism and disruption."[10] However, it can be argued that, in the essence of Islam, the protection of innocents comes first, which is part of the Islamic understanding of absolute justice. Therefore, applying justice should not cause another injustice. The movement avoids disruption because of possible transgressions on the rights of innocents like women and children who have nothing to do with that injustice.

The Gülen movement is considered an apolitical movement, yet it has contributed to the development of a democracy and multiparty system in Turkey by encouraging political participation. For example, in the 2011 general election and the 2010 constitutional referendum in Turkey, the movement, particularly through its women's platform for democracy, reached out to more than one hundred thousand households to encourage them to vote. These two elections were highly significant in preventing possible military intervention into Turkey's democratic system. Such political contributions by the movement are generally limited to Turkey and only occur when there is a significant need for direct political action.

The core of the Gülen movement lies elsewhere. Particularly, it has made important and lasting contributions to education on a global scale. To date, the movement has established educational institutions from elementary schools to universities in more than 160 countries around the world. These institutions are established as secular education systems and follow the curriculum of the host country. Students receive a high-quality education, especially in math and science. Even though religion is not taught formally, educators act as role models for their students, and a general ethic of morality is an important element of the curriculum. Parents and students might not even know the religion of the educators, but what they surely know is the morality of the educators and the quality education being provided.

THE ROLE OF RELIGION

With this background in the wide-ranging efforts of the Gülen movement, we can now turn to the role of religion in its principles. To begin, let us look at the environment in which Gülen grew up and received his education. According to available official records, he was born on April 27, 1941.[11] His first teacher was his mother, and the first thing he learned from her was the Qur'an. He grew up hearing the chanting of the divine names, the recitation of the Qur'an, and frequently hearing verses from various poems. He himself memorized the Qur'an and learned many sayings of the Prophet as well as many poems. On one occasion, during an interview with Gülen in 2004, I learned that he could recite over one thousand couplets by heart; I asked if it took much effort to memorize all of these, and he replied, "I learned them from the cultural environment and the overall milieu of my generation."

The environment in which he grew up was a mystical one. His father, a self-educated farmer who later became an imam, was a mystic and lover of the Prophet and his companions. Other scholars and mystics, particularly the Naqshbandi Sufi master Muhammad Lutfi (d. 1956) and one of the first great modern Muslim intellectuals, Bediüzzaman Said Nursi (d. 1960), had great influence on Gülen's spiritual life. Both Lutfi and Nursi were well versed in Islamic mysticism. The first was a great poet, and the latter was a great author of over one hundred treatises that were commentaries on verses of the Qur'an. Although Gülen was, and still is, curious about Western literature and has read many Western philosophers, such as Jean-Jacques Rousseau (d. 1778) and Émile Zola (d. 1902), the real religious influence that he received was from Muslim mystics. He is well versed in the commentary of the Qur'an, in the sayings of the Prophet, and in the history of Islam, particularly the era of the Prophet known in Islamic history as the era of bliss. There is no doubt that this Islamic mystical environment shaped Gülen's understanding of religion. Although the entirety of Gülen's life could be usefully examined, in the current context we must limit our analysis to a few highly salient fragments.

He was a preacher and an imam by training. He led the prayer in the mosque to which he was appointed by the Directorate of Religious Affairs, and he preached regularly on Fridays. His highly moving and influential sermons and lessons attracted thousands to the mosque. He commented on the Qur'anic verses, elaborated on the companions of the Prophet, spoke on the exemplary life of the Prophet Muhammad and prophets before Islam, and taught Muslims to be self-critical. Gülen has been an important example of a charismatic leader as defined by Robin Theobald: "The leader has a mission or message which in some way harmonizes with the basic needs, hopes, desires, ambitions or fears of his followers."[12]

We do not know if Gülen had envisioned such a large movement when he emerged as a leader in the 1980s. Nevertheless, it is evident that the principles and mystical elements of Islam have contributed to the growth of the founder as well as to the movement. Religion in general and certain particular elements of religion, such as sincerity, have functioned as an engine for the movement. In other words, as Nursi said when criticizing young Turks for their apathy toward religion, "Religion is the life of the life, both its spirit and its foundation."[13] We should note that sincerity in the Islamic mystical tradition is the spirit of religion—that is, one must act with good intention, only for the sake of God, with no personal advantages. Gülen describes such people as "sacrificing souls," those who live for others rather than for themselves. It seems to me that this Islamic principle has been at the heart of many of the movement's achievements. I shall detail these in the following paragraphs.

It is believed that all social movements confront the problem of motivating their participants to make and maintain a commitment to a collective cause. One can argue in the case of the Gülen movement that this problem is minimized. The participants are greatly motivated to sacrifice their time, their comfort, and even their financial resources. There is no doubt that Islam plays an important role in such sacrifices. It is true that material benefits may motivate people to a certain extent, yet spiritual gains, such as the pleasing of God, are a much greater motivating factor. The power of this motivation is well accepted by scholars of social movements: "Perhaps the most potent motivational leverage that a social-movement can enjoy is the alignment of its cause with the ultimacy and sacredness associated with God's will, eternal truth, and the absolute moral structure of the universe."[14] This well describes the participants' motivation in the Gülen movement.

This power of motivation is clearly seen when one makes a comparison between teacher participants in the schools that are run by the Gülen movement and schools that are run by the Republic of Turkey in Central Asia. Teachers and professors employed by the government receive a generous salary, but those who are employed by the Gülen movement receive a very modest stipend. Both groups are assigned to teach in poverty-stricken areas, but it is noteworthy that those teachers who are well-paid government employees will ask for transfers and leave their teaching posts rather quickly because of the difficult conditions of life in the region.[15] The Gülen movement teachers, who see their jobs as a sacrifice and aim at the service of people, which eventually leads to the pleasing of God, stay and thrive in their positions. Such motivation contributes to the success of the schools even though the teachers are paid a minimal salary and suffer through the same poverty they find around them. Such commitment has been one of the greatest accomplishments of the movement, not only in Central Asia but also throughout the world. This idea is captured by Martin Luther, who is purported to have said at the Diet of Worms, "My conscience is captive to the Word of God. . . . Here I stand. I cannot do otherwise." In other words, people who act for the sake of God and make pleasing God the goal of their actions will see worldly rewards to be minor compared to their high aspirations. This encompassing approach, rooted in the pleasing of God, includes respect, compassion, and service to all creatures of God. Gülen often repeats a saying of the Prophet, "God bestows His mercy to His servants who are merciful." This is also stated in Gülen's definition of religion, which is considerably different from some classical definitions. According to Gülen, "Religion is the title of a deep relationship and love toward all creation in God's name."[16] It is evident that love and compassion, which are deeply rooted in the religion of Islam, are the foundation of any successful movement, and the Gülen movement is no exception.

At this juncture, a question may arise. Why would a movement rooted in the religion of Islam be so interested in such diverse areas of activism? There are two primary answers. First, the elements of the movement's activism are related to its understanding of the broad nature of Islam. The second is related to the universality of Islam, which considers human beings to be the

supervisors of the universe. Therefore, any activism that relates to the betterment of humanity is included in the area of interest of the movement. A
quote from Gülen gives a sense of the importance of human beings to the
movement: "To love and respect human beings only because they are human
beings is an expression of love and respect for the Creator. If one loves only
those who agree with him or her, then that is not considered a real love and
respect. On the contrary, it is selfishness and idolizing one's self."[17] One can
argue that the people in the Gülen movement are propelled by religious convictions and that, whatever they do, they are expected to do it for the sake of
God. As Nursi says, "Work for God, act for God, meet each other for God,
then the minutes of your life will become years."[18] Religion helps to institute
the very substance of the movement, including its philosophy, identity, strategy, and even its approach to current issues.

The terminology employed by the Gülen movement has strong theological implications in Islam. For example, a Qur'anic verse speaks of Satan as
the enemy of human beings: "Lo, devil is an enemy for you, so treat him as
an enemy" (35:6). This Qur'anic concept of enemy, which is equated with the
devil, is employed by the movement for some social problems such as ignorance, poverty, and disunity. The movement sees these problems as enemies
just as the devil is an enemy in the Qur'an. The struggle against these enemies should, of course, be appropriate to the nature of the enemy. Therefore,
a struggle against ignorance is to be fought with knowledge through educational institutions. A struggle against poverty is to be fought with the arts,
which include technology, agriculture, and trade. A struggle against disunity is to be fought by improving unity and harmony within the community.
All of these enemies are addressed in the Qur'an. For example, to overcome
ignorance, the Qur'an commands, "Read" (96:1). To overcome poverty, the
Qur'an commands, "Give charity" (2:43, 83, 177, and 5:55). To overcome disunity, the Qur'an reminds human beings that they are all created from one
male and one female, with no superiority of one over the other. They are
created to know each other rather than to fight each other (49:13).

Several other religious factors that contributed to the activism of the
movement can be cited in this context. It can be argued that the most important factor frequently emphasized and understood as an essential ingredient
of the movement is sincerity. A short work on sincerity, taken from the writings of Nursi, is expected to be read at least once a fortnight; in it, the purpose of actions is described as "only to have the pleasing of God." If God
wills, He will make others pleased with your actions as well. Therefore, all

actions should be done sincerely for the sake of God. Another religious factor is a strong devotion to God, which connects the people of the movement and brings them to a shared value. Perhaps this is the engine of persistent activism, emphasized by Gülen when he says, "I have devoted myself to this cause, I have forbidden to myself to think anything other than this. I know this is not objective, not for everybody, but this is my way. I am a weak person, I cannot carry two things on my shoulder, I am carrying only one thing, which is my cause to serve God through serving humanity."[19]

Another important religious factor in the movement is the emphasis on quality human beings. Throughout the writings of Gülen, one can see descriptions of the type of people he wants in his movement. He believes that, without them, success is impossible. Summarizing the importance of these factors, sincerity and quality human beings, Gülen says:

> When the basic elements of sincere friendship penetrate the outer and inner senses and faculties of heroes of nearness to God, they save such people from partial thoughts about things and events, causing them to reach the horizon of unity in all their sensations, impressions, perceptions, considerations, logical or rational comments, and evaluations. These heroes are raised, each according to their own capacity, to a comprehensive observation of things with their reason, mind, senses, consciousness, hearts, and secrets [another inner faculty], and this causes them to observe through the telescope of their outer and inner senses indescribable scenes, multifarious but one within the other, and bearing the stamp of the same One Maker.[20]

Sociologists generally agree with Gülen's focus on having quality people in the movement and the importance of their values on a movement's success. Stephen Hart says, "These [values and views of reality] are appropriated, transformed, and then used by movements to guide their activities and also to articulate movement purposes and garner support."[21] People in the Gülen movement allow the values most important to them to guide and grow the movement, which is one reason for its popularity and significant achievements.

In talking about the role of religion in the Gülen movement, it is necessary to examine the powerful role that the sacred text, the Holy Qur'an, plays. The Qur'an is the eternal message of God—for the past, for today, and for tomorrow. Unlike some other books of Divine revelation, its audience is not limited to one group of people, nor is its inspiration limited to a certain period of time. Such sacred transcendence is a source of devotion as well as motivation. The Qur'an connects its readers to the realm of the unseen, the realm of eternity. Therefore, there is a world beyond this material world that is the real destination of all human beings, emphasized in about one third of the Qur'an. By implementing such faith in the heart of individuals, the Qur'an helps with the rectification of the character. This contributes to the growth of quality human beings, who are essential elements for the success of the movement. This faith in the afterlife and in the transcendent sacred source is what some scholars of social movements refer to when they speak of timeless truths, which are "believed to exist above and beyond the temporal, mundane, material world that we observe empirically."[22] The Qur'an, through its recitation and contemplation, has a powerful role in mobilizing people to do good works. For example, it addresses all human beings when it says, "Vie with one another in good works" (2:148).

The Qur'an also provides a daily inspirational source against any possible hopelessness or frustration. Many principles of the Gülen movement, such as the principle of working for justice and nonviolence, are inspired by the teachings of the Qur'an, emphasized in the verse "Peace is better" (4:128). Despite the fact that Gülen himself was imprisoned and persecuted, he never sought retaliation but instead promoted peace. It can be argued that this practice was taken from the Qur'an. For Gülen, the Qur'anic verse "No soul shall bear another's guilt" (6:164) closes all doors of violence and constitutes a central principle for the movement's philosophy of nonviolence. This is because violence cannot usually be limited to the criminal; many innocents are also affected by actions of violence. Theologically speaking, an individual may be a criminal, but his or her close relatives may be perfectly innocent. Therefore, any violence might transgress on the rights of those innocents.

The Qur'an inspires creative thinking, as well. To give one example, during the military coup of 1980 the government tried to take control of all private foundations in Turkey. For Gülen, this meant that many of his schools and dormitories, which were nonprofit institutions, would be taken over and run by the government. This was troubling him but, while reciting the Qur'an, he became inspired. In Sura 18 is a story about Moses and a friend, Khidr, who were traveling on a ship. Khidr bored a hole in the boat, an act that upset Moses. When asked why he had vandalized the boat, Khidr replied that the oppressive ruler of their destination confiscated all perfect ships. The hole in the boat, therefore, saved the ship from being confiscated by the ruler, and the poor people who owned the boat were able to keep it. Inspired by this story, Gülen decided to start construction next to each of his schools and dormitories. When the government officials saw the construction and realized that taking them over meant paying for the construction, they let Gülen keep them.

Like the Qur'anic texts, powerful narratives about the Prophet and his companions are some other religious factors that play a great role in the movement. These narratives are often presented in the form of poems and songs. Generally, devotion and spiritual strength are emphasized. For example, Gülen's famous poem, known as "The Rose of Medina" (*Medine'nin Gülü*), is repeatedly recited and has been widely spread through social media. To give a sense of Gülen's emotional and powerful narratives, here is a stanza of his poem in which he addresses the Prophet:

> I wish I could sit with your love and stand up with your love constantly.
> I wish I could rise like a spirit and wander in your horizon
> So that I could find a way to flow into your heart
> I wish I could sit with your love and stand up with your love constantly.[23]

This type of imaginative narrative provides at least two things. One is solidarity in the community at a macro level by creating a shared identity for those who love the Prophet. Second, it provides a spiritual strength at a micro level. Many individuals, including some famous Turkish musicians, have used these narratives as part of their music.[24] This unifying strength at the micro and macro levels turns into social actions through the sacrifice of individuals. Gülen describes these people as those who prefer the comfort of others over their own comfort and those who live to make others live well.

In both his poems and his prose, Gülen uses powerful, mystical terminology such as "heart," "passion," "burning," and "separation." All these terms have been frequently used by Sufi masters when they complain about their separation from the beloved. The beloved can be the Sufi master, sometimes the Prophet, and occasionally God. For the Prophet, Gülen uses the phrase, "The rose of my heart." As an example of his emotional prose narratives, one may refer to Gülen's famous Friday sermons as well as sermons on the occasion of the feast of the end of Ramadan, Eid al-Fitr, and the feast of sacrifice, Eid al-Adha. Although Gülen no longer gives these sermons, in the 1980s he used the pulpit very powerfully but also wisely. Through the large crowds his sermons attracted, he helped to create a level of peace and unity between conflicting political groups in the country, namely nationalists and communists. He strongly advised his admirers to calm tensions between these groups. These spiritual ingredients of the movement are missing from many political movements of our time. Due to the lack of this spiritual dimension, political demonstrations and protests become more important than activities designed to strengthen individuals spiritually. Political movements that do not involve spiritual elements may be more inclined to violence. It can be argued that Gülen's early sermons were the seeds for today's flourishing Hizmet movement and its peace-building efforts.

A brief analysis of one of Gülen's speeches to his inner circle that recently became available on his official website shows us how Gülen takes inspiration from the spiritual tradition of Islam.[25] The speech is entitled "Black Clouds and a Call for Collective Prayer." In this forty-minute speech, Gülen invites people to pray for peace and asks for a collective prayer to end conflicts around the world and in his home country, Turkey. He refers to the traditional prayer to end drought, a prayer well documented in the manuals of Islamic jurisprudence as an inspiration for the prayer to end conflicts. According to Islamic tradition, when a region or country has a drought, all members of the community go out and open their hands to God with the utmost level of humility, asking God for rain. The Prophet Muhammad humbled himself in this way, and sometimes even before the Prophet lowered his hands the rain would come. Gülen suggests that Muslims should be inspired by this prophetic tradition and use the same prayer to end violence and conflicts in their regions and around the world collectively. It is well known in the Islamic mystical tradition that, when any prayer becomes a collective expression, it receives greater recognition from the Divine. This is not to say that Gülen neglects strategic planning developed by think tanks and scholars of sociology, psychology, and political science to find solutions to certain conflicts. Indeed, the two go together—prayer and planning.

In conclusion, the religion of Islam, with its great spiritual strength, includes many parts. In the Gülen movement, these parts—sacrifice, eschatology, sincerity, living for others, meditation on the sacred texts, and prayer—are connected and function together like the engine of a machine. The movement's apolitical understanding of religion, which is considerably different from modern political Islamic movements, is the compass that directs its activities and goals. All the dimensions discussed above with regard to the motivation of the Gülen movement invalidate the criticisms of those who say that the movement looks for materialistic benefits and political positions. Working for material benefits instead of spiritual fulfillment would be—for people of the movement—like choosing tin over gold. On one occasion, some opponents of the movement claimed that if Gülen declared his candidacy for the Turkish presidency he would be elected. When Gülen heard of this, he responded, in regard to the effect it would have on his spiritual life, by saying: "That would be a demotion for me."

NOTES

1. See, e.g., Zeki Saritoprak, "Fethullah Gülen: A Sufi in His Own Way," in *Turkish Islam and the Secular State: The Gülen* Movement, edited by M. Hakan Yavuz and John L. Esposito, 156–69 (Syracuse, N.Y.: Syracuse University Press, 2003).

2. Fethullah Gülen, *Beyan* (Izmir: Nil Yayinlari, 2012), 83.

3. See Yusuf Akçura, *Üç Tarz-ı Siyaset*, edited by Enver Ziya Karal (Ankara: Turk Tarih Kurumu, 1976). Numerous books on the late Ottoman period have been written. The best concise introduction to this period is M. Sukru Hanioglu, *A Brief History of the Late Ottoman Empire* (Princeton, N.J.: Princeton University Press, 2008).

4. John Locke, *Epistola de Tolerantia: A Letter on Toleration*, Latin text edited by Raymond Klibansky, translated by J. W. Gough (Oxford: Clarendon Press, 1968), 131, 125.

5. Stephen Hart, "The Cultural Dimension of Social Movements: A Theoretical Reassessment and Literature Review," *Sociology of Religion* 57, no. 1 (1996): 99.

6. Ünal Tanık, "TUSKON, kadın hareketi başlatıyor," *RotaHaber* (Feb. 20, 2013), http://haber.rotahaber.com/tuskon-kadin-hareketi-baslatiyor_346090.html. An abbreviated translation of this article was published as "An In-depth Interview with TUSKON President Meral" (Feb 20, 2013), http://hizmetmovement.blogspot .com/2013/02/interview-with-tuskon-president-meral.html.

7. Wendy Kristianasen, "Turkey's Growing Trade Network," *Le Monde Diplomatique, English Edition* (May 2011), http://mondediplo.com/2011/05 /09turkeytrade.

8. Abu Abdillah Muhammad bin Yazid al-Qazwini ibn Maja, *Al-Sunan*, edited by Muhammad Fuad Abd al-Baqi (Beirut: Dar Ihya al-Turath al-Arabi, 1975).

9. Christian Smith, "Correcting a Curious Neglect, or Bringing Religion Back In," in *Disruptive Religion: The Force of Faith in Social-Movement Activism*, edited by Christian Smith (New York: Routledge, 1996), 14.

10. Ibid., 6.

11. However, there is some dispute about the actual date and year of his birth. For more discussion of this, see Marcia Hermansen's chapter in this volume.

12. Robin Theobald, "The Role of Charisma in the Development of Social Movements," *Archives de Sciences Socials des Religion* 49, no. 1 (Jan.–Mar. 1980): 85.

13. Bediuzzaman Said Nursi, "Sozler," in *Risale-i Nur Kulliyati* (Istanbul: Yeni Asya Yayinlari, 1996): 1: 328.

14. Smith, "Correcting a Curious Neglect, or Bringing Religion Back In," 9.

15. Mahmut Akpınar, "Yurt dışındaki devlet okulları," *Millet* (Jan. 27, 2015).

16. Fethullah Gülen, *Olcu Veya Yoldaki Isiklar* (Criteria or Road Signs) (Istanbul: Nil Yayinlari, 2001), 27.

17. Fethullah Gülen, *Cag ve Nesil I* (Istanbul: Nil Yayinlari, 2011), 43.

18. Bediuzzaman Said Nursi, *Lem'alar* (Istanbul: Sözler Yayinevi, 1997), 23.

19. See http://tr.fgulen.com/content/view/20956/11 (my translation; accessed June 4, 2015).

20. See http://fgulen.com/en/fethullah-gulens-works/sufism/key-concepts-in-the-practice-of-sufism-3/26549-sincere-friendship (accessed June 4, 2015).

21. Hart, "Cultural Dimension of Social Movements," 88.

22. Smith, "Correcting a Curious Neglect, or Bringing Religion Back In," 6.

23. Fethullah Gülen, *Krik Mizrap* (Izmir: Nil Yayinlari, 2011), 347–48; my translation.

24. See, e.g., Sami Özer, "Fame in This World Is Nothing; May God Give Us Fame in the Next," *Sunday's Zaman* interview with the Turkish musician Sami Özer in *Today's Zaman* (Aug. 5, 2012), http://www.todayszaman.com/ramadan_fame-in-this-world-is-nothing-may-god-give-us-fame-in-the-next_288611.html (accessed June 4, 2015).

25. See http://www.herkul.org/index.php/bamteli/bamteli-arsiv/9800-kara-bulutlar-ve-dua-seferberligine-cagr.

FIVE

Building Bridges

GÜLEN PONTIFEX

Simon Robinson

OVER THE PAST TWO DECADES, an academic subdiscipline has arisen that might almost be called "Gülen studies." It has generated great numbers of global conferences looking at different aspects of Gülen's thinking and the phenomenon he founded, the Hizmet movement. In turn, this has given rise to many research projects looking at the philosophy and practice of the movement. In this chapter, I will lay out some of the key features of this movement that has excited so much interest and will set these in the contemporary global context. In the first part, I briefly consider a sociological analysis of the Hizmet movement, noting that it does not fit easily into any conventional typologies. I then suggest some reasons for this, including Gülen's holistic approach, his synoptic thinking, and the plural identity of the movement. I note that this enables the movement to effectively build bridges across many different divides: religious and secular, different cultures and faiths, and different academic disciplines, practices, and theories.

I then suggest that central to the building of these bridges is dialogue of a particular kind, which sets the movement apart from many other attempts

---

The Gülen movement, Simon Robinson contends, is not a "sect" or a "cult," as some critics have called it, but is a special social form organized to encourage its adherents to participate creatively in a world marked by pluralism among religions and, often, hostility among them. Religious forces and movements tend to define themselves over against all others, inventing enemies and either keeping a distance from them or attacking them. Robinson, professor of Applied and Professional Ethics at Leeds Beckett University, here explores the origins of the Hizmet phenomenon and demonstrates that, though it is inspired by Sufi mysticism, its leaders and members conceive of their work not as agents of conversion but, after the model of Fethullah Gülen, as builders of bridges toward people in other religious movements and among secular forces alike.

at interfaith and intercultural dialogue. First, the dialogue involves critical examination of the ideas, values, and practice in the movement and beyond. This reflects Gülen's concern for the development of scientific thinking, both as a means of developing critical thinking and consciousness of the wider environment and as the call of God to sustain and develop this. The second aspect of dialogue has been the practice of accountability, the capacity to give an account of ideas, values, and practice beyond the movement both to other key social and religious actors and to the wider society. The third aspect of Gülen's dialogue is based on creative response to God. This is where the meaning of *hizmet* (service) begins to surface strongly, the ongoing service as vicegerents of creation. This suggests a responsibility shared by the religious and nonreligious alike. The question of any dialogue, then, is how to enable that creative response and how to share in a universal responsibility that transcends any particular faith. For much of the Hizmet movement, education, care, and business become the foci around which this response is negotiated. The chapter concludes with the argument that dialogue bridging the areas noted above is also key to the continued health of the movement. Such dialogue embodies the practice of the key sets of virtues—intellectual, spiritual, and ethical.

THE NATURE OF THE HIZMET MOVEMENT

Major concerns have been raised about the purpose and identity of the Hizmet movement. In 2008, Gülen came out on top in a poll on the world's leading intellectuals, organized by *Prospect* magazine.[1] It was noted that the number of people from Turkey voting for Gülen increased after the poll was highlighted in the the the Gülen-inspired newspaper, *Zaman*. So was there something sinister here, with willing followers being manipulated? Conspiracy theories abound in Turkey, as in any major Islamic movement, and thus it has been a short step to see the movement, at various points, as funded by the CIA, Iran, or even the Turkish state.[2] Or, other critics have suggested, perhaps this is an Islamist movement, designed to subvert the Turkish secular state by stealth, through building an Islamic middle-class power base. The many accusations are rehearsed elsewhere.[3] Other perspectives suggest the evidence points to a group that is transparent, open to critique, and concerned for the common good.[4] So what kind of a group is it?

Sociological analysis[5] might attempt to place the Hizmet movement into a typology of religious groups. Three in particular have been suggested: a sect, a "neo Sufi brotherhood," or a neo-fundamentalist movement, sometimes referred to as a cult.[6] Definitions of these different types have changed over time; for the purpose of this chapter, I will focus on broad definitions.

In the first of these typologies, it is hard to see the movement as either a formal "church" or a sect. The movement works against institutional formalization. There is no central hierarchy or related organizational system of bureaucracy.[7] On the contrary, it is more like a network with different groups spread across Turkey and the world. These include media outlets such as the *Zaman* newspaper, various groups in Turkey, including the Journalists and Writers Foundation,[8] a Teacher's Foundation, and the Confederation of Businessmen and Industrialists,[9] and various related groups spread across the world. These are all focused on developing dialogue around education and social responsibility, and on developing creative responses to need, resulting in as many as a thousand Gülen-inspired schools and universities around the world. The development and spread of these educational institutions is not centrally planned but comes as a result of dialogue between different parts of the movement about priorities and resources. Hence, cases have to be argued critically about the funding of educational projects. This suggests distributed and shared leadership. The theological dynamic here is precisely to move away from any sense of ownership or centralized power. Service to God transcends any institutional manifestation and can only be focused on the attitude and action of service. Hence, the focus is purpose, not the person who is leader. I will test this more critically in reference to cults below.

Sects tend to be defined in terms of their tension with the founding church or institution. They are moving onto a new path. Membership is not formalized, and members tend to come and go. Again, it is not clear that the Hizmet movement can be seen simply in this light. Certainly there seem to be no clear boundaries, but it does not define itself exclusively in terms of tensions with any higher or founding institution. Given the fact that there is no particular institution in Islam to be in tension with, Muhammed Çetin notes that one Islamic view of a sect is that it enacts a new, possibly deviant form of Islam.[10] It is not clear that the Hizmet movement could fall into that category, given that Gülen's stress is radical, in the sense of going back to the roots of Islam, with a strong focus on the Qur'an. His focus is on orthodox thinking and on how this works in practice. It is this stress on practice that makes the movement distinctive.

The movement is influenced by the Sufi tradition; hence it might be seen as a Sufi order. However, classical *tarikat* Sufism would require initiation and involve esoteric religious practices and arcane terminology.[11] This is the opposite of a movement that aims to make itself clear through it actions. Erol Gulay notes that Gülen also goes against the traditionalist Sufi paradigm by playing down the role of a Sufi master as mediator between the disciples and God.[12] Gülen sees himself as an inspirational leader but claims no formal authority. Rather, he points to the infinite wisdom of the Qur'an and the many different ways of accessing that.[13] Nonetheless, Gülen and the movement are characterized by a strong neo-Sufi theology that stresses holism, combining a strong affective spirituality with reflection on the Qur'an and the stress on action in one's social context.

Perhaps, then, the movement can best be seen as a cult or New Religious Movement (NRM).[14] NRMs have received bad press in recent decades due to negative examples. However, cults are not aggressive or problematic per se. On the contrary, they may fulfill many different needs, including self improvement, the desire to make a difference in life, a sense of purpose and direction, companionship and a sense of belonging, structured community, guidance, and a sense of self-worth and hope, all of which can be claimed by the Hizmet movement. Cults involve groups that are generally smaller than sects and are characterized by focus on the fulfillment of affective needs only by that group. Hence, members are given great attention upon joining the group such that they feel unconditionally accepted. The strength of the bond is then tested by the group in terms of both ensuring orthodoxy of belief and being involved in spreading the influence of the group. The continued love and care of the group becomes dependent on the person accepting the ortho-dox beliefs and taking a full part in evangelism and recruiting new members. From this emerges the reality of an exclusive and conditional community: you are only valued if you sustain this commitment to the group. In one sense, then, the cultic experience keeps the person in a form of a conforming child, with no responsibility for decision making or sense of autonomous agency.[15]

Conditionality is also associated with polarized thinking, and thus we see the member of the cult gradually turning his or her back on the outside world and viewing it as the source of evil, leading to conflict with the families of converts to the NRM in question. Conditionality is related directly to the incapacity to handle the plurality and ambiguity of the "other." Hence, the cult member will tend to see the family as accepting the conditions of the cult or not, as either good or bad.

The dynamics of dependence in a cult are also rooted in the perception of the leader of the NRM as the source of truth and, by extension, the ground of faith. The leader thus cannot be questioned and is most often not accountable. All of this leads to a judgmental ethics based on strict adherence to conditions and rules. It is not surprising that cults tend to have small numbers of members, that they are not transparent (indeed, are secretive), and that they focus on orthodox thinking rather than public or practical action. In extreme cases, they are associated with myths and rites that are antirational and even subversive, leading to violence.[16]

The Hizmet movement differs markedly from a cult in several ways. First, it is not small. Second, Gülen does not take on the directive role of a cult leader. On the contrary, he points to the primacy of the scriptures—and the imperative of service—and stresses the responsibility of the individual or the different groups within the movement to develop ideas and practice, to put flesh on the obligation to serve. There is no doubt that Gülen remains a charismatic leader and that members of the movement hold him in the highest respect.[17] However, he consistently avoids attempts to institutionalize power, to perceive him as the source of all truth, or to view him as taking responsibility for the movement. Hence, Gülen himself specifically denies that the movement can be termed the Gülen movement or that the schools developed by the Hizmet movement can be described as his.[18]

In a recent sociological study of the Hizmet movement, Joshua Hendricks argues that the movement is "ambiguous" and that this ambiguity is strategic.[19] This concept of strategic ambiguity emerges from the organizational theory of Eric Eisenberg.[20] This suggests that organizations foster ambiguity of meaning for several reasons. If the aims and objectives of an organization are ambiguous, for instance, then this might enable leaders to deny responsibility for actions. Equally, ambiguity in communication about aims and objectives might enable different, quite distinctive groups to work together within an organization. It is not the place of an overview to address this argument in detail. However, three things are worth noting at this stage. First, there is a lack of conceptual clarity about Hendricks's use of the term "ambiguity." He applies it, for instance, to Gülen's denial of any formally organized efforts to develop new schools or other enterprises. However, it is not clear that leadership which addresses broad ethical and theological issues and intentionally argues that individuals and groups should take responsibility for how service is put into practice is necessarily ambiguous. On the contrary, this is based on a model of agreement around general principles and an interpretation of these in practice. This gives rise to different expressions of any principle. Second, ambiguity is often seen as a negative idea, and strategic ambiguity in particular can be viewed as intrinsically unethical precisely because it suggests deception.[21] This sets up wider discussion about the nature of integrity as well as the integrity of organizations and leadership, which Hendricks does not sustain, largely because he does not develop an analysis of organizational ethics. Third, in the debates about leadership and organization are issues that point the need for a more profound analysis. For instance, there is positive ethical ambiguity at the heart of much religious thinking on leadership and service. One example of this is the servant leadership model, which argues, in some cases, that service should be carried out in ways that do not draw attention to the actions of the leader,[22] instead focused on virtues such as humility. This raises major questions of how ambiguity relates to contemporary views about the ethical primacy for transparency and accountability, where attention is precisely drawn to the good works of the person or group. This is a difficult tension to hold but cannot be viewed as a form of deception.

Such points suggest the need for a more nuanced view of the Hizmet movement. Even the briefest of attempts to place the movement in traditional religious categories fails. It contains elements of all these types and can be seen to be the development of different traditions as well as a simple orthodox Islamic group. It does not, as Hendricks notes, have the characteristics of an institutional bureaucracy, and the different formal groupings within the movement are not organized under the direct leadership of Gülen. It has a unifying leader and focus but has diversity within the movement. It sees the search for truth as a continuing reflective and creative activity, with God at the center. At one level, this reflects the familiar tension between religious institutional identity, with its concern for growing and sustaining the organization, and core spiritual purpose and personal development, with its concern for personal response. To explore this further requires some consideration of Gülen's thought.

GÜLEN'S THINKING

Gülen's writings begin to reveal why neither he nor the movement can be placed in narrow categories. In particular, his thinking is holistic and synoptic, based in a plural identity. It is focused in spirituality (indebted to Sufi mysticism), rational critical reflection (focused in science), tradition and theology (focused in the Qur'an), and practice.

Central to this is the idea of *hizmet,* which involves service with a great stress on continual action. Responsibility makes action critical, and Gülen contrasts passive submission with active service. *Hizmet* is about embodying the inner awareness of God in practice. It is based on spirituality and thus the consciousness of God and his call. Hence, piety is "this-worldly": "Those who always feel themselves in the presence of God do not need to seclude themselves from people."[23] The human agency of the response to God is based on a holistic and dynamic anthropology that brings together emotion, spirit, rationality, and action: "God did not create people only to have them become passive recluses, activist without reason and spirit, or rationalists without spiritual reflection and activism."[24]

For Gülen, *hizmet* involves the ceaseless responsibility of putting values into practice. This is focused in the example of the Prophet as a man of action, who "stressed learning trading, agriculture, action and thought. Moreover, he encouraged his people to do perfectly what he did, and condemned inaction and begging."[25]

The focus for the believer is not salvation but rather to please God, "thinking only of his approval in everyday speech, behaviour and thought."[26] This means that the person is engaged without ceasing in particular activity, always asking "Oh my Lord, what else can I do?" Gülen inevitably stresses then the importance of individual discipline, including good time management and well-planned activity. This is all part of what it means to be responsible. The more that such responsibility is practiced in all contexts, the more that this leads to increased responsibility; "more blessings mean more responsibility."[27]

If the response of *hizmet* is holistic, it is also synoptic, making connections between the different aspects of meaning in practice, including connections between disciplines often seen as in conflict, not least the relationship of science and critical thinking to spirituality. Key to this is Gülen's thinking about creation. God created the world and appointed humanity to be the vicegerent.[28] Humankind is thus responsible for the management of creation and, in this sense, stands in for God, as deputy, but also stands before him. Hence, humanity is both responsible with God and accountable to God for the world in its fullness.

In order to fulfill this responsibility and trust God has made available all possible resources:

If humanity is the vicegerent of God on Earth, the favourite of all His creation, the essence and substance of existence in its entirety and the brightest
mirror of the Creator—and there is no doubt that this is so—then the Divine
Being that has sent humanity to this realm will have given us the right, per-
mission, and ability to discover the mysteries imbedded in the soul of the
universe, to uncover the hidden power, might and potential, to use everything to its purpose, and to be the representatives of characteristics that
belong to Him, such as knowledge will and might.[29]

All resources are to be used to fulfill the divine purpose. The task of the
vicegerent is not simply to believe in God or to worship but to understand
"the mysteries within things and the cause of natural phenomena, and therefore to be able to interfere in nature."[30] "Interference" is less the domination
of creation and more the protecting of the harmony of the ecosystem and
using its resources for the common good. The vicegerent thus becomes a co-
creator with God, servant but also lover.[31]

Key to awareness and appreciation of the environment, and its proper use, is
science. This is not something that is seen as autonomous or against religion.
Rather, science reveals the laws of nature and, by implication, helps us to see the
purpose of creation. This clearly shows why Gülen, despite being firmly a crea-
tionist (i.e., he believes in God's literal creation and rejects the theory of evolution), is concerned about science as an essential part of his educational work.

The response to God's call involves free will. The person chooses to respond to God and, in particular, chooses how he or she will maintain the
balance of the environment, sustain the balance between the environment
and humanity, and make the most of the resources given in creation, all for
the benefit of humanity and all with a purpose of raising the level of civilization for everyone. This requires continual critical reflection on "purpose" in
context—hence, again, the need to use science. Such a continual reflective
process, of course, cannot be simplistic, or even univocal, for two reasons.
First, it is not clear that science per se can determine purpose. God's purposes are a matter of value rather than scientific truth. Science may support
and confirm that value but cannot ultimately determine the value. Second,
any judgment about purpose, or about the scientific support for purpose,
will inevitably be contested. Hence, there is need for continual debate
around the understanding of purpose. The practice of vicegerency, then, is
teleological, social, and dialogic, with responsibility shared for creation.

This reinforces identity, which is developed through the exercise of free will
in making decisions about the social and physical environment, something

similar to Charles Taylor's deep decision making.[32] Gülen points up the need to assert responsibility within that relational framework, precisely to avoid a loss of agency:

> By undertaking particular responsibilities through continuous acting and thinking, by facing and bearing particular difficulties, almost in a sense by sentencing ourselves to these, even though it may be at the expense of many things, we always have to act, to strive. If we do not act as we are, we are dragged into the waves caused by the thrusts and actions of others, and into the whirlpools of the plans and thoughts of others, and then we are forced to act on behalf of others. Remaining aloof from action, not interfering in the things happening around us, not being a part of the events around us and staying indifferent to them is like letting ourselves melt away, like ice turning to water.[33]

The stress on *hizmet* makes the movement distinct from that of Said Nursi, who, though not arguing against service, did not see it as a foundational principle. The stress on *hizmet* also opens up the movement to the public sphere. Any testing of the movement's ideas involves reflection on action and whether or not it embodies the ideas. *Hizmet* also therefore opens the movement to critical dialogue with other perspectives and to the possibilities of shared responsibility and action beyond the movement. Hence, for instance, the thinking about creation can be distinguished from perspectives such as that of Hans Jonas and others who have an essentially anthropocentric view of sustainable development.[34] Gülen's care of creation is not based on responsibility for future generations so much as responsibility to God. At the same time, both perspectives share a deep concern for the ecosystem and can work together for this good.

This, in turn, leads to a stress on plural identity, something not surprising in a Muslim thinker proud of his Anatolian identity and from a nation with an Islamic majority that is also capitalist. The Muslim is also a citizen. This moves beyond an individualistic view of citizenship and into one of citizenship as mutual responsibility, and thus as essentially social in expression. Gülen, in this vision of citizenship, sees the importance of a civil society and of the responsibility of the Muslim to contribute toward that civil society, not simply to focus on the Muslim community. This understanding involves several elements. First, he accepts a view of the common good that all can own.[35] Second, it is a short step from a view of the common good to one of human rights. As Ozcan Keles argues,[36] Gülen provides a basis for human rights in the Qur'an. Third, this is reinforced in Gülen's educational philosophy as developing universal values and virtues. In this, education becomes a critical means to the development of citizens. Education has to be founded on science, language skills, and educational excellence if it is to enable the development of people who can take leadership roles in business and society. In all this, it becomes possible for Islam to take its place in a post-modern age as key for the development of society.[37] Fabio Vicini notes that through the stress on action, and therefore the public nature of the Islamic responsiveness, Muslims are able to share responsibility for and debate about practice and underlying world views.[38] Hence, Gülen can focus on the *dar al-hizmet* (abode of service), with the Muslim as part of a creative dialogue about society.[39] This sense of responsibility for society extends to concern for peace and even for democracy itself.[40] In other words, the Muslim as citizen is not simply to accept the legal framework in which he finds himself but must work toward democracy as an ideal of the state and as a framework for civil society.

Central to the ongoing work of the movement is the provision of schools and, more recently, the support of universities. Given Gülen's thinking, it should be no surprise that these schools are not focused purely on Turkish or Muslim identities but have been developed across the world, fostering the national identities of the countries in which they are based.[41] In some cases, the schools have a minority of Muslims. In the Philippines, for instance, where there has been conflict between Christians and Muslims, one school accepted students and staff from both religions. In this case, the school moved beyond a narrow educational focus to becoming part of the development of civil society in a conflict or post-conflict situation.

Again, key to these schools is the development of the sciences and of universal values and virtues. The sciences enable critical reflection and ensure that science is not seen as antithetical to religion. The universal values include tolerance and justice, and they provide the basis for virtues that are central both to learning and to moral identity. Important for these is the consciousness of responsibility for responding to God's call. This is "a prayer, a supplication which is not rejected, and a powerful source for further alternative projects."[42] At times, this is seen as a "vast love for all creation,"[43] combining elements of *agape*, an all-embracing love, and eros, a creative love.[44] This leads to a strong sense of tolerance,[45] accepting difference but also calling everyone to creative action. Included among other virtues is that of purity of heart or intention (*ikhla*).[46] This is a response to God not based in secondary motivations, such as fear, self-interest, or even the interest or defense of the movement, but in simply pleasing God. Michael Graskemper also notes the virtues of excellence (striving to be the best) and commitment, in addition to service.[47]

The development of such virtues, in turn, is based in the plural community of the schools, which connect the families, the local community, and even businesses. The business leaders who are part of the movement work together to fund the development of the schools.[48] This activity becomes part of their *hizmet*—part of their corporate citizenship and their contribution to civil society. Responsibility in this requires cooperation and a negotiation of shared responsibility. Such negotiation recognizes resources and limitations, in the light of a sense of shared responsibility, and begins to identify how the common good can be effected in context. As noted above, the negotiation of responsibility takes the work well beyond a narrow view of religion. The development of a school in an area of conflict, for instance, moves the center of concern away from evangelism to response to need, and in turn it involves other stakeholders as co-creators in the development of peace.[49] This takes the business world into partnership with community and politics, and it thus affirms the idea of corporate citizenship. Again, holding the plurality of identity is critical. Business leaders are still primarily concerned about their business success, just as schools are focused on academic excellence. They are also citizens and, in Turkey for instance, Muslims and Anatolian Turks.

The action of the movement is also seen in the creation of a series of media outlets—primarily newspapers and television—placing it in the public sphere. This further enhances the core dynamic of being at home in the public realm and seeking to influence discussion in the secular society but also reciting the authentic voice of Islam. As a result, these outlets once more stress key universal values such as hard work, compassion, and justice.

The distinctive blend of spirituality, synoptic thinking, and plural identity, focused on the action of *hizmet*, points then to a complex and dynamic movement that does not rest on an institutional identity but constantly looks to fulfill the responsibility of vicegerent. What sustains this, bridging the different cultures, is dialogue.

DIALOGUE

At the heart of the Hizmet movement's philosophy and action is dialogue. Gülen's stress on spirituality, rationality, and action in the public realm inevitably takes this dialogue out of a narrow range of interfaith dialogue to intercultural dialogue. This has led to many different groups, such as the Intercultural Dialogue Center,[50] the Dialogue Society in London,[51] and the development of dialogue platforms, not least the Abant Platform of the Journalists and Writers Foundation. These efforts have brought together intellectuals, activists, journalists, and leaders of different groups. In 2007, the Abant Platform developed intra-dialogue in Turkey between the Sunni and the Alevi minority.

Dialogue is central to all the thought and action noted above, focusing on three interconnected aspects: consciousness of creation and the call to care for it, giving an account of thought and action, and initiating creative action. In the first of these, dialogue is essential to the development of consciousness of the environment and its nature in relation to God. Dialogue further enhances relationships with the other who shares responsibility for that environment. In one respect, it reveals the sameness of the other, something focused on in the interfaith dialogue platforms and through stress on universal values. It also focuses on difference and, with that, the importance of tolerance, again central to Gülen's thinking. Such dialogue also helps the development of a realistic and truthful assessment of the data in any situation. It enables the development of agency. It demands articulation of value and practice, which clarifies what we both think and do. Dialogue itself develops critical thinking. Even just the different perspective of the other questions and sharpens one's own values and core concepts.

This dialogue becomes even richer in light of Gülen's holism, synoptic thinking, and plural identity. The dialogue is not simply around ideas, and therefore does not lead to a dangerous stress on the defense of ideas. Samuel Huntington's thesis that Islam and the West are focused in a clash of civilizations is precisely located in such a pattern of defense and attack.[52] A holistic perspective, however, involves getting to know the self and other in mutual relations to plural culture, involving feelings as well as ideas, all focused on responsive action. It involves mutual challenge and mutual learning, with an outcome not of defense but of action. This approach, and not the defense of right thinking, is what pleases God. Hence, such dialogue primarily involves genuine engagement with the other, whether this "other" is a person, project, or place. It does not result in the assertion of the organization's location or identity in the public realm.[53] All of these elements demand that this pattern of ideas and actions involves being responsible not simply for critical thinking but also for the feelings that emerge around any sense of identity or around core values.

In the second aspect, dialogue can be seen as the key means of advancing accountability. In one sense, this involves dialogue as the major means of ensuring transparency. Writers such as William Park suggest that the movement is not institutionally transparent.[54] In a way, this is true. With many different groups involved in the movement, it is hard to see how responsibility can be worked through in a simple or linear way. However, the dynamic of dialogue itself embodies transparency, precisely because it requires all parties to give an account of their meaning and practice and thus be held accountable for it. Also, in many of the conferences organized over the past decade, this has involved an openness to critiques from different perspectives, not least in dialogue around the role of women in and governance of the movement.[55]

Such transparency enables the movement to give an account to society in general, and this is an important development of dialogue beyond simple bilateral relationships. It is not a free flow of meaning between participants, such as David Bohm's theory of dialogue.[56] Rather, the dialogue is focused on shared accountability to God and the global environment, and with that accountability to many different stakeholders, from the state to religion to other nations. This multiple accountability, which has echoes of Mikhail Bakhtin's focus on the interplay of many different voices,[57] demands an awareness of the different stakeholders and is held together by the stress on *hizmet*. There are also echoes of Paulo Friere's view of dialogue (as nondirective) in the way that leadership is dispersed in the movement.[58]

Dialogue also demands the development of commitment to the self and the other.[59] It is not possible to pursue dialogue without giving it space and time to develop, and this in turn demands a nonjudgmental attitude. Commitment to the self and the other is also essential if the potential critique of values and practice is to emerge from articulation and reflection. The practice of dialogue enables listening and, with that, empathy, appreciation, and responsiveness.[60] We learn about the other as well as ourselves only if we are open to both. This deepens any sense of accountability to the other in the dialogue. Dialogue itself also sets up a continued accountability with those involved. This is partly because it sets up a contract, formal or informal, that establishes expectations that are continually tested by that dialogue.

In the third aspect of dialogue, the stress is on action. Gülen suggests that we do not have to reach absolute agreement before working through the shared issues such as ignorance, poverty, and discrimination in society.[61] On the contrary, these issues provide a shared area of concern and, along with shared values, can be worked through regardless of differences. The stress on action strengthens the holistic framework. Action tests the accountability and commitment of those involved in the dialogue. Being accountable for actions also involves testing the actions against purpose and meaning. The actions themselves then become the basis for reflection on meaning. Such reflection becomes the basis for the development of integrity, connecting the different voices and practice.

Dialogue about creative action also enables the development of shared responsibility, not simply the recognition of shared interests. This leads to the negotiation of responsibility, exemplified in the way that businesses develop decisions around funding the work of the movement. This is very different from Jürgen Habermas's view of dialogue based on developing conceptual consensus.[62] The effect of dialogue is to extend the imagination and develop creativity. It shows what is possible, especially where responsibility is shared, and so increases the capacity to respond. In this respect, such dialogue enables the development of hope.[63] Hope can be characterized as the capacity to envision the future in a positive and creative way, and C. R. Snyder suggests that it involves agency, support, and pathways to action.[64] The first element of dialogue enables a sense of agency, personal and collective, in the participants as they develop clear understandings of purpose and identity around knowledge of ideas, values, and practice in relation to the social and physical environment. The stress on action looks to the development of pathways. Through the use of imagination and the negotiation of responsibility, pathways embodying core values are created. The commitment to action-based dialogue further enhances a sense of support and genuine engagement with the issues.

Such dialogue embodies the development of responsibility, which Gülen casts as universal responsibility.[65] This involves responsibility "for the creation of events, nature and society, the past and the futures, the dead and the living, the young and the old, the literate and the illiterate, administration and security. . . . Everybody and everything."[66]

Universal responsibility is not a simplistic moral responsibility, involving apportioning blame for everything, but implies proactive responsibility for engaging the past, present, and future, itself involving the practice of the key virtues—intellectual, spiritual, and ethical—such as practical wisdom, justice, and tolerance. Such dialogue is distinctively suited to peace building, involving creative openness to the other.[67]

CONCLUSION

The title of this chapter suggests that Gülen's thought is that of a bridge builder (*pontifex*) and that the Hizmet movement embodies such building. I have argued that, far from the identity of the Hizmet movement being problematic, it is focused on holism, synoptic thinking, and plural identity in the context of responsive service. There are institutional elements to the movement in the different groups that compose it, but it is the action-centered dialogue that sustains the movement as a whole. The dialogue at the heart of the Hizmet movement shows it "means business" and provides a dynamic of transparency that seeks an account of ideas, values, and practice that are critically tested, conceptually and empirically. It opens the dialogue to all parties so that plural perspectives can test each other. This context takes interfaith dialogue beyond the narrow and anodyne confines of discussions about theological concepts between religious leaders or theologians. It leads a dialogue of "engagement" rather than "location" (simply focusing on the identity and significance of the movement), cross-cultural dialogue, and trans-faith rather than simply inter-faith dialogue. The stress on practice and shared responsibility takes seriously the plural identity of the movement as Turkish, Muslim, and "global" in respect to citizenship, making the movement at home in the modern and post-modern worlds.

Poising a movement on such dialogue is, of course, a risky business. This is partly because it involves a constant learning process. The learning itself develops accountability as critiques are responded to openly.[68] This involves dialogue both inside and outside the movement. It is the bridges of service that sustain the movement, not any hierarchy as such. The moral and spiritual force is in the action, supported by appropriate organization. In a sense, that is why Gülen's leadership has been so important in enabling the movement to continually look both inwards and outwards. This dynamic means that the Hizmet movement and Gülen himself can be seen as being on a journey. In itself, this precludes any simplistic assessment of the Hizmet movement organization or of Gülen's thinking, not least because, in light of political and religious challenges,[69] no one can be sure of how either will develop.

In 2007, I was fortunate to visit Gülen and discuss some of these issues. At one point, I asked him what will happen to the movement when he dies. His response was simple. There is no planned structural response, no succession plan. Instead, he gave an answer that inhabited the "middle way" of practical wisdom and faith. He simply shrugged his shoulders and said that this would not be a cataclysmic event: "What will happen? They will pray." In other words, in his view, the answer will be found not in institutional organization but in dialogue with God and others who focus their response on the approach of *hizmet*.

NOTES

1. Eshan Masood, "A Modern Ottoman," *Prospect*, July 26, 2008.
2. William Park, "The Fethullah Gülen Movement," *Middle Eastern Review of International Affairs* 12, no. 3 (2008): 1–11.
3. See, for instance, http://turkishinvitations.weebly.com/repression-in-the-name-of-tolerance.html.
4. Ishan Yilmaz et al., ed., *Peaceful Coexistence: Fethullah Gülen's Initiatives in the Contemporary World* (Leeds: Leeds Metropolitan University Press, 2007).
5. Ernst Troeltsch, *The Social Teaching of the Christian Churches* (Chicago: Chicago University Press, 1981).
6. Erol Gulay, "The Gulen Phenomenon: A Neo-Sufi Challenge to Turkey's Rival Elite?" *Critical Middle Eastern Studies* 16, no. 1 (2007): 37–61.
7. Muhammed Çetin, "The Gülen Movement: Its Nature and Identity," in *Muslim World in Transition: Contributions of the Gülen Movement*, edited by Ishan Yilmaz et al., 377–90 (Leeds: Leeds Metropolitan University Press, 2007).
8. See http://www.gyv.org.tr.
9. Known as TUKSON; see http://www.tukson.org.
10. Çetin, "The Gülen Movement," 378.
11. Ibid.
12. Gulay, "The Gulen Phenomenon."
13. Ibid., 57.
14. Eileen Barker, *New Religious Movements: A Practical Introduction* (London: Her Majesty's Stationery Office, 1989).
15. Simon Robinson, *Spirituality, Ethics and Care* (London: Joanna Kingsley, 2008).
16. Çetin, "The Gülen Movment."
17. Park, "The Fethullah Gülen Movement."
18. Michael Graskemper, "A Bridge to Interreligious Cooperation: The Gülen-Jesuits Educational Nexus," in *Muslim World in Transition: Contributions of the Gülen Movement*, edited by Ishan Yilmaz et al., 622–31 (Leeds: Leeds Metropolitan University Press, 2007).
19. Joshua Hendricks, *Gülen: The Ambiguous Politics of Market Islam in Turkey and the World* (New York: New York University Press, 2013).
20. Eric M. Eisenberg, *Strategic Ambiguities: Essays on Communication, Organization, and Identity* (London: Sage, 2006).

21. Jim Paul and Christy A. Strbiak, "The Ethics of Strategic Ambiguity," *Journal of Business Communication* 34 (1997): 149–59.

22. See the recent coverage of this in Simon Robinson and Jonathan Smith, *Co-Charismatic Leadership: Critical Perspectives on Spirituality, Ethics and Leadership* (Oxford: Peter Lang, 2014).

23. Fethullah Gülen, *Prophet Muhammad: Aspects of His Life,* vol. 1 (Fairfax, Va.: The Fountain, 1995).

24. Fethullah Gülen, *Key Concepts in the Practice of Sufism: Emerald Hills of the Heart* (Rutherford, N.J.: The Light, 2004).

25. Gülen, *Prophet Muhammad,* 105.

26. Fethullah Gülen, "A Brief Overview of Islam," *The Fountain* 45 (2004): 4–6.

27. Fethullah Gülen, *Essentials of Islamic Faith* (Fairfax, Va.: The Fountain, 2000), 133.

28. Qur'an 2:30.

29. Fethullah Gülen, *Toward a Global Civilization of Love and Tolerance* (Rutherford, N.J.: The Light, 2004), 122.

30. Ibid.

31. Ibid., 124.

32. Charles Taylor, *Sources of the Self* (Cambridge, Engl.: Cambridge University Press, 1989).

33. Fethullah Gülen, *The Stature of Our Souls* (Somerset, N.J.: The Light, 2005), 96.

34. Hans Jonas, *The Imperative of Responsibility* (Chicago: Chicago University Press, 1984).

35. Fabio Vicini, "Gülen's Rethinking of Islamic Pattern and Its Socio-Political Effects," in *The Muslim World in Transition,* edited by Ishan Yilmaz et al., 430–44 (Leeds: Leeds Metropolitan University Press, 270).

36. Ozcan Keles, "Promoting Human Rights Values in the Muslim World: The Case of the Gülen Movement," in *The Muslim World in Transition,* edited by Ishan Yilmaz et al., 683–708 (Leeds: Leeds Metropolitan University Press, 2007).

37. Ali Ünal and Alphonse Williams, *Advocate of Dialogue: Fethullah Gülen* (Fairfax, Va.: The Fountain, 2009).

38. Vicini, "Gülen's Rethinking of Islamic Pattern," 441.

39. Ishan Yilmaz, "Dynamic Legal Pluralism in England: The Challenge of Postmodern Muslim Legality to Legal Modernity," *Journal of Ethnic and Migration Studies* 28 (2002): 2.

40. Keles, "Promoting Human Rights Values," 701.

41. Park, "The Fethullah Gülen Movement," 5.

42. Gulen, *The Stature of Our Souls,* 95.

43. Ibid., 32–33.

44. Robinson, *Spirituality, Ethics and Care.*

45. Gülen, *Toward a Global Civilization.*

46. Thomas Michel, "The Theological Dimension of the Thought of M. Fethullah Gülen," conference paper, October 7, 2010, Felix Meritis, Amsterdam, http:// fethullahgulenforum.nl/files/Mapping_the_Gulen_Movement.pdf#page = 58.

47. Graskemper, "A Bridge to Interreligious Cooperation."

48. Yasien Mohamed, "The Ethical Theory of Fetullah Gülen and Its Practice in South Africa," in *The Muslim World in Transition,* edited by Ishan Yilmaz et al., 552–71 (Leeds: Leeds Metropolitan University Press, 2007).

49. Selcuk Uygur, "Islamic Puritanism as a Source of Economic Development: The Case of the Gülen Movement," in *The Muslim World in Transition,* edited by Ishan Yilmaz et al., 176–86 (Leeds: Leeds Metropolitan University Press).

50. See http://www.gyv.org.tr.

51. See http://www.dialoguesociety.org/.

52. Samuel Huntington, *The Clash of Civilizations and the Remaking of World Order* (New York: Touchstone, 1998).

53. Ian Markham, *A Theology of Engagement* (Oxford: Blackwell, 2003).

54. Park, "The Fethullah Gülen Movement."

55. Helen Ebaugh, *The Gülen Movement: A Sociological Analysis of a Civic Movement Rooted in Moderate Islam* (London: Springer, 2009).

56. David Bohm, *On Dialogue* (London: Routledge, 1996).

57. Mikhail Bakhtin, *The Dialogic Imagination: Four Essays* (Austin: University of Texas, 1981).

58. Paulo Friere, *Pedagogy of the Oppressed* (London: Penguin, 1972).

59. Graskemper, "A Bridge to Interreligious Cooperation."

60. Ibid.

61. Fethullah Gülen, "Sorumluluk Suuru," *Yeni Ümit Magazine,* July–Sept. 29, 1995.

62. D. De Bolt, "Dialogue: Greek Foundations and the Thought of Fethullah Gülen and Jürgen Habermas," conference proceedings of *Islam in the Contemporary World: The Fethullah Gülen Movement in Thought and Practice,* Rice University, Houston, Nov. 12–13, 2005.

63. Robinson, *Spirituality, Ethics and Care.*

64. C. R. Synder, "The Past and Possible Futures of Hope," *Journal of Social and Clinical Psychology* 19, no. 1 (Spring, 2000): 11–28.

65. This echoes the post-Holocaust stress on universal responsibility in Zygmunt Bauman, *Postmodern Ethics* (Oxford: Clarendon, 1994), and Emmanuel Levinas, *Entre Nous: On Thinking-of-the-Other* (New York: Columbia University Press, 1998), the existentialist writings of Jean-Paul Sartre, "Existentialism," in *Basic Writings in Existentialism,* edited by G. Marino, 46–59 (New York: The Modern Library, 2004), and the grand spiritual statements of Fyodor Dostoevsky, *The Grand Inquisitor* (Indianapolis, Ind.: Hackett, 1993).

66. Gülen, *The Stature of Our Souls* , 95.

67. John Paul Lederach, *The Moral Imagination* (Oxford: Oxford University Press, 2005).

68. Ebaugh, *The Gülen Movement.*

69. See, e.g., Christopher de Bellaigue, "Turkey Goes Out of Control," *New York Review of Books,* Apr. 3, 2014, http://www.nybooks.com/issues/2014/apr/03 (accessed June 2, 2014).

SIX

Ethics in the Theory and Practice of Hizmet

Radhi H. al-Mabuk

THIS CHAPTER WILL FOCUS ON answering two questions. The first is: Since Fethullah Gülen and the Hizmet movement have much to say about morality and ethics, does one promote ethical discourse independently of various versions of Islam? The second question is: Can other religious systems or nonreligious networks learn from the movement? More specifically, I will first describe how Gülen and the Hizmet movement derive their understanding of morality and ethics from the primary and secondary sources of Islam. Their ethical understanding will be examined in terms of how ethics is enacted or applied. The chapter will then focus on similarities and differences of how ethical discourse is promoted by Gülen and the Hizmet movement compared to other versions of Islam. In the rest of the chapter, I will examine and describe ways other religious systems or nonreligious networks can learn from the ethical discourse and ethics-in-action of Gülen and the Hizmet movement.

I begin by posing the question that many have raised: What is the secret behind the broad, deep, and rapid influence of the Hizmet movement over

---

Not every member of an organization can live up fully to the ethical ideals propagated by that group's founders and leaders, and Muslims of all sorts are aware of the limits of their achievements. However, those who would appraise the Hizmet movement in its personal and larger contexts will ask what those ideals are, so that the relative achievements can be measured. We have asked Radhi al-Mabuk, professor of Education at the University of Northern Iowa, to summarize and set forth the ethical patterns and intentions, which he here does systematically and clearly. Some descriptions of how Hizmet ideals get lived out may sound unrealistic to many readers, but there need be little doubt as to what members of the movement expect of each other and themselves. Al-Mabuk clarifies what is expected and probes the reasons for ethical living in a movement whose very name focuses on "service."

diverse people on almost every continent of the globe? The answer lies in the ethical foundation upon which the movement rests and from which it derives inspiration and direction. The ethical base of the movement drives its tripartite mission or ethical interests: alleviating poverty through helping the poor and needy as well as through relief efforts; eradicating ignorance through educational initiatives; and promoting unity through intercultural and interfaith dialogue. So, what are the moral values that have motivated and continue to guide and inspire the work of this colossal transnational civic movement? And, where do these moral precepts come from?

The ethical base draws upon the primary and secondary sources of Islam. The primary sources consist of the teachings of the Holy Qur'an and the sayings and actions of Prophet Muhammad. The secondary sources include the thoughts and actions of the close and loyal companions of the Prophet and the spiritual guides that adhered to the true teachings of the Prophet. The ethical nutrients that nurture Hizmet are supplied chiefly by the writings, sermons, and counsel of the spiritual guide of the movement, Gülen— or Hocaefendi, as he is lovingly and endearingly called by the followers of the movement. Gülen's thoughts and teachings are deeply rooted in the teachings of the Holy Qur'an and the divine teachings and lived life of Prophet Muhammad. He also follows the example and counsel of the close companions of the Prophet and the spiritual guides that have followed in their footsteps. Gülen discerns that the ultimate objective of Islamic ideals is to help the individual to become perfect, refined, and self-actualized. Toward this aim, Gülen not only explicates but also leads by example the Islamic ethical principles and dictates. Although an original thinker, Gülen is very much practitioner-oriented, not a theoretician, when it comes to ethics. That is, he is most concerned with translating ethical precepts and virtues into proper actions, often preceding words with actions or at least matching words with deeds. In this respect, Gülen heeds the admonition of the following Qur'anic verses: "O you who believe, why do you say what you do not do? Great is hatred in the sight of Allah that you say what you do not do" (As-Saf, verses 2–3).

In no realm other than ethics is a Muslim called to match words with actions. Gülen fully understands that the singular and most central mission of Prophet Mohammed's message is to refine and complete the ethical ideals in order to perfect human character. To achieve this lofty divine mission, Prophet Muhammad taught humanity about ethics through actions. As Muslims believe, his lived life offers the perfect human model for developing excellence and virtue. They must emulate this model in all aspects of their lives. Indeed, Gülen follows the example of the Prophet and offers his insights and experiences to the Hizmet movement. His aim, following central teachings of Islam, is to strengthen the inner and spiritual dimension of the adherents so that they develop the qualities and qualifications to be vicegerents of God, to whom the angels were commanded to bow down. Later in this chapter, I will elaborate on the specific ethical ideals and qualities such as sincerity, honesty, humility, trustworthiness, tolerance, love, forgiveness, compassion, selflessness, and peacemaking that Gülen strives to instill in the followers of Hizmet. First, however, we must discuss the sources that inform Hizmet's ethical interests.

PRIMARY SOURCES OF ETHICS IN THE THEORY OF HIZMET

At the heart of Islamic ethics is the utter and unwavering belief that God is the Creator and source of all goodness, truth, and beauty, and that the ultimate responsibility of human beings is to submit to His will reverentially. Human beings are the responsible, dignified, and honorable agents of the Creator. They are God's appointed vicegerents on earth. Humans are so dignified by God that He put everything that is in the heavens and on the earth in their service. Humans are entrusted to do good and spread goodness in their lives and guard against corruption, evil, and wickedness. Hence, commitment and devotion to ethical ideals ensure that the human is honoring his or her mission of upholding good in this life.

Prophet Muhammad put much emphasis on the value and task of cultivating refined manners and character. The following *hadiths*, or sayings of the Prophet, underscore the centrality of refined manners in Qur'anic ethics:

The Prophet said: among the Muslims, the most perfect, as regards his faith, is the one whose character is excellent. (Al-Tiridhi, Hadith 628)

The best among you are the best in character (having good manners). (Sahih Al-Bukhari, Hadith 8.61)

Do you know the things which most commonly bring people into paradise? It is fear of Allah and good character. (Al-Tirmidhi, Hadith 4832)

The prophet said "I guarantee a house in the surroundings of Paradise for a man who avoids quarelling even if he were in the right; a house in the middle of Paradise for a man who avoids lying even if he were joking; and a house in the upper part of Paradise for a man who made his character good." *(Sahih Al-Bukhari, Hadith 5.104, narrated by Abdullah Bin Amr)*

In Sunan Abu-dawood, Hadith 4782, narrated by Abu Umamah, we read:

The most beloved to me amongst you is the one who has the best character and manners.

There is nothing heavier than good character put in the Scale of a believer in the Day of Resurrection.

The messenger of Allah said: By his good character a believer will attain the degree of one who prays during the night and fasts during the day.

ETHICS IN THE PRACTICE OF HIZMET

In order to understand the ethical ideals in the practice of Hizmet, it is helpful to think of the individual as operating at both ends of the spectrum within the following four arenas.

Obligatory to Supererogatory

Within this realm, an individual fulfills the obligatory rituals and deeds, and, by so doing, he or she is motivated to do good works for others. The act is still performed out of a sense of religious duty. If, however, the deed is performed out of love, then it falls within the supererogatory or *ihsan* domain. Before, during, and after performing the deed, the person's goal should be to seek God's pleasure only. If one engages in nonobligatory acts such as feeding the hungry and attending to the needy without regard for recognition or publicity, and if he or she does it anonymously, the act is said to be a supererogatory one. The Arabic word *ihsan* comes the closest in meaning to the word *supererogatory*, and it refers to deeds that are beautiful, proper, and suitable. The ethic of *ihsan* serves as an inspiration for Muslim piety, especially for Sufis. In the Hizmet movement, members are implored by Gülen individually and collectively to seize every opportunity to give of their time, effort, and money to help others without expectancy for reward, approval, or any material gain.

The young men and women in Hizmet who take up teaching responsibilities in faraway lands are an example of this obligatory-supererogatory ethical dimension. Teaching, for most faith-inspired groups, is a sacred act; some deem it an obligatory duty, whereas others welcome it with enthusiasm. In the latter case, teaching is seen as a divine favor and opportunity bestowed upon the dutiful servant. The servant, in turn, undertakes the duty with reliance on God for guidance, insight, and assistance to perform the act in the best and most complete manner possible. That is, he or she hopes to do the work with the utmost sincerity and purity of intention. Gülen goes so far as to teach that, at the highest point of sincerity in worship, the individual's aim is not Paradise but the pleasure of God. Gülen's point is in line with the third kind of worship that Imam Husain, grandson of the Prophet, described: "Some people worship God, coveting His rewards. This is worship of merchants. Some people worship God, fearing His punishments. This is worship of slaves. Some people worship God, thanking His blessings. This is worship of the free superior persons."[1]

Inner and External Dimensions

The inner dimension has been the focus of many scholars and spiritual masters. The heart is where the inner dimension is believed to operate, and it drives the entire human personality. The Sufis accord the inner dimension of the human a prominent and significant status. If the maintenance of the heart is neglected, then the heart is very likely to get sick, corrupt, and become a playground for evil tendencies. With ongoing service, watchful observation, and disciplined dedication, the heart is cleansed, purified, and brought closer to its Creator. The Qur'an uses the word *taqwa* to refer to one's vigilance against moral peril as it equips believers with the ability to control the inner thought that produces human action. Under the watchful eye of *taqwa,* the self-injurious or handicapping thoughts and impulses are redirected and transformed into positive and self-enhancing ones.

For the Sufis, the heart is the intrapersonal space where the inner self performs its mystic contemplation and comes into union with God. It is the gate to Divine love and knowledge. Gülen differs from the Sufis in that he stresses, in addition to the *intra*personal side, the *inter*personal dimension. Gülen asserts that "the inner and outer dimensions must never be separated."[2] Thus, one's contemplation and self-purification must be manifested outwardly in the form of good deeds and selfless service to others. Put differently, an individual's intrapersonal spirituality must materialize into an altruistic and tangible social action.

In striving to blend and integrate the two dimensions, the individual's self-purification regimen and aim must include attainment of sincerity of intention. Every act of worship a person performs must be predicated on the authentic and true intention of doing it for the sake of God. By so doing, a person will not expect monetary or moral rewards for the good deeds and services one undertakes. The reward is the pleasure and satisfaction one derives from doing good things, and doing them to please God and God only. Doing so may not be easy in an environment that thrives on and basks in human rewards and recognition. It takes the inner discipline of self-abnegation to reach the level of selflessness. This is the ultimate goal that Gülen teaches his followers to achieve.

Closely aligned with sincerity is the virtue of truthfulness, which also starts and springs from within and has direct effect on those who are genuinely striving to be truthful to God. This ethic is another jewel in the crown of a refined character, which Gülen covered in his book *Key Concepts in the Practice of Sufism*.[3] It is an ideal that was exemplified by all of the messengers of God, and one that they instructed their disciples to do. Like sincerity, truthfulness requires synergy between the outer and inner dimensions of the individual. When harmony of the two dimensions is achieved, the person's actions become infused with sincere intention, and the words and actions accord with the degree of belief the person has attained.

In speaking about truthfulness, AbdurRahman Mahdi mentions that Imam Ali, the cousin and son-in-law of the Prophet, pointed out the impact of truthfulness on others by saying, "Whosoever does three things with regards to people, they will necessitate three things from him: whenever he speaks to them he is truthful; whenever they entrust him with something he does not betray them; and whenever he promises them something he fulfills it. If he does this, their hearts will love him; their tongues will praise him; and they will come to his aid."[4] These words reflect an ethic that is essential for members in any movement, faith-inspired or not. It promotes trust among the members of the movement and, in turn, the movement with the communities they serve. Others will regard the members and the movement as trustworthy and reliable. The Prophet exemplified this ethic even before he received the revelation. The people of Mecca used to call him Al-Amin, the trustworthy one.

Concern for the Local and the Global

This dimension, often referred to as "glocal" in Hizmet circles, refers to the dual focus of the movement on immediate concerns and issues in the local community as well as on the needs beyond the community and outside the borders of one's country in a warm embrace of all humanity. It is this ethic that so appeals to people who encounter Hizmet for the first time—its ready tendency to demonstrate its "social conscience" and to share its blessings enthusiastically with others. Members of the movement have expressed their sympathy for the suffering of others by providing relief help and attending to the poor and needy both in Turkey (the original context of the Hizmet movement) and in Central Asia, Southeast Asia,*** the Balkans, Africa, the Middle East, and many other parts of the world. In essence, contributing to the well-being of the world has become the concern and ambition of Hizmet. Building bridges of friendship and goodwill with the peoples of the world is a daily activity and project for the Hizmet movement. Hands are extended and arms are stretched to embrace and welcome anyone who is willing to engage in dialogue and cultural exchange.

In the "glocal" context, the underlying ethic is derived from this saying of Prophet Muhammad: "The best amongst you is the person who serves other people." Worthy of emphasis is the Prophet's reference to "people," which includes Muslims and non-Muslims alike. From this teaching, the movement takes its "glocal" ethical dimension. In fact, Gülen describes the world as the stage of God's love. Going beyond one's geographical boundaries and familiar settings takes courage as well as intrapersonal and interpersonal skills. One must cultivate and nurture good character and disposition to be able to develop durable human relations, especially with people who have different cultures, languages, traditions, and customs as well as religions. Also, one must persevere and always be buttressed by faith and hope in the face of difficulties. Fatimah Abdullah maintains that engaging in the global stage requires ethical attributes such as mercy and its attendant manifestations of love, empathy, compassion, tolerance, and forgiveness.[5] These are the lofty human tools that would enable "servants of the globe" to surmount the potential hardships invariably and inevitably encountered along the way.

Concern with the Temporal and Eternal

The fourth and final ethical spectrum of Hizmet speaks to one's actions in this life and one's hopes and yearning for the afterlife. In this arena, sincerity, faith, patience, and other related dispositions and virtues are put to the test as the meaning of life and one's purpose in it are pondered. Gülen asserts that the "purpose of our creation is obvious: to reach our utmost goals of belief, knowledge, and spirituality; to reflect on the universe, humanity, and God, and thus prove our value as human beings. Fulfilling this ideal is possible only through systematic thinking and systematic behavior."[6] Faith propels the Hizmet volunteer to continue on the path with contentment that one is serving others for the sake of God. As hardships and obstacles arise, the volunteers rely on their sincerity and purity of intention so that their efforts are performed for the sake of God and they are awarded for their efforts whether they succeed or not. Buoyed by feelings of love and tolerance, Hizmet volunteers put these ethics into action by absorbing potentially harsh words and behaviors from critics or antagonists. They understand that serving others in this life can indeed be arduous work and that hard work pays off greatly—if not in this life, then surely in the hereafter.

Hizmet volunteers willingly, willfully, devotedly, and thoughtfully undertakes assigned or chosen duties in the movement and considers it their calling and source of joy and happiness. It is also thought of as a means to eternal life in heaven, which explains why the volunteers forsake some comforts and materialistic gain in this life. To them, this life is temporary, and its alluring comforts are fleeting and short-lived. The life worth sacrificing for is the next, the eternal one.

ETHICAL INTERESTS: ETHICS IN ACTION

The above four arenas of ethical life are demonstrated in the three major initiatives that define the Hizmet movement: waging war against poverty, ignorance, and disunity. These three challenges were identified by Said Nursi in the early twentieth century as the causes of backwardness in Turkey and other parts of the world. Gülen builds on Nursi's diagnosis of the social ills and tirelessly thinks of ways to address and eradicate them through various initiatives and programs carried out by the Hizmet movement throughout the world. The first initiative and largest of the three is seen in educational institutions, media outlets, and publications. The second is manifested in relief efforts and helping the needy. The third is promoting peace and unity through intercultural and interfaith dialogue. In these three domains, the Hizmet movement puts its ethical ideals into practice. We will examine the specific ethics involved in each.

War on Poverty

The peaceful Hizmet movement is opposed to war but, when it comes to poverty, wages a thoughtful and aggressive war to eradicate it. Expressions of "killing poverty" or "waging war against poverty" appear in old and new Islamic writings. Imam Ali, the Prophet's cousin, said, "If poverty were a man, I would have killed him!" Poverty robs humans of their humanity, and thus it is the greatest enemy of humanity. Combating it, therefore, is the highest ethic. By attending to the basic needs of the poor, hopeless, and helpless, humanity is restored. Humanity becomes healthy, hopeful, and whole again.

For Hizmet, caring for the poor is a central ethical imperative. Those who contribute funds for the poor, those who prepare food and serve them, and on-the-ground relief workers who lend a rescuing hand all demonstrate ethics in action. The Hizmet servant, more so in this domain than in any other, is implored to render this holy service with deep devotion and the intention of pleasing God. The obligatory-supererogatory, temporal-eternal, local-global, and internal-external considerations and motivations offer Hizmet volunteers an opportunity to reinforce and strengthen their belief, sincerity, and love for humankind.

The fight against poverty within Hizmet is exemplified in the humanitarian work of the Kimse Yok Mu (which means, Is Anybody There?) aid organization, which was officially inaugurated in 2004. In the relatively short period of its existence, Kimse Yok Mu has helped thousands of people in Turkey and in at least forty-two other countries. The work started after the 1999 earthquake in Turkey that claimed the lives of many people. A Turkish television program by the name of Kimse Yok Mu on Samanyolu Channel gradually transformed into an aid association in 2002 and was formally recognized as a humanitarian aid organization in 2004. Its aims epitomize the highest ethical ideals. Those aims, shared on its seventh birthday, included aid for disasters, aid for health, aid for education, aid given during holy occasions, individual aid programs, aid for Africa, and Sister Family Aid. The Sister Family Aid is focused on addressing family needs in Turkey and will undoubtedly globalize just like Hizmet's other initiatives.

Through its war against poverty, Hizmet is guided morally and ethically by the Islamic primary and secondary teachings, which exhort Muslims to provide compassionate care for the poor everywhere. One must not only sympathize with the suffering of the poor but also go beyond affects and cognitions to action—conscious and sincere action.

Crusade against Ignorance

Eradicating ignorance by providing educational access to people is the largest of the three initiatives of the Hizmet movement. This initiative was the original emphasis of the movement and is expected to remain one of its central aims. The importance of education is highlighted in the following words of Gülen: "If you wish to keep the masses under control, simply starve them from knowledge. They can escape such tyranny only through education. . . . [T]he road to social justice is through adequate, universal education."[7] Also, educational institutions including prekindergarten through grade 12 as well as higher education are believed by Hizmet to be the key to solving the poverty and disunity issues that are pervasive in the world. Until 1980, Hizmet focused on building schools in Turkey and Central Asia. Hundreds of schools were opened in former Soviet republics such as Kazakhstan, Kyrgistan, and Turkmenistan, and then the movement extended the educational project to other countries in Europe, North and South America, Africa, and Australia. The movement is willing to provide access to education wherever possible. Highlighting the importance of education, Gülen said that what society needs is not more mosques but more schools.

There are many striking features of Hizmet schools, including the high academic achievement of its students owing to the selfless devotion and effectiveness of their teachers and school administrators. The teacher expresses the Islamic ethic by enlightening and opening minds and hearts. Another feature is Hizmet's philosophy of blending science with spirituality. The curriculum used in almost every Hizmet school is a governmental and often a secularly based one. The openness and versatility of the Hizmet movement allow it to function extremely well in secular settings.

In addition to schools and universities, Hizmet's educational efforts expanded to the realm of media through encouraging and establishing media organizations to disseminate information and serve as a means of educating people. Professional, intellectual, and cultural organizations were established for the purpose of promoting knowledge and cultural exchange.

The single most important ethic that threads through all of Hizmet's educational activities is selfless service, which, when unpacked, comprises love, compassion, sincerity, devotion, and goodwill. Service is the outward illumination of these internally active ethical dynamics. The Hizmet teacher is an exemplary model for students and is both a teacher of content knowledge as well a shaper of character. The teacher inculcates in students an ethic of responsibility for self and others, which, in turn, passes the spirit of service onto the young generation. Students in Hizmet are gradually given opportunities to practice and internalize the ethic of service.

It is through this kind of education that Hizmet infuses and inspires ethically guided attitude and behavior in students, which Gülen envisions will produce the Golden Generation—a generation that will carry the torch of knowledge and Islamic ethics and lead others to the path of goodness, happiness, and advancement. Through their selfless and ethically guided actions, they will eradicate evil, ignorance, and disunity and create a peaceful world for all of humanity.

Combating Disunity

Hizmet has been described as a civic movement without borders. Of course, borders invariably exist in the world, whether they follow or create lines in the physical or geographical setting or are cultural or psychological in dimension. To operate in a bordered world, one needs the means to transcend those boundaries. The Hizmet movement does this by trying to extend its arms to embrace all fellow human beings. This takes a willingness and ability to reach out and connect with others. Gülen identifies two ethics: tolerance and dialogue as indispensible tools to waging peace and promoting unity. He recognizes that the path to unity among communities and people of the world is fraught with difficulties. It is "heart" work, and as such Gülen instructs the Hizmet volunteers to be heart-full and compassionate while engaging in goodwill and peace building. The operational directive that Gülen gives to the Hizmet peace-wagers is this: "Without hands against those who strike you; without speech against those who curse you."

The most common vehicle for promoting unity in the Hizmet movement has been through interfaith/intercultural dialogue. The overarching impetus for such dialogues is the profound belief of Gülen and Hizmet in the harmony, collaboration, and peaceful coexistence among civilizations. This position is decidedly a rational and natural reaction to the clash-of-civilizations theories that have become popular in the past decade. The Hizmet movement believes that world peace and harmony are not only possible but inevitable, and all must strive toward this humanitarian goal. The capacity for people to change for the better is always basic to assumptions in the movement.

International, national, and local conferences dealing with interfaith and intercultural dialogues have been convened by Hizmet on almost every continent. Seminars, presentations, and other efforts to engage in dialogue with people of different faith traditions and cultures are ongoing. These efforts have been productive and effective. For example, in an interview with the *Chicago Tribune's* John Kass, Greek Orthodox ecumenical patriarch Patrik I. Bartolomeos spoke very highly of Gülen's and Hizmet's efforts in promoting dialogue and building bridges among cultures in Turkey and around the world. Referring to his friend as Hocaefendi, the patriarch said, "He builds bridges, and religion should build bridges. This is why we need the dialogues. Not to have religious fanatics who divide people. The idea is to bring people of faith together for the benefit of humankind."[8]

Gülen has talked about a Golden Generation of heroes and heroines who, though they come from different cultural and religious backgrounds, would be united in their goal of achieving world peace through dialogue. Hizmet, according to Walter Wagner (an adjunct professor of World Religions at Moravian Theological Seminary in Bethlehem, Pennsylvania) "is the start of that generation of dialoguers and doers."[9]

Within this ethical interest of promoting unity, the temporal-eternal, glocal, inner-outer, and obligatory-supererogatory dynamics are operative. The Hizmet volunteer must mobilize the ethics of love, mercy, goodwill, and tolerance to perform the needed work with sincerity and dedication.

CONCLUSION

With the four ethical realms (inner-outer, obligatory-supererogatory, local-global, and temporal-eternal) and Hizmet's three ethical interests or imperatives (education, alleviating poverty, and promoting unity) in mind, we turn now to answering the two main questions posed at the beginning of the chapter. First: Does one promote ethical discourse independently of various versions of Islam?

The general answer is in the affirmative, with certain conditions. The different versions of Islam will dictate the scope of the ethical ideals one embraces and actualizes. Some versions or interpretations of Islam may emphasize education and compassionate concern for the poor as long as the audience and recipients live in one's immediate locality or are of the same faith. According to this version of the Islamic ethic, charitable work starts at home and may not extend beyond it. The ethical precepts may be performed out of a sense of strict or grim obligation, carried out for the sake of one's own salvation (earning more blessings), and done for the sake of earning enough credits to enter Paradise. Such ethical discourse gravitates toward the limited, parochial, and self-centered. Such a view would be considered incomplete by many Muslim scholars, Gülen certainly among them. He would argue that the sphere of Islam is the entire world, its message of mercy is for all humanity, and thus one's concern must be for all human beings.

Some versions of Islam may carry out humanitarian and educational missions for political gains and to expand one's group or party's influence. Hizmet is decidedly apolitical and insists on and persists in being a civic movement without borders.

The second question is: Can other religious systems or nonreligious networks learn from the Hizmet movement? Again, the answer would be "yes." In particular, they can learn from the comprehensive and global vision of Hizmet's projects. The ethic of selfless service, the name and the spirit of the movement, is inspiring. Service shows the ideals of a movement, and even a cursory review of Hizmet reveals an organization that is always in action. The members are expected to be thoughtfully engaged and involved in the various outlets, branches, networks, initiatives, and programs of the movement throughout the world. Others can learn from the brotherhood and sisterhood that bind the members of the movement to each other and to others in their communities. The generosity, truthfulness, genuineness, and sincere goodwill that members of Hizmet share with their fellow citizens of the world are endemic. Thus, others can learn from Hizmet's program of ways of shaping human character and giving it purpose and meaning. Moreover, others can join hands with Hizmet and collaborate with it in the gigantic task of solving the world's problems. Hizmet's Kimse Yok Mu has sounded the call for collaboration as follows: "We build bridges made of mercy for the world. Is there anybody who says, 'Here I am!?'"

NOTES

1. "Sayings of Imam Husain," compiled and translated by Syed Zainulabedin Razavi, http://www.imamreza.net/eng/imamreza.php?id=9917.

2. Thomas Michel, "Sufism and Modernity in the Thought of Fethullah Gülen: A Class or a Dialogue of Values?" *The Muslim World* 95 (2005): 345.

3. Fethullah Gülen, *Key Concepts in the Practice of Sufism: Emerald Hills of the Heart* (Rutherford, N.J.: The Light, 2004).

4. Quoted in AbduRahman Mahdi, "The Virture of Truthfulness: The status and Rewards of Truthfulness," http://www.islamreligion.com/articles/424 /viewall/ (accessed Oct. 23, 2014).

5. Fatimah Abdullah, "Teaching Islamic Ethics and Ethical Training: Benefiting from Emotional and Spiritual Intelligence," *International Journal of Humanities and Social Science* 2, no. 3 (2012): 224–30.

6. Gülen, *Key Concepts in the Practice of Sufism*.

7. T. Michel, "Gülen as Educator and Religious Teacher," paper presented at the Fethullah Gülen Symposium, Georgetown University, April 2001.

8. John Kass, "With Faith and Hope, Turkey Builds a New Identity," , *Chicago Tribune*, Apr. 11, 2012, http://articles.chicagotribune.com/2012-04-11/news/ct-met-kass-0411-20120411_1_orthodox-christians-halki-turkey.

9. W. Wagner, "The Worldwide Repercussions of Incitement to Hatred and Violence," paper presented at A Decade After 9/11: Incitement to Hatred and Violence on the Basis of Religion or Belief Conference, New York City, Sept. 28, 2011, http:// www.peaceislands.org/portfolio/the-worldwide-repercussions-of-incitement-to-hatred-and-violence.

SUGGESTIONS FOR FURTHER READING

Ansari, Abdul Haq. "Islamic Ethics: Concept and Prospect." *American Journal of Islamic Social Sciences* 6, no. 1 (1989): 81–91.

Arslan, Faruk. "The Hizmet Movement of Canada's Limitations and Weaknesses for a Healthy Dialogue." *Consensus* 35, no. 1 (2014): 1–9. http://scholars.wlu.ca /consensus/vol35/iss1/5.

Barton, Greg. "Preaching by Example: Global Philanthropism and Civil Religion." Paper presented at Global Perspectives on the Religious, Cultural, and Societal Diversity in the Balkans: Fethullah Gülen Experience as a Model and Interfaith Harmony in Albania, London School of Economics, England, 2007.

Gülen, M. Fethullah. *Prophet Muhammad: Aspects of His life*. Vol. 1. Fairfax, Va.: The Fountain, 2000).

———. Toward a Global Civilization of Love and Tolerance. Rutherford, N.J.: The Light, 2004.

Hashi, Abdurezak Abdulahi. "Islamic Ethics: An Outline of Its Principles and Scope." *Revelation and Science* 1, no. 3 (2011): 122–30.

Kamali, Mohammad Hashim. *Exploring the Intellectual Horizons of Civilizational Islam*. Selengor, Malaysia: ARAH Publications, 2009.

Michel, Thomas. *A Christian's View of Islam: Essays on Dialogue*. Maryknoll, N.Y.: Orbis Books, 2010.

———"Fighting Poverty with Kimse Yok Mu." Paper presented at the Islam in the Age of Global Challenges: Alternative Perspectives of the Gülen Movement Conference, Georgetown University, Washington, D.C., 2008.

———. "The Theological Dimension of the Thought of M. Fethullah Gülen." In *Mapping the Gülen Movement: A Multidimensional Approach Conference, 7 Oct. 2010*. Amsterdam: Felix, 2010.

Nanji, Azim. "Islamic Ethics." In *A Companion to Ethics*, edited by Peter Singer, 106–18. Oxford: Blackwell, 1991.

Rayan, Sobhi. "Educating toward Values." *Islam and Civilizational Renewal* 2, no. 3 (2011): 468–81.

Siddiqui, Ataullah. "Ethics in Islam: Key Concepts and Contemporary Challenges." *Journal of Moral Education* 26, no. 4 (1997): 423–31.

Tahir, Ali Raza, and Muhammad Sohail. "The Concept of Ethical Life in Islam." *Interdisciplinary Journal of Contemporary Research in Business* 3, no. 9 (2012): 1360–69.

Toguslu, Erkan. "Gülen's Theory of Adab and Ethical Values of Gülen Movement." In *Muslim World in Transition: Contributions of the Gülen Movement*, edited by Ishan Yilmaz et al., 445–58. Leeds: Leeds Metropolitan University Press, 2007.

Vicini, Fabio. "Gülen's Rethinking of Islamic Pattern and Its Socio-Political Effects." In *Muslim World in Transition: Contributions of the Gülen Movement*, edited by Ishan Yilmaz et al., 430–58. Leeds: Leeds Metropolitan University Press, 2007.

SEVEN

Gülen as an Educator

Tom Gage

"THOUGHT DOES NOT CRUSH TO STONE." This deceptively simple line embodies an understanding of how truth resists antagonistic forces, endures time's erosion, and reigns eternal, like a diamond emerged from dross. The line comes from the poem "Adamant" by the American Theodore Roethke. In many ways, the adamantine truths of Fethullah Gülen's philosophy have prevailed over several decades and today are most evident in successful schools inspired by him around the world. Like Roethke, Gülen is a poet. He is a "philosopher of education" in the sense of how that phrase denoted, in the nineteenth century, a Ralph Waldo Emerson or others who strongly influenced the thinking and action of both administrators and teachers of students. Gülen is a theologian, a scholar of Sufism, and one who is deeply influenced by the poet Rumi. For four decades, Gülen's words have challenged thousands in a similar manner to the way President John F. Kennedy's inaugural address summoned fellow Americans to "Ask not what your country can do for you but rather what you can do for your country." However, for Gülen, the call to action becomes "what you can do for humanity."

As is made plain throughout this volume, Hizmet is a Turkish-based movement with a global impact. Its dual character is never more evident than in its commitment to education. The presence of schools sponsored or influenced by Fethullah Gülen and his followers has for decades been visible and vivid in Turkey, but now schools motivated by the concepts associated with *hizmet* (service) are prospering, and their numbers are growing in nations far from Turkey, including in North America, where Muslims are in the minority. Tom Gage (professor emeritus of English at Humboldt State University) accounts for the accent on teaching and research in these schools and connects the educational ideas and ideals of Hizmet with the larger cultures, wherever they are found.

Those thousands inspired to serve are identified collectively as the Hizmet movement, the Turkish word in this book's title, which denotes selfless service to humankind. Among Hizmet's many fields of service, and foremost in the public's attention, is education.[1] Gülen's influence on education in the United States has recently attracted coverage in the media, some of it misleading and even distracting from his peace-building educational mission.[2] His approach deserves careful examination and fair representation, which this chapter is intended to provide.

Gülen's impact on education needs to be differentiated into several endeavors. First among these are the schools, both public and private, at elementary, secondary, and tertiary levels. Another important division of his efforts includes tutorial assistance for poor students from remote areas who are adapting to urban universities. Third is encouragement of projects that highlight student achievements in science, like the Olympiad, and in writing, like the Youth Platform, which celebrates young authors from the United States as well as many international high schools. The topics of these essay contests often focus on peace making.[3]

This discussion entails an account of the positive effects of the philosophy of Gülen on education around the world, along with a review of critics' charges, covering the situating of Gülen in the context of literary genre theory. The first Gülen-inspired schools were in Turkey, where he began teaching near Izmir, opposite the Aegean Isle of Chios where Homer composed. From there, schools began to appear elsewhere, including across Asia, Turkmenistan, Uzbekistan, and Kyrgyzstan, south to Cambodia and the Philippines, and throughout Africa, such as in Nigeria, Burkina Faso, Ethiopia, Morocco. The astonishing spread of Gülen's influence extends to South Africa and Europe (particularly France, the Netherlands, Germany, and Ireland) and to the Americas (especially Mexico, the United States, and Canada).

Some Gülen-inspired schools are private and tuition-funded, like Brooklyn's Amity School. Others are publicly supported, and still others are innovative hybrid programs adjoined to schools in public districts. In every case, both private and public schools are nondenominational and do not include teaching religion. This fact is key, and its importance warrants exposition, since some critics misunderstand and other misrepresent the Hizmet schools as challenges to the separation of church and state. Because the U.S. constitutional tradition does not allow for public education to include religious practices and accents, the "separation" concern is more focused there, but it has also been raised in other locales such as Kosovo and Australia. We shall deal with some of these concerns later in the chapter.

In this writer's view, Gülen's name will someday be included among other international educational philosophers who have deeply influenced American education, like the Italian Maria Montessori and the Russian Lev Vygotsky. To this point, Gülen is recognized for the ways he advances and elaborates a fusion of Eastern and Western humanism, one that is undervalued today.

Nasser D. Khalili, an Iranian entrepreneur and now a citizen of the United Kingdom, claims that "Islamic art and culture has made a huge contribution to the West."[4] Scholars in many fields acknowledge the huge debt that the West owes the Muslim world, whether in the sciences, the arts, medicine, or concerning the very cosmos.[5] It is from this heritage that Gülen derives his teachings in order to benefit learners across the world. Those who acknowledge that most Greek science entered Europe from Arab lands merely credit Muslims as transmitters, but Muslims were and are far more than mere cultural transmitters. For instance, although the West inherited much from an attenuated classical past, its curriculum is fused, mostly unconsciously, with the Islamic tradition, where its participation in providing a common cultural ground is not generally understood.

Those people educated in the U.S. and European elementary and secondary schools may not have been introduced to the ways that Christian art and literature of the Middle Ages and early Renaissance melded Roman and Islamic cultures; the latter is not often credited or understood. Another way to consider the amalgam of modernity is that the West acquired the products of Greek genius as they were upgraded and extended by Muslims from the tenth through the sixteenth centuries.

Over that time, such as during the Renaissance and under the influence of figures like Petrarch, this classical heritage was recognized as a sole cultural source, as if "the grandeur that was Rome" should receive all the credit for civilization's march forward. To tease out but one illustrative paradox, consider Aristotle's "Poetics." The only source used was first translated into Latin from Arabic a few years after Columbus set sail. Then, a decade later, it was translated back into the supposedly seminal Greek of Aristotle.

Authors like Chaucer, in *The Canterbury Tales,* or Dante, in *The Divine Comedy,* acknowledged the importance of Ibn Rushd, among a host of other Muslim scientists. Like the education of Montessori, a Christian, or of Vygotsky, a Russian Jew, Gülen's teaching of only the *temsil* (secular) subjects is commensurate with that practiced in public, tax-funded schools in the United States today. We note how today's elementary and secondary school curriculum is not only the *temsil* subjects of music, grammar, arithmetic, astronomy, geometry, composition, and thinking but also algebra and trigonometry, which demonstrate add-ons from Muslim traditions and cultures. In practice, teaching only *temsil,* those secular sciences, in schools, as is done in Gülen-influenced schools, and teaching religion only in churches, temples, and mosques avoids infringing on the human rights of minorities and is congruent with the practices following the U.S. Constitution.

The subjects taught in schools as well as other Gülen-inspired enterprises, enumerated by Helen Rose Ebaugh's sociological analysis of the Hizmet movement,[6] are further evidence of our common heritage and, in some cases, of Western debt to Islamic innovations. Among these institutions are hospitals, banks, media outlets, disaster relief efforts, and investigative journalism. Following the Dark Ages, a newly literate Europe appropriated much from Islam by operationalizing disciplines into similar service institutions that Gülen has envisioned and has realized by his contemporary Hizmet enterprises. As Fernand Braudel wrote in his influential study of the Renaissance and Mediterranean world, "Our Middle Ages were saturated, shot through with the light of the East, before, during, and after the Crusades."[7] That light mutually illuminates Gülen's heritage and the modern world, shining still today in peace-building schools.

GÜLEN'S INFLUENCE AND THE CRITICS

This summary of innovations in the Muslim world that were imported and then developed in the West provides a key to understanding the Gülen-inspired schools and their educational projects in their diverse forms. It also opens the subject of how the media have responded to a Muslim imam influencing American education. A host of books and occasional mass media representations show how Gülen reformulated the message of his tradition to address modern needs by encouraging dialogue, tolerance, and the building of schools rather than of mosques. Beyond the world of Islam, Gülen's vision of education manifests itself at the following six levels.

First, it is a move from a passive endorsement of education, occasionally modified positively and negatively by media sensationalism, to a public embracing of those who teach and of institutions hosting interaction by its stress on commitment to and support of learners. This shift so values teachers and education that young Gülen-school graduates in Turkey[8] and, one hopes, young American graduates will soon, in increasing numbers, be pursuing careers in teaching.

Second, Gulen's vision is congruent with the earlier American traditions in which the education of children is, to a greater extent, under the aegis of local authority. Increasingly, state and federal administrations have linked student outcomes (with respect to curricular achievement components) with percentages of funding sources. From the viewpoint of those who embrace Gülen-style educational models, that is a faulty alignment. Such cost-benefit accounting, they observe, has often led to miseducation that expunges the magic of classroom learning. As money comes increasingly from more and more remote sources, the neighborhood school and its classroom teachers have less say in what is taught, how that material is taught, and how to measure learning. The sum of grade point averages via teachers' subjective assessments has been the best predictor of future successes, better than the additional expense of supposedly cheap quick-fixes by state and federal assessments that purport to save tax-payer dollars but seldom do.[9]

Third, this vision is inspiring students leaving universities and citizens at large not to invest in materialist pursuits and to give increasing priority to altruistic agencies that serve humankind. This service may require one's relocation, sometimes to remote and challenging environments; it also encourages entrepreneurs who draw on Gülen's Islamic tradition, leaders whom he valorizes, to provide needed financial support for education.

Fourth, it conceives of the family model, rather than the factory model, for education. The factory model was revealed in such educational diction as the "superintendent" who heads the enterprise and of the school setting as the "plant." The family model means involving teachers, parents, and offspring in the learning process that returns education to a rapport that necessitates shifts in its stance.[10]

Fifth, this vision sets out to realize Gülen's project of forming centers for harmonious and tolerant dialogue among all participants. This requires opting for education not as learning from delivery or debate—in which there are winners and losers—but from a symposium of mutual respect and good will for all. The language in such cases is characterized by tag lines of "yes/and" rather than "yes/but." In Gulen's vision and practice, the "yes/and" approach better bonds the learner's heart and the mind, the study of science, moral behavior, and the valuing of the past.[11]

Sixth and finally, in addition to his reliance on the past, Gülen explicitly advocates education that addresses the needs of modernity with a focus on science, humanities, digitization, and ethics. These ideas anticipate implementing goals for the post-modern classroom of computers and handheld tools that have replaced styluses, compasses, and chalkboards. For the global economy of the technological age, modernity demands new strategies for acquiring knowledge and morality in updated configurations.

Given the boldness of their proposals and approaches, Gülen, Hizmet, and Turkish Americans who are involved with education have come under scrutiny. Messages and linkages on the Internet range from adulation at one extreme to paranoia at the other. For example, a Texas network in the Houston area known as the Harmony Public Schools is cited in many of these critical reports, including a *New York Times* article and a *60-Minutes* story.[12] (Harmony emerged when several Turkish graduate students at universities in Texas found the state of science and math education to be deplorable, a situation also recognized by the U.S. Department of Education. Answering this need, they organized the Harmony charter school to provide a focus on science, math, and engineering.) Harmony has addressed allegations that the schools include *teblig* (religious topics) with responses or arguments like these: If religion has indeed been taught at any of the Harmony campuses, one would expect that in a free and pluralistic society, someone—be they students, parents, or teachers—would have reported this to the authorities. As for occasional allegations that the teaching of religion in the schools occurs but is not reported: With more than 99 percent of the Harmony student body and their parents being non-Muslim, non-Turkish Americans, one must ask, would such a practice truly go unnoticed? Allegations of teaching Islam are rooted in fear-mongering, officials at Harmony argue, with the intention of perpetuating religious and racial prejudice.[13]

Those who are critical of either Gülen or Hizmet point to, for example, the lack of transparency and accountability, plus the presumed intimidating power as well as the ineffability of the founder. Some claim that Turkish teachers in the American schools were underprepared, or that their dialects were challenging to students, and they were accused of having slipped into the United States as if to form a cell. These are allusions that reflect the climate of fear that has so often shadowed American life. Still another accusation was that the schools are staffed with faculty members who are in America on visas, but, according to the Harmony response, only 10 percent were. Criticism aimed at how public monies are spent always warrants investigation, but, in the case of Harmony Public Schools in Texas, the allegations were credibly responded to. Criticism from teacher unions needs also to be addressed, since the private character of Hizmet schools can be a challenge to unions. As a member of the American Federation of Teachers for half a century, I have good reason to be alert to this. But, in my view, the language of the majority of critical writers during the time of controversy over these issues has been full of innuendo. It hinted that investigations, both federal and local, were pending and forebode dire consequences. Since 2010, when the attacks were made, it has become clear that nothing of consequence has turned up.

In all of the attacks on Gülen schools, the words "Turk" and "Turkey" appear regularly, which is an effort to identify the education provided in the Gülen schools with the Republic of Turkey. Reflecting on my own encounters with Hizmet events since 2007, I have dealt with many Turks, as one would expect, since Gülen emerged with his earliest audience from Turkey. One of the teachers from Turkey counts more Greeks than Anatolians in his ancestry. I have met others who are several-generational Americans, one of whom can identify sixteen progenitors that include Anglo, Turk, and Native American ancestries. I have met Kurds, others from Azerbaijan, Kyrgyzstan, and Kazahkstan, a Kosovar, an Australian, and an American, part Japanese and English, who taught in Vietnam. Clearly, the Hizmet movement embraces an international membership.

Regarding other positive contributions of the movement, in the title essay of *Statue of Our Souls* Gülen enumerates the competencies needed by students who will be future leaders. In that essay, he concentrates on a variety of means to achieve integrative harmonious personalities. He describes such learned attributes that relate to "turning to science with a trio of reasoning, logic, and conscience"; pursuing knowledge of the universe; understanding with mathematics how humanity and natural phenomena relate; and appreciating art.[14] Gülen's generalizations are heuristics; further specificity only limits them, for the attributes, though general, have pragmatic implications. More concrete specifics of what should be taught are up to the schools but always in conformity with the directives of the education departments of the state. Nowhere are a society's values more codified than in its educational curricula and its assessments of such in outcomes-evaluations. Gülen-inspired schools in the United States respect the local and state authorities, and they likewise trust in the will of elected and appointed officials to serve the publically determined good.

Much of what I have stressed in this discussion may sound abstract, but I have practical aims. Let me draw upon a theoretical assessment in my book *Gülen's Dialogue on Education*; using Gülen as a center of a Venn diagram, I explore overlapping commonalities with major educational theorists, including Montessori, Vygotsky, John Dewy, Jean Piaget, and a variety of social educational constructionists.[15] In addition to these valid comparisons, Gülen accents love, openness to dialogue, respect for others, and resilience in the face of ambiguity—these being attitudinal components too rarely addressed in the educational literature. This stance and these strategies are congruent implicitly with prominent education theorists—whether conservative, like Karl Bereiter, or progressive, like Robert Reich, former U.S. secretary of labor under President Bill Clinton. Instead of a teaching model that is just the delivering of facts assessed subsequently on multiple-choice tests, the goals of teaching today include improving skills for collaboration, developing expanded and deepened system thinking, honing competence and sophistication for abstract thought, and increasing one's repertoire for experimentation, all prioritized by academics and informed by significant laypersons as well. Implicitly, Gülen values these student outcomes, which, like the powerful influence of the family, derive from a nourishing but perplexing environment.

Gülen enumerates as learned attributes—or abilities that must be acquired by those he calls "Inheritors of the Earth"—the competence to think abstractly (that is, to infer the microcosm from the macrocosm and to be able to extrapolate from the microcosm to the macrocosm), to engage collaboratively, to be well grounded in math, science, and aesthetics, to exhibit initiative; and to experiment in systemic patterning. Gülen has in mind those future highly educated leaders of business and government as well as all voting citizens of a democracy. He elaborates this last objective, which is "collaboration," in a chapter entitled "Consolation" in *Statue of Our Souls*. This he sees as an essential requisite for cooperation, whether on the part of the rulers or the ruled, by adults or young students; it is "one of the prime dynamics which keep the Islamic order standing as a system."[16] Gülen elaborates further:

> Even if a person has a superior nature and outstanding intellect[,] if they are content with their own opinions and are not receptive and respectful to the

opinions of others, they are more prone to make mistakes and errors than the average person. The most intelligent person is the one who most appreciates and respects mutual consultation and deliberation (*mashwarat*), and who benefits most from the ideas of others.[17]

As with the family's influence, Gülen values knowledge acquired when learners and teachers learn simultaneously in group work to identify, broker, mediate, and solve problems via engaging cooperatively with shared, learned strategies of how to advance a project that entails assigned stages. I contend that this thrust toward consultation, collaboration, and systems-thinking is crucial for U.S. education at every level. For too long, among those influenced by the Gülen perspective, the culture has been mired in subjective individualism, keyed to self-reliance and autonomy, concepts that have been inherited from the American past but, unless transformed and reconfigured, are ill-fitting for the global economy. Throughout the United States, specific zones of enterprise sustain catalytically our economy among world markets and are unmatched in internet technology, communications, space exploration, computer security defense, and molecular biology and biotechnology in areas like Silicon Valley, California; Atlanta, Georgia; Austin, Texas; Cambridge, Massachusetts; and Fayetteville, Arkansas. These and many other geographic pockets are composed of women and men engaged in consultation and in the above-described collaborative endeavors. To attain status in these positive zones of productivity, one must broaden any local centrisms, whether Amero-centric or Eurocentric for the multi-centrism of the global citizen. In my half-century of experiences in Turkey, I find of late many catalyzers of synergy among the Hizmet movement, those whom Gülen calls "*aksiyon insanlar*," or "people who act." These are agents whose collaboration with others makes a difference through their writing, teaching, or working as aid volunteers responding to those in need after disasters.

Gülen's foundation is love, which he sees as an attribute of altruism grossly needed in an economy that encourages and, too often, feasts on greed. These components of Gülen's educational philosophy undergird needed attitudes lacking in all the present subject disciplines. Consider, for instance, the example of education for engineering, as spelled out by Yetkin Yildirim: "In preparation for unseen challenges of the future, Gülen understands that scientists and engineers must be made accountable and aware of the ethical dimension of their work. For this reason, new models for scientific education, models that welcome the involvement of ethical and moral perspectives, must be explored."[18]

Gülen stresses positive attitudes—among several themes—as foundational in today's education, because the learner's attitude will significantly shape his or her future in the marketplace, and yet attitude cannot be measured by standard accountability testing. For several semesters at Humboldt State University in California, I investigated with both undergraduate and graduate students the causes for local employers to terminate their employees. Students interviewed more than a hundred employers in businesses along the north coast. Overwhelmingly, the data indicated attitudinal causes for firings, such as inability to deal with aged clients, lateness, not listening, dishonesty, and blaming others for errors. In rare cases, perhaps 2 percent of them, reasons for termination were because of the employee's lack of so-called skills, the acquiring of which has often been seen as the sole purpose of education. Research by the U.S. Center for Research and Development in Higher Education that focused on personality over a half-century supports the importance that Gülen prioritizes.[19] Gülen's message is to expand from the authority of the self as part of a family to being a responsible member of a larger community.

As a caveat relating to Gülen's culture, it may be wise at this point to discuss reading his philosophy in translation. I write about Gülen's education theories with the guidance of some who read him in Turkish. However, all translation misrepresents the source to a certain extent. Gülen's exposition reveals contrasting rhetorical strategies and literary genres remote to Western eyes, a thesis corroborated by recent studies of Muslim discourse.[20] Gülen's craft of composing entails different aims and audiences, depending on whom he is addressing. These are not general but specific to the *ummah,* or Muslim congregations.[21] Like, perhaps, in the case of the rhetoric of Dr. Martin Luther King, Jr., whose metaphors may appear to the jaded as flowery, Gülen's images can filter into English as awkward. For example, the word "tolerance," derived from the Turkish, implies in English hegemonic/subaltern relations. Can one ask of a street person to be tolerant? Such connotations belie the semantics of the Turkish source, which is best rendered into English as "not feeling discomfort in the presence of difference."

Along with the problem of translation, those who deal cross-culturally with Gülen's thoughts and strategies also have to address with the issue of genre. Since the advent of Mikhail Bakhtin's influential work of genre theory, scholars for the past quarter century have been called to understand how the mind compartmentalizes utterances.[22] Research of Arab autobiography and conversion narratives, analyzed by Wayne Booth, reveal distinctive features.[23] This discourse is structured in light of audience awareness and upon organizing principles foreign to structures with which Europeans are familiar. As Dwight Reynold explains: "[C]ontents of autobiographies reflect a widespread conceptualization of life as a sequence of changing conditions or states rather than as a static, unchanging whole or a simple linear progression through time."[24] He elaborates:

> Although it is filled with narratives of differing lengths, the work as a whole rejects the concept of ordering a life into a single narrative, a life "story" in the literal sense. Rather, it [Arab autobiography] derives from an intellectual methodology in which classification, categorization, and description were the ultimate tools for the acquisition and retention of knowledge.[25]

As with autobiography and conversion narratives, so it is analogically in the other expository genres that Gülen favors.

EDUCATION WITHIN THE U.S. TRADITION

In the context of intellectual conflicts in U.S. history, a particular legal and political issue calls for attention. It refers to the legacy of the American founders, who authored in 1776 the Declaration of Independence and, later, in 1787 and 1789, the Constitution with the Bill of Rights. Some political factions who today advocate a "Christian America" create the impression that these founders were all orthodox Christians trying to invent a republic that privileged their particular faith. Although most of these founders were, in fact, Christians of one sort or another, much of their thinking on constitutional and educational matters reflected their variety of religious influences as well as a desire to begin separating church from state. Some were Deists, a mix of Free Masons and those influenced by the European Enlightenment. The Evangelicals, who were dominant in the culture, had to work with and benefit from the Enlightenment figures and ideas. They allied to draft and then to adopt the Virginia Statue of Religious Freedom. The initial separation of church and state came to a head when Evangelicals of the newly liberated nation battled over taxation. Baptists rejected any idea of the new government subsidizing with their tax dollars the salaries or costs for maintaining rival houses of Episcopalian worship. The first seven

U.S. presidents belonged to this denomination, the American version of the Anglican Church of Imperial Great Britain that this ex-colony had just rejected. The First Amendment to the Constitution, which extended liberties to members of all denominations, derived not from secularists but from the religious among the Founding Fathers.[26] None willed the full expunging of religion to the extent practiced in France or Turkey, such as many ideological secularists of today advocate.

Since the 1960s, Gülen has criticized laicism,[27] the centralized administration of education, and the imposition of a national curriculum. These articulations have led to his arrest though never to a conviction of guilt for undermining the Turkish state.[28] Although Gülen has consistently raised issues about how the Republic of Turkey centralized the administration of education, he has also consistently advocated that the schooling of youth address only *temsil* subjects and, further, that schools and teachers conform to what B. Jill Carroll calls "a state-mandated curriculum and to submit themselves to state review."[29]

Some scholars, Carroll among them, consider Gülen a humanist in the tradition of Erasmus (1466–1536). Both of these thinkers reveal an openness and piety in contrast to scriptural authority as conceived in their times. Enlightened leaders of their times welcomed each, but their goals of peace were frustrated when militant members in the faith communicants embraced violence.[30] Humanists like Erasmus and Gülen likewise exegete the basic scriptures of their religions in order to apply age-tested wisdom to contemporary life, seeking peace.[31]

The word *humanism* warrants scrutiny when applied to Gülen in order to clarify ambiguities addressed by another Gülen scholar and by returning to historical origins.[32] Helen R. Ebaugh frames Gülen's interest in science and faith as complementary and compatible, and, far from being in contention, they were conceived as agencies for pursuit of knowledge to link one's outer world with inner experiences.[33] Gülen's worldview provides a context for secular learning because he "rejects religion as blind faith and criticizes those who fail to use their reason and to explore and analyze the observable universe. Therefore, he sees the necessity of reconciling faith and reason rather than disparaging either of them."[34]

The present comprehensive embrace positions Gülen in the humanist tradition that is inherent in Islam as well as in the humanist tradition from the Renaissance. Every religion entails esoteric and exoteric divisions, the latter of which at the extreme may include ultra-conservatives and fundamentalists, who, in times of crisis, come to be regarded by many as true representatives of the religion. However, humanism in many forms are also at home in Christianity, Judaism, and Islam alike, a common element in each great religion.

Since the Enlightenment, the West has increasingly emphasized secular learning while downgrading religious disciplines and approaches to knowledge. This approach does have philosophic benefits but, in the eyes of many critics, a philosophic downside as well. Today, for some interpreters, the concept of humanism connotes a reduction or abolition of the dominant station of religion. There is also the common understanding that humanism denotes a valuing of life, (that is, of humans as well as other sentient beings). In the case of *homo sapiens,* a seminal corollary is that each person warrants the opportunity to achieve his or her full potential, which for Gülen shares the ancient Aegean understanding that, in acquiring knowledge of the world, one actualizes the latent excellence of humans.

Apprehending the paradox of church and state, Gülen envisions a separation similar to that which Thomas Jefferson elaborated late in his life to clarify the intent of his fellow Founding Fathers in establishing religious freedom in the new United States. Jefferson described this discourse as a "mantle of its protection, the Jew and the Gentile, the Christian and Mahometan, the Hindoo, and Infidel of every denomination."[35] This humanism was (and is) not unique to the West; indeed, it draws from the fusion of the religious secular approaches of Islam.

Reflecting on the above, it can be said that Gülen-inspired educators and the Hizmet movement itself derive from the same historical sources as the West. Spatial differentiation, dress, and manners of expression may blur the perception of some in modern times. Although Gülen has been targeted by both the over-reactive and the well-intentioned but misinformed, the United States is already benefiting from a new ethos—which, ironically, is not so new. Gülen believes that every person is responsible for acquiring knowledge, for acting to better the world, and for holding true to adamantine verities.

In *Statue of Our Souls,* Gülen advances only those *temsil* subjects that— as implied in the metaphor of the book's title—craft a person's representation, which is in turn sculpted by good deeds. In this image, one's lasting "statue" results from (in Gülen's phrase) the emergence of *aksiyon insani,* or "the person of action," who actualizes moral behavior. After life, a person's statue remains in the form of deeds that define one's self: "ἕκαστος ἄνθρωπος ἐνὰι ὁ γλὐπτης τις ζὦ ἐις τοὐ." Translated, this means, as described by the Greek rhetorician Isocrates, that people are "the sculptor of their own life." As we read in Roethke's poem summarizing a view by Gülen of human purpose and ends, "Truth never is undone; / Its shafts remain."[36]

NOTES

1. M. Fethullah Gülen, *Toward a Global Civilization of Love and Tolerance* (Rutherford, N.J.: The Light, 2004), 193–215. See also Zeki Saritoprak, "An Islamic Approach to Peace and Nonviolence," *Muslim World* 95 (2005): 413–25.

2. Dogan Koç, *Strategic Defamation of Fethullah Gülen: English vs. Turkish* (New York: University Press of America, 2012).

3. "Gülen Institute Youth Platform," *Gülen Institute of Houston*, Apr. 2–4, 2014, http://www.gulenyouthplatform.org.

4. Nasser D. Khalili, *The Art of Islam: Treasures from the Nasser D. Khalili Collection* (New York: Overlook Books, 2000).

5. See, e.g., Hans Belting, *Florence and Baghdad: Renaissance Art and Arab Science* (Cambridge, Mass.: Harvard University Press, 2011); Tamin Ansary, *Destiny Disrupted: A History of the World Through Islamic Eyes* (New York: Public Affairs, 2009); *The Arab Influences in Medieval Europe: Folia Scholastica Mediterranea*, edited by A. Agius and Richard Hitchcock (Reading, U.K.: Ithaca Press); Jonathan Lyons, *The House of Wisdom: How the Arabs Transformed Western Civilization* (London: Bloomsbury Press, 2009); Mark Graham, *How Islam Created the Modern World* (Beltsville, Md.: Amana Press, 2006); Jon Mcginnis and David C. Reisman, *Classical Arabic Philosophy: An Anthology of Sources* (Indianapolis, Ind.: Hackett, 2007); Maria Rosa Menocal, *The Arabic Role in Medieval Literary History: A Forgotten Heritage* (Philadelphia: University of Pennsylvania Press, 1987); Salima Khadra Jayyusi, *The Legacy of Muslim Spain*, vols. 1 and 2 (Hague, the Netherlands: Brill Scholars, 1992); Lisa Jardine, *Ingenious Pursuits: Building the Scientific Revolution* (New York: Random House, 2000); Liza Jardine and J. Brotton, *Global Interests: Renaissance Art Between East and West* (London: Rasktion, 2000); Mustapha Cherif, *Islam and the Wet: A Conversation with Jacques Derrida*, translated by Teresa Lavender Fagan (Chicago: University of Chicago Press, 2008).

6. Helen R. Ebaugh, *The Gülen Movement: A Sociological Analysis of a Civic Movement Rooted in Moderate Islam* (New York: Springer, 2009).

7. Fernand Braudel, *The Mediterranean and the Mediterranean World in the Age of Philip II*, translated by Sian Reynolds (New York: Harper and Row, 1966), 797.

8. Y. Alp Aslandoğan, "Pedagogical Model of Gülen and Modern Theories of Learning," presentation at the Conference on Islam in the Contemporary World: The Gülen Movement in Thought and Practice, Southern Methodist University, Dallas, March 4–5, 2006.

9. Leonard L. Baird, *Predicting Predictability: The Influence of Student and Institutional Characteristics on Prediction of Grades* (Princeton, N.J.: College Board), Report No. 83-5, ETC RR No. 83-30, 1983m Table 7, p. 8. See also Eric Westervelt, "College Applicants Sweat the SATs. Perhaps They Shouldn't," National Public Radio, Feb. 18, 2014, http://www.npr.org/2014/18/277059528/college-applicants-sweat-the-sates-perhaps-they-shouldn-t (accessed Apr. 24, 2015). Edmund Farrell, professor emeritus of Education at the University of Texas, who served on the Willard Wirtz panel that investigated the drop in SAT scores in 1971, confirmed my assertion that GPA is equal or better (personal communication, Apr. 24, 2015).

10. Fethullah Gülen, *Pearls of Wisdom*, translated by Ali Ünal (Somerset, N.J.: The Light, 2006), 35–46.

11. Y. Alp Aslandoğan and Muhammed Çetin, "The Educational Philosophy of Gülen in Thought and Practice," in *Muslim Citizens of the Globalized World: Contributions of the Gülen Movement*, edited by Robert A. Hunt and Yüksel A. Aslandoğan, 32, 44–45 (Somerset, N.J.: The Light, 2006).

12. "Gülen Promotes Democracy," Lesliey Stahl, *CBS* (May 2012), https://www.youtube.com/watch?v=2okYwm54Qsw (accessed Aug. 1, 2013). See also Stephanie Saul, "Schools Tied to Turkey Grow in Texas," *New York Times,* June 6, 2011, and "The Gulen Movement," anchored by Lucky Severson, *Religion & Ethics Newsweekly, PBS* (Jan. 21, 2011), http://www.pbs.org/wnet/religionandethics/episodes/january-21-2011/the-glen-movement/7949 (accessed July 11, 2012).

13. Personal communication with Dr. Yetkin Yildirim, 2013.

14. Fethullah Gülen, *The Statue of Our Souls* (Somerset, N.J.: The Light, 2005), 31–42.

15. Tom Gage, *Gülen's Dialogue on Education: A Caravanserai of Ideas* (Seattle: Cune Press, 2014).

16. Gülen, *The Statue of Our Souls*, 45.

17. Ibid., 44.

18. Yetkin Yildirim, "Ethics in Engineering and Science: Fethullah Gülen's Model," presentation at the Gülen Symposium, Carleton University, Ottawa, Canada, Oct. 24, 2009. See also Elizabeth Özdalga, "Following in the Footsteps of Fethullah Gülen: Three Women Teachers Tell Their Stories," in *Turkish Islam and Secular State: The Gülen Movement*, edited by Hakan Yavus and John L. Esposito, 85–113 (Syracuse, N.Y.: Syracuse University Press, 2003).

19. See, e.g., Nevitt Sanford, ed., *The American College: A Psychological and Social Interpretation of Higher Learning* (New York: John Wiley, 1967), 805–87.

20. Ali Ahmad Said Esber Adonis, *An Introduction to Arab Poetics*, translated by Catherine Cobham (London: Saqi, 1990); Dwight F. Reynolds, *Interpreting the Self: Autobiography in the Arabic Literary Tradition* (Berkeley: University of California Press, 2001), 3–5.

21. Ali Bulaç, "The Most Recent Reviver in the '*Uluma* Tradition: The Intellectual '*Alim*, Fethullah Gülen," in *Muslim Citizens of the Globalized World: Contributions of the Gülen Movement,* edited by Robert Hunt and Y. Aslandoğan, 89–106 (Somerset, N.J.: The Light, 2006).

22. Mikhail Bakhtin, *Problems of Dostoevsky's Poetics,* edited by Caryl Emerson, with introduction by Wayne Booth (Minneapolis: University of Minnesota Press, 1984). See also Mikhail Bakhtin, *The Dialogic Imagination: Four Essays,* edited by Michael Holquist, translated by Caryl Emerson and Michael Holquist (Austin: University of Texas Press, 1981), and Mikhail Bakhtin, *Rabelais and His world,* edited by Helene Iswolsky (Bloomington: University of Indiana Press, 1984).

23. Wayne Booth, "Rhetoric of Conversion Narratives," in *Fundamentalisms Comprehended,* edited by Martin E. Marty and Scott Appleby, 367–95 (Chicago: University of Chicago Press, 1995).

24. Dwight F. Reynolds, *Interpreting the Self: Autobiography in the Arabic Literary Tradition* (Berkeley: University of California Press, 2001), 5.

25. Ibid.

26. Steven Waldman, *Founding Faith* (New York: Random House, 2008), 122–33.

27. Muhammed Çetin, *The Glen Movement: Civic Service without Borders,* with foreword by Akbar S. Ahmed (New York: Blue Dome Press, 2010), 14.

28. See James Harrington, *Wrestling with Free Speech, Religious Freedom, and Democracy in Turkey: The Political Trails and Times of Fethullah Gülen,* with an introduction by Michael E. Tigar (New York: University Press of America, 2011).

29. B. Jill Carroll, *A Dialogue of Civilizations: Gülen's Islamic Ideals and Humanistic Discourse* (Somerset, N.J.: The Light, 2007), 73.

30. Regarding Gülen, see Said Amir Arjomand, "Unity and Diversity in Islamic Fundamentalism," in *Fundamentalism Comprehended,* edited by Martin E. Mary and R. Scott Appleby, 179–98 (Chicago: University of Chicago Press, 1995).

31. Ibid.

32. For historical origins, see Edward Said, *Humanism and Democratic Criticism* (New York: Columbia University Press, 2004).

33. Helen R. Ebaugh, *The Gülen Movement: A Sociological Analysis of a Civic Movement Rooted in Moderate Islam* (New York: Springer, 2010), 34.

34. Ibid., 35. See also B. Jill Carroll, *A Dialogue of Civilizations: Gülen's Islamic Ideals and Munanistic Discourse* (Somerset, N.J.: The Light, 2007), 3–4.

35. Denise A. Spellbert, *Thomas Jefferson's Qur'an: Islam and the Founders* (New York: Vintage, 2013), 106–10, 117–20, 236–39.

36. Theodore Roethke, "Adamant," in *Words for the Wind* (Bloomington: Indiana University Press, 1965), 22.

EIGHT

Women and the Hizmet Movement

Margaret J. Rausch

CONSIDERABLE CONTROVERSY SURROUNDS the topic of gender in Islam. The U.S. media's nearly exclusive focus on negative images presented as exemplifying the circumstances of all Muslim women's lives results from the dearth of knowledge about Muslims and Islam among viewers and journalists alike, coupled with an agenda to promote fear and hatred of Muslims and to expand readership and increase profits. Acts of violence perpetrated against non-Muslims in the name of Islam by some radical reform groups, and oppressive practices targeting women in some Muslim contexts, both of which are erroneously labeled Islamic, dominate the media, whereas the vision of Islam that informs the practices, comportment, and lifestyles of most Muslims receives little or no coverage.

This chapter seeks to elucidate some of these misconceptions by examining the status and roles of women as they are understood and lived by one Muslim community—namely, the affiliates of the Hizmet movement. It

Active in and providing leadership for interfaith programs and activities in many nations and cultures, the Hizmet movement makes no secret of being committed to Islam and having its origins in Turkey. Although Fethullah Gülen is regularly identified as a Sufi mystic and scholar, he uses his position in Islamic culture as a base for promoting movements devoted to "service" and peace among believers in other faiths and, for that matter, among those who do not identify with any religion. However, one problem raised even by many who sympathize with the movement has to do with the historic and contemporary understandings of the role of women. People who know little else about Muslims "know" that it denigrates women and forces them to accept male leadership. Margaret Rausch, professor of Religious Studies at Rockhurst University, is thoroughly at home with the subject and its expressions. She systematically assesses the role of women and opens this understanding to discussion among others who want realistic and helpful discourse.

investigates Fethullah Gülen's approach to gender, as articulated in his writings and exemplified in his daily life, and its practical implementation by Hizmet movement affiliates in their daily lives and in the practices and institutions inspired by his teachings based on interviews and fieldwork observations conducted among women and men affiliates. I begin by examining various dimensions of the controversy surrounding gender in Islam and the ways scholars have approached those dimensions in general and in relation to women affiliates of the Hizmet movement.

INTRODUCTION TO GENDER ISSUES IN ISLAM

Gender is at the core of one of the most common stereotypes about Muslims held by Westerners: the notion that the oppression of women is religiously sanctioned and thus acceptable and even obligatory. This notion also constitutes one dimension of secular feminists' general rejection of religion as irreparably patriarchal. With regard to Islam, it derives from the lack of knowledge not only about Muslim women's historical and contemporary societal roles but also about the way such practices as the wearing of head coverings by women, gender segregation, gender-based divisions of labor, and polygyny are presented in the foundational sources, the Qur'an and Hadith. Perceived as religiously sanctioned by some non-Muslims and Muslims alike, these practices are frequently criticized and inextricably linked to Muslim women's submission and oppression. Moreover, these same stereotypes informed early European Christian critiques of Muhammad's multiple marriages and the distorted images of harem life in paintings and inaccurate descriptions produced by later European male artists, writers, and travelers.

Impelled by the abundant media attention and scholarly focus on gender, Islamic reformers of all stripes feel obliged to publicly articulate their views in response to, or in spite of, these stereotypes. Not surprisingly, many of these articulations, including those of Gülen, compare the historical and contemporary status, roles, and rights of women in Muslim and Western contexts. Whether addressing local, national, or global audiences, some reformers clarify that these gender-related practices are matters of personal choice. To other reformers, they are indeed viewed as religious obligations. In Iran and Saudi Arabia, for example, laws requiring women to wear prescribed forms of head coverings and restricting their mobility in the public sphere are strictly enforced. By contrast, the wearing of head coverings by women employed in the civil service or university students in Turkey was prohibited from 1982 until 2008, and it is currently banned in France for public school students, teachers, and staff, and in Germany for public school teachers. Polygyny, while illegal in some Muslim countries but permitted with formal consent by a current wife or wives elsewhere, is relatively rare except among the wealthy in Saudi Arabia, the United Arab Emirates, and parts of Africa, where it remains unrestricted.

For nearly a century, scholars worldwide—Muslim and non-Muslim alike—have sought to bring clarity to these issues. Many of them underscore the fact that women's oppression derives from cultural, social, and economic realities and that it continues to exist worldwide. Some scholarly research on the wearing of head coverings by women has documented its origins in Greece and Persia and later proliferation among Muslims (as well as Christians and Jews) in the Middle East, and subsequently worldwide. Other scholars have demonstrated that the foundational Islamic sources, the Qur'an and Hadith, do not explicitly require veiling, gender segregation, and women's seclusion and limited mobility; still others cite the same sources to assert the opposite. With regard to polygyny, most scholars agree that it initially aimed at addressing the needs of widows.

Understandings of these practices have varied widely among Muslims around the globe, as have scholarly approaches for investigating them. Whether deemed religiously sanctioned, considered matters of personal preference, or enforced by law, they have been the focus of heated debates among women complying with them, their detractors, and scholars from diverse backgrounds and fields. An important question that arises is whether or not they are necessarily emblematic of women's submission and oppression. Responses from women, who have adopted them voluntarily in increasing numbers since the 1980s, or who comply with them under coercion, vary considerably. Furthermore, the approaches and terminology employed by scholars who study Muslim women and their daily lives and religious practices have undergone considerable revision in recent decades.

The term *feminist* has been used to designate Muslim women actively seeking to improve the status, roles, and rights of women in their communities and societies, with the understanding that their activism constitutes resistance to patriarchy.[1] Furthermore, liberal secular feminist scholars such as Saba Mahmood have emphasized the need to broaden the spectrum of actions labeled feminist. Mahmood's 2005 research in particular demonstrates that the cultivation of Islamic attitudes, values, and sensibilities undertaken by the women participants in an Islamic revival movement, and the appropriation of mosques throughout Cairo by women preachers to gather and guide them, ultimately heightened the women's awareness of and sensitivity to modes for exercising agency in various daily life situations.[2] By examining the preachers' lessons and the participants' understanding and application of them in their daily lives, she demonstrated that, while on the surface they sought to cultivate postures of humility, timidity, and reticence, the resulting self-transformation was liberating as it enabled them to resist, circumvent, and discover new ways of dealing with the patriarchal structures and practices governing their daily lives. Mahmood's results reveal that key to assessing the practices of the participants in Islamic revival and other religious and social movements is a thorough grasp of their perceptions of their practices, of the self-transformative processes that they enable, and of the impact of those processes on their everyday life circumstances as well as of the principles and values that underpin them. In keeping with this approach, this chapter investigates women in the Hizmet movement affiliates' perceptions of their everyday life gender-related roles and practices, preceded by an examination of Gülen's views and the teachings on gender, education, and self-transformation that often inform them.

GÜLEN'S APPROACH TO GENDER

The central focus of Gülen's writings, and the main objective of the movement inspired by his writings and example, is service to humanity. This service is integrally linked to education, both of which are ultimately intended to promote compassion for others, social justice, dialogue, and peace as part of a broader goal of resolving major world problems. Language, thought, and action, which constitute the central tools for achieving this end, are interconnected, in Gülen's view. Trained in the Islamic sciences but also highly knowledgeable of pertinent areas of the Western philosophical and scientific traditions, Gülen is often characterized as a thinker with a moderate Islamic revival and reform agenda. This reckoning derives from his abhorrence of violence, lack of political aspirations, and openness to women's societal participation.

Gülen's writings on gender are intended to elucidate his interpretations of the Islamic sources, the Qur'an and Hadith, but also to guide movement affiliates as well as to respond to Western misconceptions. He rejects the belief that Muslim women should be treated as inferior with regard to legal testimony and inheritance. Citing Qur'an verses on these topics and the historical contexts of their revelation, he contends that the testimonies of two women were equated with that of one man in the case of financial contracts, as the latter were historically beyond women's scope of experience. That this rule also applied to rural male inhabitants who were likewise unfamiliar with urban business practices proves that it was not based on women's inferiority but instead on their lack of familiarity with the subject matter. Similarly, inheritance laws gave men twice women's portion to ensure that the men upheld their legal obligation to support their families and all needy female relatives, not to degrade women. Based on these and other rulings, Muslim women were not denied but rather guaranteed equal rights with regard to freedom of expression and socioeconomic status. Thoroughly investigating rules and guidelines, along with the historical contexts of their inception, reveals their intent to maintain and promote gender equality and social justice.

However, not all of Gülen's approaches to practices regarding women find their grounding in Qur'an verses and the historical context of their origination. He considers, for example, the wearing of head coverings to be compulsory for women, although no formal guidelines explicitly regulating practices pertaining to external appearance exist. Such practices are situated under the designation *furuat,* he explains, meaning that they are of lesser or secondary importance and are thus subject to individual interpretation, discretion, and preference. In his view, embodying such Islamic values as compassion, modesty, generosity, and devotion through daily life comportment is more important than complying with dress codes. Further, he asserts that there are no official restrictions on women's access to the public sphere in their communities and that their participation in the workforce is permissible as long as the work conditions are suitable.[3]

Freedom is a basic human right, in Gülen's view, but the misguided means for its pursuit today disturbs him. He is critical of freedom when it is defined by sexual liberty or relegates women to objects of pleasure, entertainment, and advertisement. Furthermore, he rejects the argument that men are naturally disposed to oppress women. In his view, Muslim women live free lives and have been full participants in daily life in societies that are not contaminated with non-Islamic customs. According to *Hanafi* jurisprudence, he explains, women have sometimes been permitted to serve as judges, particularly for cases on female issues, since their understanding of the latter exceeds that of men. Furthermore, he reminds readers that early Muslim women prayed in mosques together with men, led armies, engaged in business, and could voice their opposing views with regard to judicial matters at a time when Christians were debating whether women were human beings with souls or were devils. To exemplify this contrast and underscore the notable discrepancies between women's roles and status in Islam and Christianity, Gülen refers to the writings of Lady Montagu, who accompanied her husband on his diplomatic mission to the capital of the Ottoman Empire in the early eighteenth century.[4] Lady Montagu challenged contemporaneous European male scholars' inaccurate accounts of Muslim women by recording the observations she made during home visits. She praised the superior hygienic conditions of women's lives, their participation in many spheres of social life, and their right to personally possess and manage wealth and property. Gülen points out that the right to own property, though guaranteed to Muslim women from the beginning, was denied to European women until the late nineteenth century.

On the issue of polygyny, he clarifies that neither the Qur'an nor Hadith encourage Muslim men to take more than one wife. Instead, the Qur'an mentions polygyny as an option intended to protect and support women who are deserted or widowed. It requires equal treatment of all wives, which makes taking more than one very difficult, if not impossible, and therefore strongly recommends taking only one.[5]

Regarding gender roles, Gülen asserts that, while there is no obstacle to equal rights and responsibilities for women and men, they nonetheless differ. Gender roles have developed in accordance with these differences, but they should not be used as the basis for any form of gender hierarchy. Islam does not distinguish between men and women's status, he argues, since both are fundamentally human. In Gülen's view, men and women are not the same but, rather, complement one another like two sides of a coin: men are often physically stronger and more often capable of bearing physical hardship, whereas women are more compassionate, delicate, and self-sacrificing, predisposing them for bearing the responsibilities of motherhood. As he articulates it, God bestowed upon women the unique and honorable position of being the first nurturers and educators of each new generation.[6]

Education, according to Gülen, is a life-long process that begins with childhood upbringing. Although mothers are the initial and primary nurturers and educators, fathers are encouraged to provide affection, care, and guidance to their children in keeping with the Prophet's example. Both parents educate their children directly and indirectly through their words and deeds, which should reflect their values and principles. According to Gülen's writings, modeling constitutes an essential component of education during this—and subsequent—phases. As elucidated in the following excerpt, teachers (by which, though not explicitly, he includes women and men) do not simply impart knowledge:

> The real teacher . . . is occupied with what is good and wholesome. [They] lead and guide the child in his or her life and in the face of all events. . . . [A] child is cast in his or her true mould and attains to the mysteries of personality. . . . [I]magination and aspirations, or specific skills and realities, everything acquired must . . . be the key to closed doors, and a guidance to the ways to virtue. . . . [This] enables pupils to connect happenings in the outer world to their inner experience. . . . [As] intermediaries, teachers . . . provide the link between life and the self. . . . [They] find a way to the heart of the pupil and leave indelible imprints upon his or her mind. Teachers . . . will be able to provide good examples for their pupils and teach them the aims of the sciences . . . through the refinement of their own minds. . . .
>
> Educating people is the most sacred, but also the most difficult, task in life. In addition to setting a good personal example, teachers should be patient, . . . know their students well, and address their intellects and their hearts, spirits, and feelings . . . , not forgetting that each individual is a different "world."[7]

Gülen emphasizes the importance of acknowledging and developing the whole individual in all its facets. Education therefore encompasses guiding children—girls and boys—in the cultivation of essential values and principles. He advocates equal participation for women and men as parents, teachers, and pupils.

Education continues beyond formal schooling as a kind of self-transformation that occurs naturally in society, in Gülen's view. Among men and women affiliates, it entails the individual and communally supported pursuit of self-perfection, which comprises the acquisition of character traits and propensities such as self-supervision (*muraqaba*), self-scrutiny (*muhasaba*), and limiting one's relationship to material things (*zuhd*). It centers on self-renewal through emulation of peers and advanced-level affiliates. It prepares affiliates to offer service to others as a means of addressing societal problems linked to widespread animosity and lack of compassion for others, which are understood to arise primarily from excessive materialism.

Gülen envisions self-perfection as a means to revitalize compassionate acceptance of others, which is central to true humanism. His approach consists of empowering one's spirituality against one's carnal self (*nafs*) instead of shunning the material world. In his view, other people constitute equals, not opposites. Compassion, dialogue, and a mutually supportive existence are central to self-perfection and to the discovery of one's "true identity." Essential components of the process are action and thought, which are integrally linked to serving and guiding others, as articulated in the following excerpt:

> [T]he way to true existence is action and thought, and likewise the way to renewal, individual and collective.
>
> Action in this context then means embracing the whole of creation with full sincerity and resolve, aware of journeying to an eternal realm . . . ; it means expending all one's physical, intellectual and spiritual faculties in guiding the world to undertake the same journey.
>
> As for thought, it is action in one's inner world. Any truly systematic thinking entails seeking answers to all questions arising from the existence of the universe as such. In other words, truly systematic thinking is the product of a conscious mind relating itself to the whole of creation and seeking the truth in everything through its language.
>
> . . . [T]he realization of such noble aims depends on the existence of guides and leaders able to both diagnose our external and inner misery and to be themselves in constant relation with the higher worlds. . . . Thus, all the institutions of life will be remoulded. . . . Sciences will progress hand-in-hand with religion, and belief and reason combined will yield ever-fresh fruits of their cooperation. In short, the future will witness a new world built in the arms of hope, belief, love, knowledge, and resolve.[8]

Although gender is not explicitly mentioned, Gülen is addressing both men and women affiliates. In the following excerpt, he implicitly elaborates the role of language as a further dimension of self-perfection:

> Language is one of the fundamental dynamics in the composition of a culture. Language is an important tool for humankind in our efforts to better understand the cosmos and events both holistically and analytically. The more richly and colorfully a nation can speak, the more they can think; the more they can think, the broader is the span their speech can reach. Every single society leaves behind what they speak and think today for its validity to be probed, tested, and protected by future generations. In this way, a huge reserve of experience and learning are saved from being wasted; the knowledge and ideas of the past are utilized for the benefit of the present; what was

right or wrong in the past is compared with the rights and wrongs of today so that we do not tread the same path and suffer from the same errors. This is valid for all nations of the world; the capacity of a language to express a thought is related to the level of development it has achieved, and a thought can become the instrument by which the language is tuned to this level of development. From every aspect, language plays a defining role in the formation of our culture.[9]

Self-perfection is facilitated by group spiritual conversations (*sohbetler*), where more advanced men and women affiliates serve as role models and supervise the progress of novices. No formal, explicit guidelines exist for conducting *sohbetler* or for monitoring progress. Instead, Gülen's writings offer a new "language and culture" and attributes to be cultivated to create the ideal men and women models of an awaited "Golden Generation."

The members of the Golden Generation "will put might under the command of right, never discriminate on grounds of colour or race" and "unite in their character profound spirituality, wide knowledge, sound thinking, a scientific temperament, and wise activism. . . . Never content with what they already know, they will continuously increase in knowledge—knowledge of the self, knowledge of nature, and knowledge of God." They will attain "true life" by applying the attributes developed through self-perfection as follows:

> The true life is the one lived at the spiritual level. There is a mutually supportive and perfective relation between one's actions and inner life. . . . Attitudes like determination, perseverance, and resolve illuminate one's inner conscience, and the brightness of this inner conscience strengthens one's will power and resolve, stimulating him or her to ever-higher horizons. They will always seek to please the Creator and humanity . . . and enjoy orderliness, harmony, and devotion to duty in their outer worlds. At the same time, they increase the pure light of their inner worlds. . . . Their intellect can combine . . . all current knowledge . . . and thereby obtain new syntheses. They are so modest that they see themselves as just ordinary people among others. Finally, their altruism has reached such a level that they can forget their own needs and desires for the sake of others' happiness.[10]

These attributes and character traits enable spiritually advanced men and women to confront societal problems worldwide.

The resolution of these problems lies in awakening others and offering them guidance, according to Gülen. He elaborates this process as follows:

> In order to awaken the people and guide them to truth . . . those young people . . . implant hope in our hearts, enlighten our minds and quicken our

souls. . . . They will visit every corner of the world . . . and pour out their reviving inspirations into the souls of the dumbstruck people.[11]

As the excerpts cited above reveal, affiliates continuously pursue self-perfection in preparation for, but also in conjunction with, offering service and guidance to others. In Gülen's vision, all three dimensions—cultivating self-perfection, offering service, and guiding others—are equally accessible to men and women, and both genders are capable of contributing to the resolution of world problems. Most important, in Gülen's view, is that every action be undertaken in the hope of pleasing God.

GENDER IN HIZMET PRACTICES AND INSTITUTIONS AND IN AFFILIATES' DAILY LIVES

Affiliation with the Hizmet movement encompasses implementing the ideas and practices and cultivating the values and character traits advanced by Gülen in pursuit of God's pleasure. These ideas, practices, values, and character traits include the wearing of head coverings by women, gender segregation, and gender-based divisions of labor. In the context of Gülen-inspired institutions and practices as well as in everyday situations, many affiliates observe these gender-related practices. Nonetheless, their observance is considered a matter of personal preference and should not result from social pressure or coercion. Noncompliance does not hinder women's equal participation in movement activities, nor does compliance prevent them from pursuing degrees in higher education and professional careers. On the contrary, covering their hair and other body parts deemed erotic, and avoiding inappropriate contact with members of the opposite sex, enable affiliates to decide to reserve acts of amorous affection and sexuality for one's future spouse. The practices enable women to concentrate on developing other facets and attributes of their selfhood. They do not consider them to be forms of gender discrimination. The sole practice that can be viewed as discriminatory with regard to gender is women's exclusion from admission to the select circle of affiliates who undergo advanced training in the Islamic sciences with Gülen in his private residence.

Religious ritual observance and personal spiritual reflection are two occasions when gender segregation is the most strictly maintained. Many women

affiliates feel that the presence of members of the opposite sex is inappropriate and undesirable, as it would impede their capacity to adequately concentrate on the experiences encompassed by spiritual reflection and ritual
observance. These experiences are personal and emotional, and thus better
suited for the intimacy of a gender-segregated space, according to these
women affiliates. Furthermore, whereas male affiliates perform ritual prayers
as a group in unison with one of them serving as prayer leader, women pray
individually or side-by-side in small groups without designating a leader.
This is the only gender-based distinction between men and women's separate
participation in these two activities.

Both take place communally in the context of gatherings for spiritual
conversation (*sohbetler*) and retreats (*yaz kamplarι,* or summer camps). The
term *sohbet* (sing.) refers to a gender-segregated gathering for spiritual reflection and discussion commonly held once a week by affiliates. Reading aloud
from a text by Gülen or Said Nursi or watching a video of Gülen preaching
serves to stimulate this reflection and discussion. The topic of focus depends
on participants' stage of development and interest. An advanced-level affiliate, referred to as big sister (*abla*; pl. *ablalar*) or big brother (*abi*; pl. *abilar*),
leads the gathering and serves as a role model and source for answers to questions on doctrine and practice. One affiliate recalled her earliest *sohbet* experience in Turkey:

> The *abla* read from a book. It was either by Gülen or Said Nursi. We dis-
> cussed the reading and tried to figure out its implications and ways it could
> be applied to real life. *Sohbetler* are interactional. They were not lectures.
> Each woman explained what she had understood. There was a nice, harmoni-
> ous atmosphere. Sometimes we would go jogging, eat delicious food and have
> fun together after the *sohbet*. When in college, during the daytime, I was
> busy with courses and worldly issues. The *abla* kept me focused on the other
> world and the idea of struggling to be a better person. I felt like I was getting
> my spiritual food from *sohbetler*.[12]

The role of *ablalar* and the gender segregation of *sohbetler* were described by
another affiliate in the following way:

> *Ablalar* help students to improve themselves. They try to motivate them and
> help with their homework. They also try to teach them something about reli-
> gion, if possible. But the most important and beneficial way to learn some-
> thing from an *abla* is by observing her. Her attitude and behavior are more
> effective than what she says. And it is important that she is a woman, and

that the group is all women. Women can relate better to other women, and share their inner thoughts and feelings better with other women. Gender segregated gatherings have a variety of advantages.

As described above, *sohbetler* are usually followed by a light meal or snack and friendly conversation as well as other activities on some occasions. The ultimate purpose is to cultivate the attributes necessary for the self-perfection process by discussing them and observing a same-gender living role model who embodies and enacts them, but it also constitutes an opportunity to get to know and build friendships with other same-gender affiliates.

There are no official guidelines regarding attire for *sohbetler* or other movement-related activities, much less other daily life situations. However, both men and women are expected to dress modestly, and women are required to wear head coverings while performing daily prayers. Modesty for men entails wearing loose garments covering their torso from their shoulders to their knees. Short-sleeved shirts and short pants are deemed permissible, but most men prefer long sleeves and long pants even in the summer at formal events—and at informal mixed-gender gatherings. Modesty for women may vary to an even greater extent in accordance with personal preferences and depending on whether an activity or event is gender mixed or gender segregated. Many women affiliates cover their entire bodies except for their hands and face at all times, except to bathe, at bedtime, and when they are in their own homes, the homes of relatives or close friends, or in certain gender-segregated settings. By contrast, other women affiliates cover their heads exclusively during prayer. Many women affiliates choose to wear long skirts, whereas others feel that wearing pants is a satisfactory means for maintaining modesty.

Sohbetler also occur daily during *kamplar* (retreats), which are held in the summer (*yaz*) in Turkey and during the winter break in the United States. The retreats for single students in Turkey are always gender segregated. Participants need not be movement affiliates. Retreats for married students, teachers, and professionals in other fields also take place in Turkey and the United States. Affiliates usually attend as married couples, with or without families. Most activities are held in gender-segregated groups, but some family-oriented events occur. As with *sohbetler,* the activities occurring during retreats correspond to the participants' levels of advancement toward self-perfection. One affiliate described her first retreat experience in Turkey as follows:

I attended my first *yaz kamplar* while living in an *ışık evi* (movement subsidized dormitory). Every day we gathered in groups for *sohbet*, followed by different activities and snack time. I got close to the other women by sharing my feelings and ideas and enjoying fun activities with them. I learned a lot from them, especially from the *ablalar*. They explained things and guided me. More importantly, they demonstrated the behavior I was trying to learn. It is pleasant and beneficial to be surrounded by women pursuing the same goals. I cannot imagine achieving the same development and having the same enjoyment if there were guys present. I would have felt intimidated and distracted, and I would not have been able to explore so many different emotions and inner thoughts.

Bringing along a friend not affiliated with the movement is permissible, she explained further. Modesty is expected for all participants in retreats, but the degree of observance varies according to personal preference. *Yaz kamplar* constitute occasions for more concentrated doses of spiritual reflection and growth, as other distractions are absent.

Dormitories, known as *ışık evleri* (lighthouses) extend access to higher education to Turkish youth whose parents are without the necessary financial means. They are built near high schools and universities in urban centers with funding provided by movement affiliates. The *ışık evleri* offer *sohbetler* and organize *yaz kamplar* for student residents. Many students have no prior experience with or knowledge of the movement. Their residency does not obligate them to participate in the *sohbetler* and *yaz kamplar* or to be affiliated with the movement in any way. Nonetheless, many eventually become movement affiliates. A woman affiliate who is currently pursing her Ph.D. in the United States recounted her initial experiences in an *ışık evi* as follows:

My introduction to Hizmet was affected by terms used by Hizmet affiliates, such as *abla, abi* and *tevafuk* (by the will of God), which were familiar to me from childhood. In Turkey, younger cousins call older ones by their names plus *abla* or *abi* depending on gender. I was very impressed by my older cousins' knowledge. Their response to my insistence that things happen by chance was to teach me about God's will. They would say: "There is no such thing as chance. There is only *tevafuk!*" I was reminded of these childhood experiences when I stayed in an *ışık evi* during college. I knew it belonged to Hizmet and was unsure of what to expect. The *abiler* and *ablalar* were wiser than me and also spoke of *tevafuk*. I eventually grew to love it more than any other place. My *abla* always insisted that I stay at the *ışık evi* as much as possible even on weekends. At that time, my parents became prejudice[d] against Hizmet and were afraid of losing me. People told them that the Hizmet people would brainwash me. When I learned about Gülen-inspired schools worldwide, I told my parents I wanted to teach abroad. They were terrified. My father asked to speak with my *abla*. The following weekend, I brought home a DVD about the schools for him to watch. While watching it, his eyes filled with tears. He said: "You should work in a Turkish speaking country in Central Asia! They need our help!" The voice of Hocaefendi [affectionate appellation for Gülen meaning honorable teacher] recorded on CDs and DVDs was always audible in the *ışık evi*. I missed it when I went home, so I began taking home DVDs to watch with my family. At the time, I wished I could be a student and live in *ışık evleri* forever. Those were the most beautiful years of my life.

Through gender segregation and the presence of *abiler* and *ablalar,* the *ışık evleri* offer residents a morally acceptable atmosphere that is already familiar to them in some ways. In addition, they are immersed in an intimate environment where central values and ideas permeate daily life. Members of the opposite sex, such as residents' family members and repairmen, enter only on special occasions with prior notification of all residents. Male and female students in adjacent *ışık evleri* sometimes take part in gender-mixed events, but they sit or interact in gender-segregated spaces. Modesty is required in communal spaces in all *ışık evleri,* but most female students cover their heads only during prayers.

During events and activities geared toward reaching out to people outside the movement, strict gender segregation is not maintained; however, gender-based divisions of labor and other limits are noticeable. Unlike men affiliates, women affiliates rarely serve as organizers for or speakers at interfaith dialogue dinners, academic conferences, and other events, though they are frequently present. At interfaith dialogue dinners, they are often assigned seats next to their husbands or, if single, next to another woman affiliate, but they interact freely with male and female nonaffiliates seated at the same table. They also participate in meals with guests at group breakfasts, lunches, and dinners at academic conferences organized by the movement. They rarely present papers or chair panels but are present in the audience and may participate in the question-and-answer sessions. Another dimension of their participation entails greeting and handing out nametags and programs to the nonaffiliated dinner and conference guests as they arrive at these events. Thus, while such gender-based divisions of labor do not hinder women affiliates' access to public visibility and freedom to interact with both female and male guests at these events, they reserve roles and tasks typically belonging to leadership positions exclusively for male affiliates.

When questioned about their attitudes toward leadership and the possibility of women holding leadership positions in the movement, women affiliates' responses differed considerably and offered several alternative understandings of it. Some focused on leadership as a concept; others looked more critically at the tasks it entails. Interestingly, gender as a factor in choosing leaders surfaced fairly infrequently in their responses.

In fact, only three of the respondents spoke to the question of whether gender played a role in determining who is eligible to serve and who is not. The first woman based eligibility for leadership squarely on gender, connecting the assignment of leadership roles to male affiliates with an allegedly innate male capacity for the tasks characterizing it. However, she also rejected the idea that those tasks should be elevated above the kinds of tasks in which, according to her, women tend to excel, and she believed that the latter should not be viewed as passive. In addition, she underscored the fact that all of the tasks performed by affiliates are important in ensuring the success of events and activities, and she asserted that women's contributions are greatly appreciated:

> There are differences between men and women in terms of leadership, but one is not above the other one. These differences arise from their nature. Women are better at some things than men. People should work in their area of specialization. Most men are better at leadership and most women are better at organizing. Women appear to be passive, but without them most activities could not happen. They work in the background. People in the movement appreciate this a lot.

The second woman spoke indirectly to the question of gender in relation to leadership by simply rejecting the idea that a hierarchy exists within the movement and arguing that all tasks are equally important and distributed based on individual daily life situations:

> There is no hierarchy in the Hizmet movement. Everyone's task is equally important as long as one is working for the common good and not for personal gain. People make choices according to their situations.

The third woman flatly rejected the idea that the preference of men over women was the issue and instead perceived gender segregation as the deciding factor. She argued that the need for interaction among those affiliates who serve as leaders, which presupposes that all leaders be either female or male, is the reason for women's exclusion from leadership roles rather than women's lack of propensity for or ability to carry out leadership tasks:

> Having no women as administrators does not mean that they cannot do the work. It is because men and women should not mix. All of the administrators could be women, but most women are studying, working and caring for their children and have no time for that work.

She continued by providing examples of women successfully organizing and leading events—all of which, however, were intended exclusively for women. Interestingly, male respondents also rejected the idea that a hierarchy exists among affiliates and that women are unable or less or not at all disposed to serve as leaders. Thus, the notion that gender plays a significant role appears to be generally downplayed by affiliates.

The responses in a second category focus on the fact that leadership roles involve considerable responsibility, hardships, and broader repercussions for the personal lives of the male affiliates serving in them. The first respondent pointed out that leaders have a heavy workload, but she also inferred that their wives share the burden since most of them may have to postpone their pursuit of higher education or employment as a result:

> The men who organize interfaith dinners and other events are overloaded with work. Most of them are single or have wives who are not studying or working.

With a similar focus on the disadvantages of serving as a leader, the second respondent expressed relief. Holding a leadership position, as she implies in her response below, would interfere with child rearing and the pace of her studies:

> I am glad not to participate in administrative functions. I have children and I am studying. I can take good care of my kids and finish my studies faster.

The third respondent addressed questions surrounding leadership by criticizing what she refers to as "radical feminism" for devaluing the tasks performed by wives and mothers. According to her, spouses, since they are ultimately performing the same tasks but for practical reasons in different locations, are essentially collaborating and working together toward the same vision:

> These equality questions are often approached from a wrong angle. Being equal does *not* mean doing the same things. Radical feminism has devalued

women's role. We should ask: Why aren't more men running homes or cooking for movement events? People undervalue these responsibilities and elevate employment outside the home. Essentially, both groups are doing the same kind of job, but in different places, and the main reason is practicality. Administrators are responsible for large events that take weeks to organize. This requires counseling, advising and being gone from home for days. A mother cannot neglect her children and their emotional wellbeing just to compete with a man, when there are others who can do the job. Women and men have the same vision and work together, yet apart, toward that vision.

According to her, mothers' concern for the emotional well-being of her children is the main hindrance to competing with men and serving in leadership roles.

Most frequent were responses that sought to deconstruct the concept of leadership. Their alternative vision encompassed a rejection of the usual elevation of leadership roles and tasks as if they were superior in status to or required a higher level of skills than other forms of involvement in movement events and activities. According to one woman, leadership essentially conflicts with one of the core character traits that are cultivated by affiliates in their pursuit of self-perfection—namely, humility. She used Gülen's vision of leadership, and his intent to relinquish it for that reason, as an example:

No one should strive to be a leader. The best leaders are the most humble ones, who become leaders naturally because others see them as leaders. Hocaefendi [Gülen] rejects being viewed as a leader. He considers himself a servant.

The alternative view of leadership in the following response recognizes that role modeling, which is central to all forms of service performed by affiliates, can be perceived as a form of leadership:

All the men and women in the movement lead by serving as models for others to follow. You don't have to speak at an interfaith dinner to be a leader.

Echoing the underlying message of this response, another woman underscored the expertise acquired by women affiliates through higher education and the fact that this expertise is practically applied not only in child rearing but also in their interactions with their husbands. In her opinion, their contributions on both of these levels are essential in enabling the growth of the movement:

One does not need public visibility to influence others. Higher education produces strong and wise women for raising children, not only for seeking employment. It entails attaining knowledge, wisdom and a well-balanced life. For mothers, acquiring knowledge is a must. It is an invaluable resource for child rearing and community development. Women's wisdom also guides husbands in the right direction. Women are influential at the administrative level through wise interaction with husbands. Women's knowledge, dedication and willingness to execute their roles completely allow the movement to thrive and continue to grow in a sustainable manner.

In this response, the existence of a gender-based division of labor is acknowledged. However, it is perceived not as an indication of women's oppression or a hindrance to women's pursuit of higher education but rather as an arrangement for ensuring that affiliates as spouses can establish a well-balanced home environment in which to raise their children and collaborate in furthering the aspirations of the movement. In fact, the wife's "wisdom" and advice, in her view, are quintessential to the husband's ability to effectively fulfill his administrative functions, on which the movement's future depends. Thus, without officially serving as leaders, affiliates are nonetheless able to directly or indirectly guide others in their own way on different levels and ultimately have an impact on the communities and societies in which they live through the movement.

From the alternative visions of leadership presented in the above responses, it is evident that these women affiliates do not view their exclusion from official leadership positions as a hindrance to their engagement in the movement, but instead consider the role modeling that all affiliates perform in a variety of contexts as a form of leadership. They also perceive all types of service, including raising their children and pursuing their higher education and career goals, as both necessary and equally important to advancing the goals and ensuring the future success of the movement.

In their private lives, affiliates make their own choices regarding gender-based segregation and divisions of labor. As one woman affiliate articulated it, "Not everyone views Hocaefendi [Gülen] as a leader to the same extent. Some follow his guidance to a 'T,' others not much at all, and still others somewhere in between." Many women affiliates are intent on pursuing higher education and career goals. Therefore, careful reflection on priorities, conscience cooperation among spouses, and intricate management of household and child-rearing duties are a must. Although some female affiliates may have to insist on their rights, many male affiliates enthusiastically participate in the rearing, care, and supervision of their children and voluntarily shoulder various other household responsibilities. When entertaining other affiliates in their homes, some affiliates insist on the strict maintenance of gender segregation, while others do not. Whether or not unmarried women affiliates are not invited or turn down invitations depends on the perspective of hosts and guests. In either case, affiliates are willing to accommodate each other's preferences.

Gender-based segregation, division of labor, and the wearing of head coverings, even when strictly implemented, do not prevent women affiliates from pursuing the main goal of the movement, which is *hizmet* (service). *Hizmet* was summed up by women respondents as "the lens through which I view everything I do"; "a fulfilling way of life"; "the most important aim of my life"; "simply serving my family for the sake of God"; "being a good example in everything I do"; and "seeking God's pleasure in everything we do." Emphasizing sincerity and purity of intention, which, in her view, can transform the simplest act into a form of worship, another woman defined it as follows:

> *Hizmet* encompasses 1) self-development, understood as seeking peace of heart and mind and developing good character, 2) sacrifice and serving people, almost to the point of living for others' wellbeing, 3) teaching through words and 4) setting a good example. But all of these are meaningless without pure intention and sincerity. Pure intention and sincerity turn simple acts into worship.

Her definition mentions additional facets, specifically self-sacrifice "almost to the point of living for others." Those affiliates who would prefer to remain in their countries of origin but nonetheless commit to spending one or more years abroad experience this self-sacrifice the most emphatically, even if they are able to combine their movement commitments with the pursuit of higher education and career goals.

Formulated more explicitly, this dimension of *hizmet* comprises offering service to, engaging in interfaith and intercultural dialogue with, and promoting compassionate acceptance of others. It is undertaken through various means and in different contexts. The following quote illuminates the way one female affiliate understood her efforts to spread knowledge about Islam and Muslim women and consequently promote interfaith and intercultural understanding in the United States:

I am a Muslim lady with a headscarf. I came to the US alone for my MA program. I have a job and attend social activities. The first impression should be that being a Muslim lady does not isolate me from the world and is not an obstacle for my career. My situation might help non-Muslims to change the stereotypes about Muslim women (such as uneducated, slaves of men, suppressed, etc.). I also try to be a nice, moral and kind person and interact with non-Muslims as much as possible so that they notice that we Muslims are not that much different from them. I have also given public presentations and lectures about Islam and Muslim women on campus. I think they learn more from watching me than from what I say since being a living example is more influential than trying to impose your ideas.

Similarly, another respondent relates that she and her husband employ their interpersonal interaction in public to dispel misconceptions about Muslim women, specifically the way their husbands treat them, as a means to spread knowledge and promote understanding:

My husband and I usually hold hands in public in the US because we like doing it, but also because it is the image we want to project about Muslims, instead of CNN images of men walking ahead of women covered from head to toe in black.

In keeping with these two responses, both of which suggest that actions speak louder than words, another respondent underscores the importance of pursuing self-improvement both as an end in itself and as a facet of and means to prepare for performing *hizmet*:

Since participation in weekly meetings known as *sohbetler* is also viewed as part of *hizmet*, efforts toward self-improvement are considered *hizmet* indirectly. Honestly, I feel that the biggest service one can offer society is to take the time to improve oneself to a certain degree before lecturing others.

According to many women affiliates, striving to cultivate, embody, and model the values and attributes put forward by Gülen in his writings and through his living example as consistently as possible in daily life is considered as much a part of *hizmet* as actually performing acts of service. They feel that cultivating, embodying, and exhibiting them in daily life are equal in importance to the public speaking roles and administrative positions held by male affiliates. In their view, the ultimate aim of *hizmet* is to focus every thought, word, and deed on exemplifying and striving to proliferate the compassionate acceptance of others as a means to please God, alleviate suffering, and promote peaceful coexistence.

CONCLUSION

As revealed in the above examination of Gülen's vision of gender, education, and self-transformation and of the ways that Hizmet movement participants interpret and apply the ideas, intentions, and values gleaned from that vision in their practices, activities, and daily lives, their central aim is to serve others. At the core of their preparation for service is the cultivation of compassionate acceptance of others, which goes hand in hand with refining specific character traits and values. Since this process begins with the individual and his or her interaction with other affiliates, achieving clarity regarding all facets of the self is essential, to which the importance of community cannot be overemphasized. The wearing of head coverings by women, gender segregation, and gender-based divisions of labor create an optimal environment for pursuing self-perfection since they highlight the realm of human instincts related to acts of amorous affection and sexuality. Observing these practices, while seen by those who comply primarily as one means to seek God's pleasure, also facilitates reaching and adhering to the decision to reserve these acts for marriage. Gülen encourages their observance as a way to exercise modesty, but he also considers it, like daily life practices, to be a matter of personal choice. Nonetheless, he feels, as do many affiliates, that their observance enhances rather than hinders women's participation in the movement and their ability to access and advance in other domains of life.

NOTES

1. Margot Badran, "Gender Activism: Feminists and Islamists in Egypt," in *Identity Politics and Women: Cultural Reassertions and Feminisms in International Perspective,* edited by Valentine Moghadam, 202–27 (Boulder, Colo.: Westview Press, 1994); Margot Badran, "Between Secular and Islamic Feminism/s: Reflections of the Middle East and Beyond," *Journal of Middle East Women's Studies* 1, no. 1 (2005): 6–28.

2. Saba Mahmood, *Politics of Piety: The Islamic Revival and the Feminist Subject* (Princeton, N.J.: Princeton University Press, 2005).

3. M. Sait Yavuz, "Women in Islam: Muslim Perspectives and Fethullah Gülen," paper presented at the Islam in the Age of Global Challenges: Alternative Perspectives of the Gulen Movement conference at Georgetown University, Nov. 14–15, 2008, http:// gulenconference.net/files/Georgetown/2008_SaitYavuz.pdf (accessed Aug. 2014).

4. Bernadette Andrea, "Women and Their Rights: Fethullah Gülen's Gloss on Lady Montagu's 'Embassy' to the Ottoman Empire," in *Muslim Citizens of the Globalized World: Contributions of the Gülen Movement,* edited by Robert A. Hunt and Yüksel A. Aslandoğan, 161–81 (Somerset, N.J.: The Light, 2006).

5. Yavuz, "Women in Islam."

6. Maria F. Curtis, "The Women's Side of the Coin: The Gülen Movement in America, a New Turkish-American Community Taking Root," paper presented at the Islam in the Contemporary World: The Fethullah Gülen Movement in Thought and Practice conference at Rice University, Houston, Texas, Nov. 11–12, 2005, http://en.fgulen. com/content/view/2136/31/ (accessed Aug. 2014).

7. Fethullah Gülen, "Our Education System," http://www.fethullahgulen.org (last modified 2006; accessed Aug. 2014).

8. Fethullah Gülen, "Action and Thought," http://www.fethullahgulen.org (last modified 2006; accessed Aug. 2014).

9. Fethullah Gülen, "Language and Thought," http://www.fethullahgulen.org (last modified 2008; accessed Aug. 2014).

10. Fethullah Gülen, "Balancing the Spiritual and the Physical," http://www .fethullahgulen.org (last modified 2008; accessed Aug. 2014).

11. Fethullah Gülen, "The Awaited Generation," http://www.fethullahgulen .org (last modified 2006; accessed Aug. 2014).

12. All quotes appearing in this chapter were taken from interviews that I conducted with Hizmet movement affiliates between January and July 2011.

NINE

The Hizmet Movement in Business, Trade, and Commerce

Phyllis E. Bernard

THE HIZMET MOVEMENT BRINGS to ordinary commercial dealings an extraordinary focus on idealism embedded in pragmatism. Hizmet principles promoting values beyond mere short-term financial goals comport with (but pre-date) the 2010 principles announced by the United Nations Global Compact on Supply Chain Sustainability. For the U.N. and other associations of business entities now pursuing corporate social responsibility as their modus operandi, this new direction owes more to pragmatism than idealism. Acting with concern for the operating environment, including workers and their communities, makes supply-chain disruptions less likely.

The Hizmet movement, however, pursues something more. It seeks to bring morality and community service to the marketplace. Other organizations, particularly in Islamic countries, have undertaken similar goals. The

---

The Hizmet movement attracts even the attention of people who live spiritually far from Sufi Islam, which is the starting point for Imam Fethullah Gülen. Beyond the zones of "interfaith dialogue" and "education," which have been surveyed in preceding chapters, Gülen and many of his affiliates are very much at home in the worlds of business, commerce, and finance, which are alien territories to many who are steeped in sacred texts and devotionalism. Yet Gülen's critiques of the economic order and practices have attracted diverse participants. Phyllis Bernard, the Robert S. Kerr, Jr. Distinguished Professor of Law at Oklahoma City University School of Law, tried out some of Gülen's ideas in conversations that, she says, included "self-described atheists, agnostics, lapsed and practicing Catholics, secular and observant Jews, devout and disaffected Protestants, [and] some Zen practitioners." Inspired by Hizmet discourse, she also presents for comparison an option from history that she favors: Quaker capitalism. Readers do not have to belong to any of the camps she mentions to profit from her explorations of Hizmet with economic theories and practices in view.

followers of Gülen distinguish themselves in the breadth of their vision, the influence exerted by following that vision, and the energy and discipline that have sustained their efforts. Any group achieving such success in commerce will inevitably change the social order, in small ways and eventually large. This prompts some observers to view Hizmet idealism with apprehension.

The Hizmet model of capitalism does something radical: it puts people before profits. As an act of praxis—contemplation in action—the Hizmet approach continually calls on the followers of Gülen to ask in virtually every aspect of their business culture and decision making: "What is the right thing—the ethical thing—to do?"

Unlike the shareholder capitalism model of business management, the Hizmet company is not driven by pressures to achieve quarterly earnings goals so that projected dividends can be paid. Instead, this Sufi paradigm for commerce measures achievement in terms of servant leadership and stewardship—not only within the company but also in the larger community.

COMPARISONS TO QUAKER CAPITALISM

Using faith to guide business decisions may sound like folly to most Westerners. That is, until one considers, as one example, the history of Quaker capitalism, which facilitated the accumulation of immense wealth combined with efforts to uplift humanity. Barclay's Bank, for instance, was founded by devout Quakers committed to the virtues of plain living and piety. However, after several generations, those principles could not withstand the allures of modern industrialism.[1]

The English Quaker Cadbury family was famous not only as chocolatiers but also as ethical employers who sought to create a capitalist workers utopia—something that their American Quaker competitor, Hershey, also attempted. In both businesses, the overt Quaker presence eventually transmuted into early icons of modern corporate social responsibility but now are difficult to distinguish from other multinational corporations.

By comparison, the Hizmet model thus far seems to keep idealism alive among followers even as they prosper financially. Business people committed to the cause work together to underwrite projects of spiritual significance that benefit the larger public. To facilitate adherence to the movement's altruistic goals, business people organize themselves into "circles" for peer support, providing mutual encouragement, advice, and assistance.

Outsiders know little about the actual structure and day-to-day operations of Hizmet circles. Compare this to the copious records left by English and American Quakers, who had maintained since the seventeenth century stringent rules for the conduct of business, financing, and enforcement of those rules through fines. When examining the conduct of Quaker meetings that guided business dealings among the Friends, we clearly see the overarching paradigm of control to ensure truth and trust.[2]

Modern-day Hizmet circles seem more akin to bands of trusted companions sharing a quest. The Hizmet businessperson's aim is two-fold: to carry out business according to eternal verities, and to contribute substantial sums of money, labor, and in-kind donations to support Hizmet projects for health care and education. Interestingly, this quest echoes the pioneer Quaker belief that "your own soul lived or perished according to its use of the gift of life." Thus, spiritual wealth was more important than accumulation of possessions.[3]

Invariably, people who are not already followers of Gülen question both motive and method: How/why do businessmen dedicate so much of their for-profit endeavors to underwriting Hizmet philanthropy? Are their motivations benign? Are they sincere? As the Hizmet movement gains greater influence, are increasing numbers of business people attracted more to the peer group opportunities for business referrals than to fellowship with the faithful?

FRACTALS: USING THE MICRO TO UNDERSTAND THE MACRO

Such questions about the "true" nature of the Hizmet network cannot be answered by reference to the abstract model alone. The core challenge pertains to whether one can believe in the character of individuals, as shown in their works. The macro concept of pursuing virtue in business and community can best be understood at the micro level of encounters with individual members of Hizmet peer circles and their related alliances and confederations—that is, larger groupings of local circles.

The Hizmet model is a fractal, whereby the pattern at the smallest unit replicates thousands of times over, in ever-expanding extensions of the same pattern, until we see a global network of schools and cultural exchanges funded by Hizmet businessmen like the individuals interviewed below. This chapter synthesizes and expands on actual interfaith, cross-cultural dialogues among Hizmet movement members in business, trade, and commerce and among Western academics, government officials, and attorneys specializing in international commercial negotiation. These dialogues took place in Istanbul in 2009 and were supplemented with 2010 interviews involving Hizmet members from a wider range of industries and locales.

CORPORATE CULTURE: THE HIZMET APPROACH IN CONTEXT

The principled capitalism espoused by Gülen runs counter to the narrowest but most prevalent view of how to achieve "limitless economic efficiency." Namely, "[c]ultural and moral constraints should be minimal."[4] After spending time privately in dialogues and interviews with Hizmet businessmen, one gains an abiding sense that the circles offer positive reinforcement to strengthen members in their commitment to moral and cultural values that they see as enhancing, not constraining, the modernization of society.

The Hizmet movement has its critics. However, as James Harrington explains in another chapter in the present volume, when addressing attacks on Gülen and his followers one must consider the source of those attacks and the intended audience. Some negative judgments reflect political manipulation of information. Others derive from a healthy skepticism about the role of idealism, faith, and trust in commerce—challenges that might equally apply to a network of avowedly Christian businessmen in America. I shall take a more contextual view: that the Hizmet approach—while grounded in Islamic cultural values—echoes trade customs that transcend faith traditions and continents.

PERCEPTIONS AND PARADOXES: FAITH IN ACTION

Turkey's contemporary culture of entrepreneurship arose from a convergence of faith-in-action, action-against-faith, dislocations of traditional economic and political power, and tectonic shifts in class status. For outside observers new to Turkish history, the fast-moving currents of national and international policies on agriculture and industrialization, the role of the government, and the role of the private sector appear dizzying. We shall use the following reference points as the framework to discuss the Hizmet movement in business, trade, and commerce.

Although prominent and the subject of this book, the circles and confederations of Hizmet businessmen are not the only faith-based organizations that encourage Turkish businessmen to engage in private ventures while promoting the public good. Indeed, this approach to trade grows from the historical roots of many *bazaars* (marketplaces), which developed, in part, to support the adjacent *masjid* (mosque). In turn, this intertwining of commerce with charitable works facilitated the fulfillment of the obligation of *zakat,* one of the pillars of Islam.

That being said, where a government provides few services to the underclass—in terms of education, health care, or provision for the poor—charitable works inevitably assume political significance, whether intended or not.[5] The faith-inspired works of well-organized Muslims who take *zakat* seriously (similar to Christians who take seriously the obligation to tithe and to provide for the needy) can overshadow episodic or smaller scale efforts by persons opposed to religion in the public square. Businessmen openly committed to *zakat* risk being labeled as "Islamist," perhaps largely by comparison to a wholly profit-driven model of capitalism where charitable works play no role.

In the last quarter of the twentieth century, Turkey implemented policies that restructured and privatized the economy. Control shifted away from so-called "family cartels" that dominated the industrial sector and away from state enterprises widely seen as inefficient. This process created opportunities for a new generation of business leaders from "lower and middle class families" who found energy and empowerment through their faith communities.[6] Were these "Islamists" as connoted by conservative Western media and politicians? That is, were such business groups—sometimes referred to as "Islamic brotherhoods"—merely part of a political strategy to build "extensive networks of charity and philanthropy" to recruit the disenfranchised lower classes to support a new theocracy?[7]

It is intriguing to note this overlap in terminology. The term "Islamic brotherhood" might not necessarily denote a political party that American security analysts and politicians routinely identify with dangerous, fundamentalist radicals. Instead, brotherhood (small cap) can be used as a generic term to describe social and business groups that Westerners might otherwise recognize as a "lodge" or "club," similar to Rotary International. The inadvertent or intentional use of this loaded term raises the specter that Hizmet business groups pave the way for the return of caliphate "hard power" in the form of Shari'a law.

THE "SOFT POWER" OF PURPOSEFUL PHILANTHROPY

To date, however, the Hizmet movement exemplifies modern Turkey's "soft power" of sharing culture, education, and influence—teaching by example a positive model of tolerance and modernism. Its network of schools builds interethnic and inter-religious tolerance person-by-person, community-by-community, over the span of time. The soft power includes programs for cultural exchanges, bringing hundreds of American educators, students, public officials, and non-Muslim clergy to Turkey every year. Stateside, Hizmet interfaith dialogue organizations introduce Americans to Turkish hospitality as a model of Islamic moderation. Hizmet businesses provide massive amounts of financial support for these activities.

A key characteristic of businessmen inspired by Gülen is the commitment to "quality education for the development of the human person and, simultaneously, for bringing Turkey into the modern era."[8] Businessmen support these efforts through donations that average 10 percent of their annual income; many persons contribute as much as one-third of their income to support Gülen schools, hospitals, and other Hizmet activities.[9]

Solid data on the number of such institutions, beneficiaries, budgets, and amounts contributed are elusive. Other chapters in this volume address it more directly. Here, we focus on how this commitment to philanthropy grows from the Hizmet view of the role of commerce and education in society. That view sees the three elements—commerce, philanthropy, and education—as a dynamic triad that energizes the long-term effort to uplift humanity.

Interviews I conducted in 2010 among members of Hizmet provided specificity that concretized general statements found in other texts. Business colleagues in Hizmet circles support not only their local Gülen-inspired school or college but also projects overseas. They contribute money, personal time, and—it was stressed to me—prayers and friendship. One circle may adopt a school in Angola; another circle will choose a school in Haiti; and so on. These schools are open to all students, free of charge, so long as they and their parents agree to set aside traditional ethnic, class, or religious animosities in order to live and learn in a cooperative environment. Parents must also be willing to encourage the education of females and for their children to take instruction from female teachers.

As an example, businessmen of Kutahya (a rural city of fewer than 200,000 persons) contribute the equivalent of U.S. $15,000 per month to support a Hizmet school in Kyrgyzstan. This school's mission is to educate a new generation of Kyrgyz, Uzbeks, and Russians who will be less likely to tolerate or participate in long-standing violent conflicts.[10]

Such disciplined and purposeful philanthropy can trigger in some quarters a whiff of envy mixed with unabashed suspicion. Consider, for example, a description of the Hizmet movement as a sort of "cult" that is moving "increasingly mainstream"—with "tentacles" that "expand relentlessly."[11] This characterization comes from a self-described nonpartisan publication based in Israel, voicing common fears about any movement perceived as nurturing anti-Israeli sentiments. Yet, little in Gülen's statements or approach suggests an anti-Israeli agenda; rather, they promote peaceful coexistence with Israel as with the rest of the world.

A more temperate analysis recognizes that the Hizmet movement follows a path previously laid by Said Nursi and the Nur community. Gülen and his followers ultimately exceeded the Nur circles paradigm. How? The Hizmet movement consciously and continuously reached beyond locality and social station to rear a new generation of entrepreneurs who pursue principled capitalism on a global level.[12] The timing could not have been better. Viewed in historical terms, the maturing Hizmet movement in trade and commerce blended with currents that brought Turkey into the mainstream of international manufacture, mining, energy exports, and textile production.

The growth of today's global supply chains roughly paralleled growth of the Hizmet movement in commerce. Is there a connection? Perhaps. The Hizmet focus on education and ethics created a critical mass of highly educated persons able to interact fluidly with the West while honoring traditional norms. This created a path that bridged traditional and modern, secular and sacred, building capacity on all sides of the business transaction. Perhaps inevitably, Hizmet in commerce has grown to such a size that it is now viewed by many as a significant factor in Turkey's economic-political life, with influence that extends far beyond the stated, nonpartisan intentions of Gülen.

BRIDGING MODERN COMMERCE
AND ANCIENT TRADITIONS

Some years ago, most discussions about globalization accepted unquestioningly the theory that modernization (through international business deals) and secularization go hand in hand. Standardized templates of law and business practices would not only harmonize the law but also eventually nullify the impact of religion. Faith would have little effect on commerce except perhaps among the less educated, less sophisticated, lower-class masses.

Emerging reality has not tracked past theory. Globalization and modernity thrive in a secular world but do not require jettisoning cultural values rooted in religious tradition.[13] Granted, commercial transactions seeking short-term gains from episodic contractual arrangements may operate satisfactorily without focusing on deep cultural context. However, entrepreneurs seeking long-term, self-sustaining international business partners want and need more. Especially if markets involve suppliers, manufacturers, financing, or labor rooted in Islamic cultures, the businessperson seeking maximum satisfaction strives to understand the human geography of the operating environment and how to navigate through it.

Standard westernized/Americanized templates for conceptualizing business "flatten" the human terrain, enforcing a false homogeneity. Explicit reference points to "landmarks" of Western clothing, education, and technology are taken as implicit assimilation of Western material values. Not so. Islamic values embedded in culture may shape the perceptions and conduct of persons who otherwise appear thoroughly secular. The businessmen of the Hizmet movement offer excellent examples of this convergence.

THE "BRIDGE" EXPERIENCE IN ISTANBUL

In 2009, I traveled to Turkey for my second visit, the first having been sponsored by the Institute for Interfaith Dialog (IID) in Oklahoma City, Okla. I returned this time for a conference that was part of a multiyear global project sponsored by the JAMS Foundation for conflict resolution in commerce and trade. The task was to update the standard American model for teaching international commercial negotiation to address the complexity and diversity of the twenty-first century. Istanbul was an ideal location for this encounter, offering both an actual and a metaphysical bridge between non-Western spiritual traditions and Western modernity.[14]

Through the generous assistance of Orhan Kucukosman, director of the Turkish Raindrop House in Oklahoma City, arrangements were made for members of the Alliance of Turkish Businessmen in Istanbul to meet with self-selected conference participants. Although these visitors were seasoned professionals, they knew little if anything about Gülen, had generally never been in a country with the *azan* call to prayer, and most were not yet familiar with the idea of "three cups of tea" as a ritual of relationship building. (I refer here to the widespread tradition of tea and friendship in the Middle East, not merely the discredited popular book of the same name.)

This dialogue created a fresh lens by which to view the Hizmet movement. Among other things, it revealed that one's understanding of Hizmet in business, trade, and commerce would be strongly impacted by whether one already had an appreciation for Islamic cultural values, generally, and for trade, specifically. The concept of a certain line of trade as a way of life, binding together families and communities over the course of generations, is something that few Americans have encountered. Yet this is the essence of commerce in the Middle East.

The dialogues then pursued the question: "What role does your faith play in how you conduct your business affairs?"

MONETIZED VERSUS SPIRITUALIZED WORLDVIEWS

These dialogues with Hizmet members created formal opportunities for informal discussions where teachers and scholars could become learners—asking questions that otherwise might seem intrusive, and allowing more revealing responses than would otherwise be considered polite. Afterward, some conference participants described the dialogues as "moving," "illuminating," and "one of the most powerful experiences" in their memory. For most, if not all, the dialogues were a surprising, refreshing, often unsettling encounter with "the Other."

Included among the dialogue participants were self-described atheists, agnostics, lapsed and practicing Catholics, secular and observant Jews, devout and disaffected Protestants, some Zen practitioners, and many who would describe themselves as "spiritual" but not "religious." Small groups of three to five, accompanied by a Turkish translator from IID, traveled to an

Istanbul business where they met members of Hizmet local circles. (Most businessmen actually understood English but felt more comfortable having a translator available.) Approximately 50 percent of IID members are professionals and businessmen, many of whom completed education in the United States.

To comprehend the complex layers involved in a discussion of morals, culture, and business, let us focus on the quintessential business deal: testing idealism in action.

In analyzing feedback from conference participants, who were very knowledgeable and sophisticated but highly westernized professionals, I concluded that much wariness concerning the Hizmet approach derives from fundamental—and perhaps irreconcilable—differences in worldviews. The dominant Western view sees the world as wholly monetized. Everything has a price. Everything can be negotiated. The point of a business negotiation is to find what price a person will pay or accept. Period. This model does not include room for the ineffable.

When something is not already overtly a commodity—to be bought, sold, or traded—then standard commercial negotiation training teaches business people how to make it so. Intangibles such as sentiment, loyalty, identity, and values matter only insofar as they can be manipulated to achieve the one goal that matters: the best price.

The model of negotiation I have promoted in the *Rethinking Negotiation* series seeks to retire the commodity orientation.[15] The U.S. military has determined that this kind of orientation is essential to navigate the human geography of the Middle East. But, even if not dealing specifically with businessmen committed to the Hizmet movement, not everything is negotiable. Not everything has a price. Sometimes a businessperson's values—including reputation and religion—matter more than any price. The standard, monetized orientation to business deals teaches people how to negotiate (that is, how to lead people to compromise) personal values. This assumes that such values have only illusory or manipulative significance—if they are paid attention to at all.

A shift in orientation would recognize that such values actually shape the business landscape. Cultural and religious values make meaning for international trading partners, whether the unstated implications of that meaning are fully appreciated or not, and whether they involve the Hizmet movement or not.

HOSPITALITY AS BUSINESS CUSTOM
AND SACRED OBLIGATION

One of the most important lessons learned in the course of the dialogues was that Westerners seeking to understand the Hizmet movement in business must first understand Islamic cultural values as they shape the content and conduct of business dealings. It was necessary to understand that the business deal is the relationship between people, not the piece of paper on which a contract is written; that business is done among people whom you can call friend; that friendship carries with it a set of commitments much more profound than in America or Western Europe; and, finally, that the method of developing relationships in business revolves around the ritual of serving and drinking tea.

Much of the learning was contextual. Each group learned by experience the bedrock of Islamic business customs: hospitality. In Turkey, as throughout the Middle East, hospitality means far more than mere courtesy. It is an expression of sacred obligations dating to times that some believe even pre-dated Islam. Under Islam, however, these bonds and rituals gained enriched value. Hence, the "courtesies" of sharing tea are not merely secular but also sacred.

Embodied in the rituals of hospitality are fundamental principles seriously at odds with the monetized worldview of business dealings. Instead, Islamic business arrangements are formed through three key traditions: tempo, tea, and trust.

The tempo of negotiations is far slower than is usual in America and much of Western Europe. The pace allows time for parties to understand each other, their stated and unstated interests. The slower tempo allows time to consult with and consider the needs of others whose interests are affected by the transaction, which is part of the Hizmet obligation of stewardship.

Sharing tea is an icon of business transactions in Islamic cultures. Whether initiating a sale of products or services to a customer, or initiating a supplier-purchaser, manufacturing, or trade agreement, traditions dating from days of the Silk Road dictate that all business discussions begin with a pot of tea. It might be mint, apple, or black tea, or coffee, accompanied by juices and sweets. Regardless, the guest has a reciprocal obligation to accept graciously the proffered hospitality.

This social ritual serves a strategic purpose. Parties use this opportunity to gauge the level of trust essential to create a business deal that is self-enforcing, efficient, ethical, and hence profitable. In Islamic cultures, friendship—not a paper contract—binds parties in a commercial transaction. Classically, the sharing of tea can describe degrees of friendship, which also describes the qualities of relationship essential for business success: What is their depth of knowledge about each other's character? What obligations would they undertake on behalf of each other? How much trust is there?

Trust strong enough to support a sustainable commercial venture can neither be rushed nor compressed to fit an artificially limited (Western) timeframe. Timing must be relatively leisurely, a pace and measurement described proverbially according to the cups (or pots) of tea consumed during conversation that reveal character, worldview, and capacity—not capital budgets.[16]

One cup of tea represents the mere threshold of politeness owed any stranger or customer. Over the second cup (or pot) of tea, business persons explore the contours of compatibility, not only regarding each other directly but also regarding extended families and communities expected to vouch for credibility and completion of obligations. The third cup (or pot) of tea marks the threshold of a true friendship, one strong enough to merit action in reliance on the other's word alone; no written contract required.[17]

Standard guides to international business practices and travel books routinely describe tea hospitality in Islamic culture as matters of cross-cultural etiquette. But the roots run deeper than secularism alone. Arising from sacred obligations established in Islam and Buddhism, these practices on the ancient Silk Road developed a reliable merchant network extending across ethnic and religious lines, as does the Hizmet movement today.

Trust is the essential ingredient. Without trust, no business will be conducted. The higher one's earned reputation for being reliable and trustworthy, the greater value the person's name can carry. Business transactions everywhere require some degree of trust to be self-enforcing. In Islamic culture, the duty to perform extends beyond the individual to that person's extended family. Do the Hizmet circles increase the pressure and the guarantee of reliability? An outsider can only speculate.

Notwithstanding, the custom is not limited to the Middle East or to the Hizmet movement. Some Westerners still operate or remember operating on similar principles. For example, among "old school" New York City businessmen, there is a quiet but firm recognition that "pride, reputation and good will" are important in negotiations and "although . . . intangible . . . are absolutely real."[18]

Our IID host, Hossein Güzell, operates the family business Güzella, Inc., an international high fashion design and textile business. He taught his visitors by "total immersion"—demonstrating the "three T's" in action. We observed many teaching moments, which he graciously explained. But one key resource was not displayed in a manner that facilitated easy access: it was a framed poster situated across from his desk, out of the line of sight for visitors, yet directly in his view. Translated from the Turkish, "I Say to Myself (The Way of Life)" articulated principles of servant leadership that many business people might recognize, including those from humanist Western or observant Christian or Jewish backgrounds.

Güzella as a business presents a fractal pattern that demonstrates the essence of the Hizmet model in action.

Tempo

Two seemingly contrasting concepts demand equal respect: industriousness and neighborliness. The poster across from Güzell's desk reminded us: "Be punctual, straightforward and just"; "Work hard, persevere, and look at the lives of those who are successful"; "Don't waste your time. God doesn't like those who kill time." This would suggest support for a tempo and profit-driven focus similar to the fast pace and goals of Western commerce.

However, much more emphasis is placed on how to prioritize one's time, which also sets the pace to conduct work. The overarching guideline is to remember: "The things that you do today should serve today and tomorrow. The things that you do in this world should serve this world and the hereafter." In today's world, one must take the time to serve others. It is seen not only as a duty but also as a source of happiness. "Live for the other more than yourself; happiness is a perfume that makes you more aromatic if you shower it on the ones around you."

These concepts are synthesized in the Turkish understanding of neighborliness, where persons are expected never to be in such a rush that they cannot take time to show caring and compassion for others no matter how "thin" the relationship may be. Virtually everyone acts in relationship to/with others. Acknowledging this interdependency renders business in Istanbul much more like business in rural America, where, even if you do not know a person's name, you are expected to exchange greetings and engage in conversation as a sign of respect and membership in the community.

Tea

In a Western world that admires multitasking, where Tweets and text messages often constitute conversation among family members and intimate friends, the concept of taking time to give one human being undivided, face-to-face attention becomes less and less familiar. Yet this is what the ritual of tea as part of business negotiations achieves. On the surface level, the lengthy process of drinking tea together carves out time and space for people to engage in mindful conversation. In this process, people can begin to build relationships.

On a deeper level, the ritual of tea is a modern iteration of an ancient tradition, born from nomadic cultures where life depended on mutual assistance, later reinforced and given a spiritual dimension by Islam. Conference participants who visited a Turkish business host were lavished not only with tea, coffee, soft drinks, and pastries but also with full meals and gifts. This phenomenon is common throughout the Middle East. Often Westerners either take the hospitality for granted or react skeptically, questioning whether it is merely a gimmick to lay the foundation for getting the best price.

Rather, Turkish generosity springs both from sincerity and from the desire to be virtuous in the eyes of God. Hospitality is open-ended, not tied to a commercial result. This may be difficult for some Westerners to accept unless they know the deep roots of the modern practice. Turkish oral traditions describe the underlying principle, which pre-dates Islam: "If a stranger knocks at the door, s/he should be invited inside, given ample food and shelter for three days; and only at the end of three days should the cause of the visit be asked." A guest who arrives unexpectedly should be considered "a guest from God." The tradition has a touch of pragmatism, however. After three days a guest becomes family and is expected to help with chores.

More frequent than the tradition of household hospitality that confers family status upon guests is the third cup of tea, which similarly marks the crossing of a threshold. With the third cup of tea, the relationship amd the trust have built to a point of mutual obligations that extend beyond merely completing the terms of a commercial contract. They mark bonds of unquestioned loyalty and integrity—levels of performance that few Western businesses contemplate in an ostensibly straightforward business deal.

How much should one rely on these constraints, especially in regions famous not only for hospitality but also for treachery? In a follow-up visit to Turkey on a trip hosted by the IID in 2010, I addressed this issue directly with businessmen who were part of the Hizmet movement but engaged in commerce in the legendarily corrupt areas of construction and mining in Central Asia and Russia. Their answers blended idealism and pragmatism. I venture to summarize:

You cannot do business with thieves, period. Even if a deal sounds enticing initially, over time the problems that inevitably arise will outweigh any benefits.

Therefore, you need to be ready to not do business at all in some areas. So be it. Short-term profits are not worth long-term regrets.

When dealing with persons who are merely "slippery" but not treacherous, do not take a step without good legal counsel.[19]

The theme can best be summed up in the popular Islamic proverb: "Trust God, but tie your camel."

Trust

Trust in business deals in Turkish culture goes well beyond soft sentiment. Among other reasons, integrity is vital because transactions are traditionally handled based on a person's word, their reputation. Cash is the preferred method for doing business. Thousands, even millions of dollars will transfer from person to person across vast distances based solely on a verbal request. How? Why? Because the sender knows that the receiver—and the receiver's family—will fulfill the obligation no matter what. It is difficult to imagine a Western business with the same expectations about commitments.

Trust serves as a guiding principle not only outside but also inside the company. The Güzella human resources model puts into action a consultative, shared notion of power in the workplace. It sounds nearly "New Age" or classic Quaker but actually stems from a commitment to Islamic concepts of leadership. A leader, including an officer of a for-profit business, must fulfill a sacred duty of trust whereby all decisions are made with an eye toward protecting the best interests of the entire organization, as a community. Indeed, one might go so far as to identify Güzella, Inc., as an informal family—albeit a family with over 700 members.

Hizmet values show in the vocabulary used. As Güzell describes: "I do not call my employees 'workers' or 'employees.' I call them 'friends.' I eat what they eat. I believe in their honesty, so they believe in my honesty."[20] He deals similarly with business colleagues, and he has never been to court.

THE VALUE OF A VALUES-ORIENTATION

Shareholder capitalism—detached from morals and culture, seeking only to maximize short-term profit—is the antithesis of principled capitalism. And the future belongs to those who can maintain uninterrupted, sustainable supply chains. How does one achieve that? To quote Güzell: "A focus on money can only take you so far. And now such companies have maxed out. They've gone as far as a money model can take them. Now they are slipping backwards. They are having to relearn, restructure around these more lasting cultural values which have sustained other businesses for generations."[21]

I dare say that Quaker George Cadbury would agree.

NOTES

1. D. Cadbury, *Chocolate Wars: The 150-year Rivalry between the World's Greatest Chocolate Makers* (New York: Public Affairs, 2010), 122.

2. Ibid., 36.

3. Ibid., xvii.

4. B. Ozaral, "Islam and Moral Economy," in *The Sociology of Islam: Secularism, Economy and Politics,* edited by T. Keskin, 21–44 (Ithaca, N.Y.: Ithaca Press, 2011), 24.

5. A. D. Aksular, "Faith-based Organizations in the Struggle against Poverty: Deniz Feneri Welfare and Solidarity Association, Sample of Ankara Branch," Master's thesis, Department of Sociology, Graduate School of Social Sciences of Middle East Technical University, Sept, 2008.

6. G. B. Ozcan and H. Turunc, "Economic Liberalization and Class Dynamics in Turkey: New Business Groups and Islamic Mobilization," *Insight Turkey* 13, no. 3 (2011): 70.

7. Ibid., 69.

8. H. Ebaugh, *The Gülen Movement: A Sociological Analysis of a Civic Movement Rooted in Moderate Islam* (Dordrecht, Germany: Springer, 2010), 52.

9. Ibid., 59.

10. Personal interviews with members of the Confederation of Turkish Businessmen in Kutahya (Suleyman Dogan, Husein Karakuzu, and founder of the Kyrgyzstan school, Suleyman Akkay), May 26, 2010.

11. B. Park, "The Fethullah Gülen Movement," *Middle East Review of International Affairs* 12, no. 4 (Dec. 2008), www.rubincenter.org/2008/12/park-asp-2008-12-08 (accessed May 29, 2015).

12. J.F. Walton, "Horizons and Histories of Liberal Piety: Civil Islam and Secularism in Contemporary Turkey," Ph.D. diss., Department of Anthropology, University of Chicago, Dec. 2009.

13. P. Berger, *The Desecularization of the World: Resurgent Religion and World Politics* (Washington, D.C.: Eerdmans, 1999).

14. P.E. Bernard, "Reorienting the Trainer to Navigate—Not Negotiate—Islamic Cultural Values," in *Venturing Beyond the Classroom*, vol. 2 of *Rethinking Negotiation,* edited by C. Honeyman, J. Coben, and G. De Palo, 61–76 (St. Paul, Minn.: DRI, 2010).

15. Ibid.

16. The following quote also applies to Turkey: "A good personal relationship is the most important single factor in doing business successfully. . . . In the end, personal contacts lead to more efficiency than following rules and regulations." M.K. Nydel, *Understanding Arabs: A Contemporary Guide to Arab Society,* 5th ed. (Boston, Mass.: Nicholas Brealey, 2012), 10–11.

17. The convention of "three cups of tea" can expand to "three months of meals" if needed to build sufficient trust among the parties. See H. Alon and J.M. Brett, "Perceptions of Time and Their Impact on Negotiations in the Arabic-speaking World," *Negotiation Journal* 23, no. 1 (Jan. 2007): 55, 60.

18. D. Rose, "Ulysses and Business Negotiation," in *The Negotiator's Fieldbook: The Desk Reference for the Experienced Negotiator,* edited by A.K. Schneider and C. Honeyman, 711–14 (Washington, D.C.: American Bar Association, 2006), 714.

19. Personal interviews with Suleyman Maltas (Kutahya, May 27, 2010) and Metin Sagil and Eyup Kaynak (Istanbul, May 25, 2010).

20. Personal interview with Hossein Güzell (Istanbul, May 18, 2009).

21. Ibid.

TEN

The Sacred and the Secular in the Hizmet World

Ihsan Yilmaz

DESPITE THE TOP-DOWN AGGRESSIVE secularization policies of the Kemalist state, religion in Turkey has not disappeared and is unlikely to do so. In total opposition to the Kemalists, the Islamists would stress the influence and role of religion in the political realm. The understanding of the Hizmet movement on state/religion/society issues stands between these two extremes in a creative way.

There are quite a few versions of secularism(s): inclusive, passive, tolerant, liberal, benevolent, moderate, evolutionary, weak, ameliorative or principled-distance secularism, *laïcité plurielle, positive, de gestion,* and *bien entendue,* in opposition to strong, intolerant, statist, exclusive, assertive, aggressive, or malevolent secularism.[1] In passive secularism, the secular state plays a "passive" role and, while avoiding the establishment of any religions, allows for the public visibility of religion.[2] In assertive secularism, the state tries to exclude religion from the public sphere in addition to playing "an 'assertive'

Two terms, "sacred" and "secular," have become code words for complex realities in many cultures. In few places on the global scene are controversies over both terms more intense and fateful than in Turkey, the original base of the Hizmet cause. There is no doubt that this movement is rooted in "the sacred," rich as it is in devotion to scriptures, devotions, and ethical discourse. There is also no doubt that its environment in Turkey has provided one of the best case studies of "the secular," which in this case has meant a studied and severe attempt to rule out any devotion to "the sacred." Ihsan Yilmaz, professor of Political Science at Faith University Istanbul, brings a scholarly perspective that promotes fairness and on-the-scene experience, and he helps to ensure an informed representation of Hizmet's religious implications. He takes great care to define the variations on the Turkish scene and thus provides angles of vision for interpreting the aspirations of Hizmet and the conflicts promoted by its more stringent and powerful critics.

role as the agent of a social engineering project that confines religion to the private domain."[3] In Turkey, though the Kemalist state has been assertively secularist, the ruling Justice and Development Party (AKP) and the Hizmet movement are passive secularists.[4]

Emerging from the context of the modern history of the Turkish republic, Hizmet's "contribution is one that has developed and matured through engagement with both ideological 'secularism' and political 'Islamism.'"[5] The border-transgressor[6] Hizmet movement skillfully inhabits religious and secular worlds simultaneously, is in critical engagement with them, and blurs conventional political lines on the hotly debated issue of state/religion/society issues, challenging the rudimentary typologies.

KEMALISTS, ISLAMISTS, AND GÜLEN

The concept of civil religion has its roots in the eighteenth-century Enlightenment, particularly in the thought of Jean-Jacques Rousseau. The Rousseauian understanding of civil "religion" was an instrument that would be used to ensure allegiance to the state through a sort of "secular" faith. Émile Durkheim also wrote about civil religion, but his was a bottom-up civil religion unlike the Rousseauian top-down construct. Robert Bellah's understanding of religion is similar to Durkheim's in the sense that it has a bottom-up focus but it is much more "religious";[7] he has underscored that America was exceptional in melding religion and nationhood. In the Turkish case, the Kemalists combined Rousseauian and Durkheimian approaches. On the one hand, the Turkish state wanted to use the already existing religion as a helping hand with a Durkheimian mentality;[8] on the other hand, with a Rousseauian approach, it tried to create a top-down new version of civil religion that I call "Lausannian Islam." By using this term, I want not only to emphasize the fact that the Kemalists tried to create an official version of Turkish Islam within the borders of Turkey as defined by the Lausanne Treaty in 1923 but also to imply that, by deferring to the spirit of the Lausanne Treaty, this Turkish version of Islam jettisoned Islam's transnational and inter-religious dimensions.[9] For instance, Lausannian Islam did not care about inter-religious dialogue until Fethullah Gülen and the Hizmet movement took the initiative in this area.[10] To subordinate religion to the political establishment, the Kemalist state endeavored to manufacture a state version of Turkish Islam, in which there is already no conflict between the religion and Turkish modernity that covers the modern nation-state, secularism, and democracy.[11] All imams and preachers are employed by the state's Directorate of Religious Affairs, and, other than these civil servants, private imams, preachers, sermons, religious education, and tutoring are not allowed. All texts of the Friday sermons are written in the directorate headquarters in Ankara and have to be read verbatim throughout Turkey by more than 80,000 imams and preachers who are state employees. The directorate is so precious for the Kemalist establishment that even today, according to the Political Parties Law, political parties are not allowed to offer any change in the directorate's constitutional status. Asking for any modification is legal grounds for a closure case. This is understandable, given that its role, as defined by the Kemalists, "has been to control and to shape Islam in accordance with the needs of the secular nation-state to the effect of creating a secular, modern, national, official Lausannian-Islam."[12] Kemalist hegemony tried to create a normalcy centered on the Lausannian-Islam or a Bourdieuian secular/nationalist/religious *doxa* by using the directorate in addition to several other Gramscian apparatuses such as the organic intellectuals, media, and schools. All other public Muslim religious manifestations that did not conform to Lausannian Islam were demonized, vilified, and even criminalized. During the AKP period, this has not changed much, and further research is needed to analyze the recent "Islamist" developments.

Lausannian Islam envisages a Muslim type that adores the state and is secularist, Turkish nationalist, and Atatürkist. A good Lausannian Muslim is one who does not have any transnational cultural aspirations and who accepts that the state, not the ulema or the Sufis, knows best about religion. A Lausannian Muslim practices his religion either privately at home or in a mosque but not in the public sphere, and he does not base his arguments or demands on religion.[13]

The Kemalists' ideal citizen is encapsulated by the acronym LAST, which is similar to WASP (White Anglo-Saxon Protestant). LAST stands for Laicist, Atatürkist, Sunni, Turk. Laicist does not mean a secular-minded person; rather, it refers to a person who is aggressively secularist and is not pleased with public manifestations of Islam even though he does not care much about other religions' public visibility. Atatürkism is a softer version of Kemalism, and, as long as one loves Mustafa Kemal Atatürk, deeply respects him, and does not think he made mistakes, one is considered an Atatürkist.[14] To be a first-class citizen, one needs to be a nonpracticing Sunni Muslim who belongs without practicing[15] and an ethnic and nationalist Turk. All others outside of these parameters are not fully trusted by the Kemalists and their state. Non-Muslims, practicing Muslims, non-Atatürkists such as leftists and liberals, Alevis, and Kurds have always been discriminated against by the Kemalist state whenever these identities become manifest in the public sphere.

The state has worked hard to socially engineer these perfect citizens or "LASTmen," and the directorate has been given an important role in this Rousseau-Durkheimian project.[16] As a matter of fact, recent research by Nezir Akyeşilmen has shown that the directorate's Friday sermons focus on concepts such as "country, nation, national and Turk."[17] In 150 Friday sermons between 2003 and 2005, the directorate chose "the love of God" only 5 times as the main topic, whereas "the love of the country" was chosen 6 times. The words "country, nation, national and Turk" were used 263 times, but "human rights, equality, freedom and Islamic brotherhood" were mentioned only 29 times.[18] The word "war" was used 135 times in a positive sense, such as "one must sacrifice one's life for some noble values and national honor"; it was negatively referred to only 9 times.[19]

Being children of "Kemalistan," Turkish Islamists also shared the Kemalist (Rousseauian) idea of top-down social engineering and a Jacobinist state-centric view of religion. They envisaged a top-down religio-cultural transformation after coming to power by democratic means.[20]

In contrast to the Kemalist and Islamist attitudes toward religion/state relations, Gülen's ultimate concern in this life focuses on the hereafter, spirituality, and worship.[21] He strongly argues that Islam is more than a political ideology: "When those who have adopted Islam as a political ideology rather than a religion in its true sense and function, review their activities and attitudes they claim to be based on Islam, especially political ones, will discover that they are usually moved by personal or national anger, hostility, and other similar motives."[22] He understands the problems and challenges facing Muslims in the contemporary age, and he deals "with them but he does not believe that politics is the most effective way to do so in the twenty-first century."[23] Gülen's *ummah* "is a transnational socio-cultural entity, not a Utopian politico-legal one."[24] He "does not see the world in political terms and does not draw imaginary boundaries."[25] Gülen "eschews politics in the belief that it leads to social divisiveness and distraction from the essential issues of values and principle. In fact, the movement opposes the creation of political parties founded on religion in general, believing that they end up compromising or contaminating religion and that they only serve to create social strife damaging to the position of religion in society."[26]

He advocates working "in the interests of domestic social transformation by striving to outperform rivals in the market, rather than to overcome them in political confrontation."[27] Thus, he opposes the ideology of Islamism:

> This vision of Islam as a totalizing ideology is totally against the spirit of Islam, which promotes the rule of law and openly rejects oppression against any segment of society. This spirit also promotes actions for the betterment of society in accordance with the view of the majority. Those who follow a more moderate pattern also believe that it would be much better to introduce Islam as a complement to democracy instead of presenting it as an ideology. Such an introduction of Islam may play an important role in the Muslim world through enriching local forms of democracy and extending it in such a way that helps humans develop and understanding of the relationship between the spiritual and material worlds. I believe that Islam also would enrich democracy in answering the deep needs of humans, such as spiritual satisfaction, which cannot be fulfilled except through the remembrance of the Eternal One.[28]

Gülen has repeatedly stated that there is no particular model for either the method of election or the system of administration. He explains, "[I]n Islam it is not possible to limit the concept of governance and politics into a single paradigm, unlike the principles of faith and the pillars of Islam."[29]

Gülen underscores that the Qur'an is not a political book or project:

> The Qur'an is a translation of the book of the universe. . . . It is an explanation of the reflections of the divine names on earth and in the heavens. It is a prescription for the various problems of the Islamic world. It is a guide for bliss in this life and in the life to come. It is a great guide for the travelers in this world moving towards the hereafter. It is an inexhaustible source of wisdom. Such a book should not be reduced to the level of political discourse, nor should it be considered a book about political theories or forms of state.[30]

He emphasizes that "Islam does not propose a certain unchangeable form of government or attempt to shape it. Instead, Islam establishes fundamental principles that orient a government's general character, leaving it to the people to choose the type and form of government according to time and circumstances."[31] According to Gülen, fundamental Islamic political principles are a social contract and election of a group of people to debate common issues.[32] He puts it that, "[i]n Islam, ruling means a mutual contract between the ruler and the subject and it takes its legitimacy from the rule of law, and from the principle of the superiority of the law."[33] He is of the firm opinion that "it is impossible to prove in any way that Islam opposes democracy."[34]

Some have argued that the Hizmet movement is also a political movement. Yet this depends on what one means by "politics." On this, I agree with Graham Fuller:

> There is no doubt that the movement quite explicitly aspires to transform society through transformation of the individual, a process that could ultimately lead to collective calls for the creation of national and social institutions that reflect belief in a moral order. In a very loose sense, it is possible to call this a political project if we consider any attempt to transform society to be a political project. But I would argue that it is just as much a social and moral project. Indeed, the term "political" loses its meaning if applied equally to all efforts to transform society, regardless of means. Promotion of change through teachings, education, and information does not really become political until it formally and institutionally enters the political process.[35]

It must be added that, even though the Hizmet movement is not engaged in daily politics but works in the realm of civil society, it has concerns, of course, that need to be addressed in the political sphere. For instance, for the sake of more freedoms, the movement has been lobbying for the European Union accession project of Turkey and for a new democratic constitution. Moreover, unlike the Islamists, Hizmet never legitimizes politics in the name of Islam. Even though Gülen has been discouraging his followers from entering politics, in the final analysis, in this movement of volunteers, individuals have the freedom to enter daily politics in their individual capacity, not as representatives of Hizmet or Islam. If they enter politics, they will be expected to jettison any representative role they might have within Hizmet.

GÜLEN ON RIGHTS, FREEDOM OF RELIGION, AND SECULARISM

While explaining the Islamic theological reasons why people are responsible for their own fate, Gülen also talks about free will and freedoms:

> Islam considers a society to be composed of conscious individuals equipped with free will and having responsibility toward both themselves and others. . . . The Koran (13:11) says: "God will not change the state of a people

unless they change themselves [with respect to their beliefs, worldview, and lifestyle]." In other words, each society holds the reins of its fate in its own hands. The prophetic tradition emphasizes this idea: "You will be ruled according to how you are." This is the basic character and spirit of democracy, which does not conflict with any Islamic principle. As Islam holds individuals and societies responsible for their own fate, people must be responsible for governing themselves.[36]

Gülen is an advocate of Shatibi's *Maqasid al Shari'a* (Major Objectives of Islamic Law): "[R]eligion, life, reproduction, the mind, and property are basic essentials that everyone must protect. In a sense, Islam approaches human rights from the angle of these basic principles."[37] He emphasizes that:

> Islam upholds the following fundamental principles: 1. Power lies in truth, a repudiation of the common idea that truth relies upon power. 2. Justice and the rule of law are essential. 3. Freedom of belief and rights to life, personal property, reproduction, and health (both mental and physical) cannot be violated. 4. The privacy and immunity of individual life must be maintained. 5. No one can be convicted of a crime without evidence, or accused and punished for someone else's crime. 6. An advisory system of administration is essential.[38]

Gülen is a staunch advocate of human rights, political participation, protection of minority rights, and the participation of individuals and society in decision-making institutions:

> Everybody should be allowed to express themselves with the condition that no pressure should be made on others through variety of means. Also, members of minority communities should be allowed to live according to their beliefs. If these sorts of legislations are made within the norms of international law and international agreements, Islam will have no objection to any of these.[39]

On secular law-making, Gülen makes it clear that "[i]n Islam, the legislative and executive institutions have always been allowed to make laws. These are based on the needs and betterment of society and within the frame of general norms of law. On domestic issues in the Islamic community and its relationship with other nations, including economic, political and cultural relations, Muslims have always developed laws." [40]

He claims that, in a real secular system, everybody can and should be able to freely express and live his or her religious sentiments and ideas.[41] In

Gülen's thinking, "[R]eligion is not reduced to a private or personal affair, but can have a collective character and can freely intervene in society. Believers can publicly express their faith, organize, and develop diverse activities."[42] This conforms to the Habermasian understanding of religion in the public sphere. Gülen asserts that, if secularity could function as it is in the West, nobody would reject it.[43] He does not see any contradiction between Islamic ideals and a democratic republic, as it is a system that can protect freedoms, human rights, and dignity: "A true republic is a form of rule by elevated spirits and is the most suitable for humanity's honor. . . . The republic can be the mother or governess of freedom, for it nurtures and raises generations in love with freedom. . . . As our spirit, which has an innate desire for freedom, rejects all forms of domination, it reacts to any limits to be placed on its freedom of thought, behavior, and expression."[44]

He underscores that Islam "recognizes right, not force, as the foundation of social life."[45] In his view, Islamic principles of equality, tolerance, and justice can help democracy to reach its peak of perfection and bring even more happiness to humanity.[46] With regard to religious freedom, he is unequivocal: "As for those who don't believe in Islam, leave them to their own understanding and lifestyle, for Islam's commands are obligatory only for Muslims. If there is anxiety that people will be forced to do this when Islamic principles are carried over into public life, it should be understood that such a forceful act is not Islamic."[47]

Gülen does not oppose the idea of mutual autonomy of state and Islam.[48] He argues that, "[i]f a state . . . gives the opportunity to its citizens to practice their religion and supports them in their thinking, learning, and practice, this system is not considered to be against the teaching of the Qur'an. In the presence of such a state there is no need to seek an alternative state."[49] He "advocates a total separation between the religious and political in contemporary Muslim societies. He thinks that the domination of the state over religious affairs has greatly harmed the cause of Islam in the present time and thus advocates the freedom of the religious realm from political authority."[50] In Gülen's thinking, one can also find traces of what Alfred Stepan calls "twin tolerations."[51] First of all, Gülen makes clear that "Islam has nothing to do with theocracy."[52] He continues that, if human rights including freedom of religion are respected by the state, then there is no need for an "Islamic" state. He has made it clear that "one can practice authentic Islam without needing to live in an Islamic political system."[53] In his view, "If a state . . . gives the opportunity to its citizens to practice their religion and supports them in their thinking, learning, and practice, this system is not considered to be against the teaching of the Qur'an. In the presence of such a state there is no need to seek an alternative state."[54] With regard to religious demands in the public sphere, he advises self-sacrifice: "If the religious people are thinking of living peacefully in this country, they should not contribute to the expansion of the conflict by challenging the fragile issues. Peace in a society can be achieved by mutual self-sacrifice. It seems better to leave some issues to the interpretation of time."[55] It is obvious that, in such an understanding, there is room for Stepan's toleration: religious authorities must "tolerate" the autonomy of democratic parliaments without claiming any constitutionally privileged prerogatives to mandate or veto legislation and public policy.[56] Without labeling it as such, Gülen seems to talk about twin tolerations in a speech that he made many years ago: "If secularity is understood as the state not being founded on religion, hence it does not interfere with religion or religious life; and as the faithful living his religion does not disturb others; and furthermore if the state will accomplish this task in a serious neutrality, then there is no problem." [57]

CONCLUSION

Until the sudden eruption of religion into the public sphere in many parts of the world in the late 1970s and early 1980s, a relatively widespread consensus had existed in the sociology of religion discipline over the privatization thesis.[58] Since then, it has been realized "that differentiation did not necessarily mean that religion would remain in its assigned place in the private sphere and not enter the public arena." [59] Some scholars, such as José Casanova, have argued that during the course of the past few decades a process of "deprivatization" of religion has taken place in the world, and even though a historical process of religious differentiation has occurred in the West, institutional differentiation does not necessarily result in the marginalization and privatization of religion.[60]

Casanova divides the modern democratic polity into three—state, political society, and civil society—and he argues that in principle there can be public religions on all three levels.[61] But, in his view, only public religions at the civil society level are compatible with the modern principle of citizenship. By contrast, in his elaboration on John Rawls's political theory, in particular concepts of the "public use of reason" and "translation provisio," Jürgen Habermas has objected to this restrictive idea of the political role of religion and argued that, other than the state level, public visibility of religions could be allowed at civil society and political society levels.[62]

Rawls argues that "reasonable comprehensive doctrines, religious or non-religious, may be introduced in public political discussion at any time, provided that in due course proper political reasons—and not reasons given solely by comprehensive doctrines—are presented that are sufficient to support whatever the comprehensive doctrines are said to support."[63] In response, Habermas emphasizes that "religious communities and movements provide arguments for public debates on crucial morally-loaded issues and handle tasks of political socialization by informing their members and encouraging them to take part in the political process."[64] However, each time they have to "find an equivalent in a universally accessible language for every religious statement they pronounce" as part of the duty of civility.[65] This epistemic burden results in a sort of self-censorship. It is obvious that "many religious citizens would not be able to undertake such an artificial division within their own minds without jeopardizing their existence as pious persons."[66] Habermas concludes that "the liberal state, which expressly protects such forms of life in terms of a basic right, cannot at the same time expect of all citizens that they also justify their political statements independently of their religious convictions or world views. This strict demand can only be laid at the door of politicians, who within state institutions are subject to the obligation to remain neutral in the face of competing world views."[67] Citizens must agree "that only secular reasons count beyond the institutional threshold that divides the informal public sphere from parliaments, courts, ministries and administrations."[68] Religious citizens, too, can agree to this "institutional translation provisio" without splitting their identity into a public and a private part when they participate in public debates and discourses. Thus, they should "be allowed to express and justify their convictions in a religious language if they cannot find secular 'translations' for them."[69]

A convergence between Gülen's idea that passive secularism is compatible with Islam and a Habermasian understanding of religion in the public sphere can be observed. This convergence could even amount to an overlapping consensus, to use Rawls's concept. Here, a secularist (Habermas) agrees with an Islamic scholar (Gülen) that religion could be practiced in the public realm, that religious demands could be made in the public sphere, and that the state is equidistant to all religions.

Gülen's conception of Islam-friendly democracy is key to understanding his approach to sacred and secular relations. He does not see a contradiction between Islam and democracy, and he reasons that Islam establishes fundamental principles that orient a government's general character, leaving it to the people to choose the type and form of government according to time and circumstances. With regard to state/society/religion issues, he has argued, unlike the Islamists, that passive Anglo-Saxon secularism which guarantees human rights and freedoms, including freedom of religion, could provide a wider framework for Muslims to practice their religion comfortably where other religious minorities also benefit from human rights. In his view, the faithful can comfortably live in secular environments if secularism is religion-friendly and understood as the state not being founded on religion. Hence, it does not interfere with religion or religious life, and the state is equidistant to all religions in a neutral manner. It can be argued that Gülen's approach to sacred/secular relations is similar to the First Amendment of the U.S. Constitution ("Congress shall make no law respecting an establishment of religion, or prohibiting the free exercise thereof") since he has highlighted that Islam does not need a state to survive and that civil society or the civilian realm in liberal-democratic settings is sufficient for its individual and social practice. This understanding of "Islamic secularism" or "twin tolerations" resonates with Habermas's "religion in the public sphere,"[70] which argues that the faithful can have demands based on religion in the public sphere and that, in the final analysis, it is the legislators' epistemic task to translate these demands into a secular language and enact them accordingly.

NOTES

1. Veit Bader, "Beyond Secularisms of All Sorts," in *The Immanent Frame: Secularism, Religion and the Public Sphere*, 2011, http://blogs.ssrc.org/tif/2011/10/11 /beyond-secularisms-of-all-sorts/ (accessed Apr. 30, 2015).

2. Ahmet Kuru, "Passive and Assertive Secularism: Historical Conditions, Ideological Struggles, and State Policies toward Religion," *World Politics* 59 (2007): 571.

3. Ibid. See also Charles Taylor, "Modes of Secularism," in *Secularism and Its Critics,* edited by Rajeev Bhargava, 31–53 (Delhi: Oxford University Press, 1999).

4. Kuru, "Passive and Assertive Secularism," 582.

5. Paul Weller and Ihsan Yilmaz, *European Muslims, Civility and Public Life: Perspectives On and From the Gülen Movement* (London: Continuum, 2012), xxii.

6. Klas Grinell, "Border Thinking: Fethullah Gülen and the East-West Divide," in *Islam and Peacebuilding: Gülen Movement Initiatives,* edited by John L. Esposito and Ihsan Yilmaz, 43–62 (New York: Blue Dome Press, 2010).

7. Robert Bellah, "Civil Religion in America," *Dædalus, Journal of the American Academy of Arts and Sciences* 96, no. 1 (1967): 1–21.

8. Ihsan Yilmaz, "State, Law, Civil Society and Islam in Contemporary Turkey," *The Muslim World* 95, no. 3 (2005): 387–89.

9. Ihsan Yilmaz, "The Last of the 'LASTmen' and the New Constitution," *Today's Zaman,* Mar. 15, 2012, http://www.todayszaman.com/columnist-274316-the-last-of-the-lastmen-and-the-new-constitution.html (accessed Mar. 26, 2012).

10. Yilmaz, "State, Law, Civil Society and Islam," 404–5.

11. Ibid., 388.

12. Ibid., 389.

13. Yilmaz, "The Last of the 'LASTmen.'"

14. Ibid.

15. Danièle Hervieu-Léger, "The Case for a Sociology of 'Multiple Religious Modernities': A Different Approach to the 'Invisible Religion' of European Societies," *Social Compass* 50, no. 3 (2003): 287–95.

16. Yilmaz, "The Last of the 'LASTmen.'"

17. Nezir Akyeşilmen, "Diyanet Hutbelerinde İnsan Hakları (Human Rights in Diyanet's Sermons)," *Hülasa* 1, no. 1 (2011): 19–21.

18. Ibid., 21.

19. Ibid., 20.

20. For details, see Ihsan Yilmaz, "Beyond Post-Islamism: Transformation of Turkish Islamism Toward 'Civil Islam' and Its Potential Influence in the Muslim World," *European Journal of Economic and Political Studies* 4, no. 1 (2011): 245–80.

21. Paul Tillich, *Systematic Theology* (Chicago: University of Chicago Press, 1951), 211.

22. Fethullah Gülen, "An Interview with Fethullah Gülen," translated from Turkish by Zeki Saritoprak and Ali Ünal, *Muslim World* 97 (2005): 455.

23. I. M. Abu-Rabi', "Editor's Introduction" to Nevval Sevindi, *Contemporary Islamic Conversations: M. Fethullah Gülen on Turkey, Islam, and the West,* edited by Ibrahim M. Abu-Rabi', translated by Abdullah T. Antepli, vii–xiv (Albany: State University of New York Press, 2008), xi.

24. Ihsan Yilmaz, "*Ijtihad* and *Tajdid* by Conduct: The Gülen Movement," in *Turkish Islam and the Secular State: The Gülen Movement,* edited by M. H. Yavuz and J. L. Esposito, 208–37 (Syracuse, N.Y.: Syracuse University Press, 2003), 235.

25. John L. Esposito and Ihsan Yilmaz, "Gülen's Ideas on Freedom of Thought, Pluralism, Secularism, State, Politics, Civil Society and Democracy," in *Islam and Peacebuilding: Gülen Movement Initiatives,* edited by John L. Esposito and Ihsan Yilmaz, 3–15 (New York: Blue Dome Press, 2010), 4.

26. Graham Fuller, *The New Turkish Republic: Turkey as a Pivotal State in the Muslim World* (Washington, D.C.: United States Institute of Peace Press, 2008), 58.

27. J. D. Hendrick, "Globalization, Islamic Activism, and Passive Revolution in Turkey: The Case of Fethullah Gülen," *Journal of Power* 2, no. 3 (Dec. 2009), 343.

28. Gülen, "An Interview with Fethullah Gülen," 452.

29. Ibid., 454.

30. Ibid., 456.

31. Fethullah Gülen, *Essays, Perspectives, Opinions* (Somerset, N.J.: The Light, 2006), 14.

32. Ibid., 17.

33. Gülen, "An Interview with Fethullah Gülen," 450.

34. Ibid., 451.

35. Fuller, *The New Turkish Republic*, 59.

36. Fethullah Gülen, "A Comparative Approach to Islam and Democracy," *SAIS Review* 21, no. 2 (2001): 135.

37. Fethullah Gülen, *Advocate of Dialogue: Fethullah Gülen*, compiled by Ali Ünal and Alphonse Williams (Fairfax, Va.: The Fountain, 2000), 134.

38. Gülen, "A Comparative Approach to Islam and Democracy," 134–35.

39. Gülen, "An Interview with Fethullah Gülen," 451.

40. Ibid., 450.

41. Fethullah Gülen, *Hosgoru ve Diyalog Iklimi*, edited by Selçuk Camcı and Kudret Ünal (Izmir: Merkür Yayınları, 1998), 282, quoted in Ebru Altunoğlu, "Fethullah Gülen's Perception of State and Society," Master's thesis, Department of Political Science, Boğaziçi University, Istanbul, 1999, p. 104.

42. Altunoğlu, "Fethullah Gülen's Perception of State and Society," 104.

43. Fethullah Gülen, *Fasıldan Fasıla III* (Izmir: Nil AŞ, 1996), 133.

44. Gülen, *Advocate of Dialogue*, 147.

45. Gülen, "A Comparative Approach to Islam and Democracy," 137.

46. Ibid.

47. Gülen, *Advocate of Dialogue*, 63–64.

48. Yilmaz, "Beyond Post-Islamism," 262.

49. Gülen, "An Interview with Fethullah Gülen," 451.

50. Abu-Rabi', "Editor's Introduction," xi.

51. Alfred Stepan, "The World's Religious Systems and Democracy: Crafting the 'Twin Tolerations,'" in *Arguing Comparative Politics*, edited by Alfred Stepan, 213–53 (Oxford: Oxford University Press, 2001), 218–25.

52. Gülen, *Advocate of Dialogue*, 65.

53. Abu-Rabi', "Editor's Introduction," x.

54. Gülen, "An Interview with Fethullah Gülen," 451.

55. Mustafa Armağan and Ali Ünal, eds., *Kozadan Kelebeğe: Medya Aynasından Fethullah Gülen* (İstanbul: Gazeteciler ve Yazarlar Vakfı Yayınları, 1999), 76, quoted in Altunoğlu, "Fethullah Gülen's Perception of State and Society," 69.

56. Stepan, "The World's Religious Systems and Democracy," 213–17.

57. Armağan and Ünal, eds., *Kozadan Kelebeğe*, 108, quoted in Altunoğlu, "Fethullah Gülen's Perception of State and Society," 103.

58. Inger Repstad and Pal Furseth, *An Introduction to the Sociology of Religion* (Aldershot: Ashgate, 2006), 97.

59. Ibid.

60. José Casanova, *Public Religions in the Modern World* (Chicago: University of Chicago Press, 1994).

61. Ibid., 219.

62. Jürgen Habermas, "Religion in the Public Sphere," *European Journal of Philosophy* 14, no. 1 (2006): 1–25.

63. John Rawls, "The Idea of Public Reason Revisited," *Chicago Law Review* 64, no. 3 (1997): 777.

64. Habermas, "Religion in the Public Sphere," 7.

65. Ibid.

66. Ibid., 8.

67. Ibid., 8–9.

68. Ibid., 9.

69. Ibid., 10.

70. Habermas, "Religion in the Public Sphere."

ELEVEN

Political Implications of
the Hizmet Movement

James C. Harrington

EVEN THOUGH THE HIZMET MOVEMENT views itself as a proponent of civil society, its work certainly has political ramifications, both in Turkey where it originated and, to a lesser degree, in other areas of the world where it operates. It is a faith-based movement, although scrupulous in presenting itself as having no religious agenda at all, being strictly a humanitarian enterprise.

Religious-based movements seldom display themselves as proponents of democracy, tolerance, inclusion, and dialogue. Many religious groups historically have oppressed, even killed others in the name of their "truth." This is not to say, however, that religion is always the motivating factor in the strife and conflict perpetrated in its name. Quite often, it is a convenient tool manipulated by political and economic forces to accomplish their goals.

Hizmet is different. Associated with religious scholar Fethullah Gülen, it is a leading moderate Islamic reform movement in Turkey. It is a distinctly Western-oriented, contemporary blend of mysticism and hospitality, drawn

---

Although Fethullah Gülen concentrated on the religious and philosophical theories that have became central to the Hizmet movement, he also—by design and inevitably—was drawn into the world of practical politics. He has characteristically kept some distance from formal political parties and expressions, but his involvement in civic culture has often led him to be critical of existing political structures and those who administer them in Turkey. Similarly, he necessarily had to involve himself with attempts to bring elements in the political order into line with humane concerns. Such endeavors drew strong opposition among the political leaders who ruled Turkey—and among those who rule it today. James Harrington, former adjunct professor of Law at the University of Texas, deals in this chapter with the emerging political spheres where Gülen, as reformer, was suspect and where, as visionary, he has attracted followings that help him project a more open political scene than that favored by those in authority.

from the country's deep Sufi tradition that promotes education, science, modernization, and technology for their benefits to society.

Although business entrepreneurs, middle-class people, and students shape the Hizmet nucleus, it attracts a larger group of adherents within Turkey and has a grassroots following. Gülen promotes a cosmopolitan, multinational, and multicultural Turkish identity that appeals to his compatriots, and his non-nationalist views and steadfast stand against terrorism resonate with moderate Turks, who reject Islamic extremism.

The Hizmet movement also has attracted non-Muslim followers. There is no accurate account of how many people are active in Hizmet to some degree or other, but it clearly has considerable supporters worldwide. There is little question that Hizmet has greatly affected Turkey's politics and has helped build civil society in a country once dominated by military and autocratic regimes.

This chapter focuses on the cultural, intellectual, and institutional projects promoted through Hizmet. It also looks at the movement's part in bringing greater democracy to Turkey and its interactive role in Turkey's efforts to join the European Union. That long (and still incomplete) accession process culminated in the constitutional referendum in 2010 that overwhelmingly adopted civil liberty protections, improved the judicial system, expanded economic and social rights, and created legal accountability for previous coup d'état leaders.

This overview covers Turkey's recent history, how and why Hizmet has become a force in civil society, and Hizmet's interaction with current political realities, including how Turkey's former prime minister and current president, Recep Tayyip Erdoğan, has become a foe of civil liberties and of Hizmet.

TURKEY'S HISTORICAL CONTEXT

A quick historical synopsis of modern Turkey is critical to understanding the political and social importance of Hizmet and its projects for helping democratize that nation. Kemal Atatürk founded the Republic of Turkey in 1923 and served as president until his death in 1938. He had emerged as a brilliant Turkish military commander and nationalist rebel leader, and he led the armed struggle to liberate Turkey from the Allies' occupation after defeating the Ottoman regime in World War I.

Atatürk initiated an ambitious array of political, economic, and cultural reforms. An admirer of the Enlightenment, he sought to transform the country into a modern, democratic, and secularist nation-state. The principles of his reforms fall under the rubric of "Kemalism," the "six pillars" or "six arrows" of which are republicanism, populism, nationalism, secularism,[1] statism, and revolutionism.

Atatürk's presidency is a stunning saga of modernization, matched in few other nations. With indefatigable energy and a sometimes heavy hand, he moved the country to a new political and legal system, made both government and education secularist, gave equal rights to women, replaced Arabic with the Latin alphabet for writing the Turkish language, Westernized personal attire, and advanced the arts and sciences.

Even though Atatürk admonished the armed forces not to meddle in politics, Turkey has had the historical misfortune of a series of military coups d'état since its first democratic elections in 1950. There have been three "hard" coups (1960, 1971, and 1980), in which the military seized direct control of the government, and a "soft" or "post-modern" coup in 1997. These coups severely thwarted the country's path toward democracy and weakened the institutions of government and civil society.

The 1960 overthrow was ruthless and bloody. The junta executed the country's first democratically elected prime minister, Adnan Menderes, two of his ministers, and thousands of others—and prominently published a photograph of Menderes on the gallows. Many more victims suffered torture and imprisonment. Menderes was very popular and had served two terms in office, but the strongly secularist military fretted over his populism. Even though he was apparently a nonobservant Muslim, the military painted him as attempting to transform the country into a theocratic regime.

The 1971 overthrow, known as the "coup by memorandum," which the armed forces delivered in lieu of sending out tanks, came amid worsening domestic strife and violence. The military forced the government to resign, and it installed its own prime minister to form a new administration. Many people, especially intellectuals across the political spectrum, underwent investigation, prosecution in special martial law courts, torture, and imprisonment for their political views. Many others perished or languished in jail.

The 1980 military regime came during a period of intense conflict among student groups that fought each other for political reasons. Thousands of youth died. The armed services stabilized the situation and assumed political power, but they never explained why they had to take over the government rather than simply quell the violence. The coup was brutal, bloody, and broad. Thousands were put to death or tortured. A constituent assembly drafted a new constitution, which voters approved in November 1982 as the only way to move again toward democracy, however slowly. Martial law gradually lifted, but effective military oversight continued.

The 1997 unarmed coup overthrew a coalition government headed by the Islamist-leaning Welfare Party. It received the "post-modern coup" moniker because, different from earlier coups, the military merely flexed its muscle and directed the outcome. The military attempted to eliminate all religiously motivated movements deemed a threat to the secularist regime. It was a sophisticated, bloodless, and effective operation.

Apart from meddling in politics, the armed forces over time developed their own economic prowess, evolving into a "mercantile military," a military/industrial complex showcase. In particular, the Turkish Armed Forces Foundation became emblematic, receiving subsidies and tax exemptions from the government and increasing its economic strength.

Two contemporary, protracted, and complex trials, "Ergenekon" and "Sledgehammer (Balyoz)," have been ongoing in Turkey, dealing with interactive corruption among the military, banks, and corporate enterprises (including some media outlets), allied as the "Deep State." The cases, which began in 2008 and 2010, respectively, have revealed continuing scenarios of wide-ranging political machinations and even a prospective coup. Some of the extensive allegations involve conspiracy activity against Gülen and Hizmet.

Despite the interruption of the 1997 post-modern coup, Turkey had begun its transition from an authoritarian regime toward liberal democratization under Turgut Özal, who served as prime minister of Turkey and then as president until he died under suspicious circumstances in 1993. Özal transformed Turkey's moribund economy into a powerhouse by beginning privatization of many state enterprises and moving the country to an export-led drive toward free enterprise.

THE HIZMET MOVEMENT AND GÜLEN

Other chapters in the present volume have detailed many aspects of the career of Gülen and of the Hizmet movement, but I believe it will be helpful in this political context briefly to consider salient aspects of the movement insofar as they bear on its underlying philosophy and impact on politics and civil society, both in Turkey and in the larger global community. They also help explain why Hizmet has gained political traction in Turkey.

Gülen is the movement's spiritual "soul." He is a prolific writer, widely read, self-educated, and respected as an intellectual. He has lived in the United States since March 1999, when he came seeking medical attention and eventually took up residence in a secluded rural retreat in Pennsylvania. However, his relocation has not diminished his influence.

As we have seen in other chapters, the thought of Kurdish scholar Said Nursi (1877–1960) on accommodating Islam to modern life and harmonizing science and religion greatly influenced Gülen, although he rejected Nursi's intense nationalism. Nursi's understanding of Islam, upon which Gülen built, combined Islamic values with advocacy of human rights, democracy, the rule of law, secularism with respect for religious rights for all, regard for cultural diversity, science, and ecumenical dialogue. Nursi himself suffered decades of arrest and imprisonment and harassment for his modern views.

Sufi ideas also course through Gülen's thinking. One belief—that God, humanity, and the natural world are all linked—has practical consequences, such as its stress on loving and respecting humanity and the natural world as one would God, regardless of people's faith or lack thereof.

Gülen has attempted to present a moderate Islam to Jews and Christians and, in turn, to present those other religions to Muslims. He was the first Islamic leader to have formal discussions with the Alevis, Christians, and Jews in Turkey, and he weathered fierce criticism from hard-line co-religionists for meeting with those outside their Islamic tradition.

Science and technology are important to Gülen, and he views the underdeveloped condition of many Islamic countries to be a result of their neglecting contemporary scientific knowledge. He sees no conflict between reason and revelation. For him, the Qur'an does not contain all that is necessary for scientific understanding, but each informs the other.

Gülen's personal charisma goes hand-in-hand with good organization by his followers and an appealing message that one can be at home in the modern world and still embrace traditional values like faith in God and community responsibility. He often notes that 95 percent of religion is about one's personal life and that community advancement comes through progress in one's spiritual life. Social leadership—that is, civil society—is more important than political leadership.

Gülen is credited with more than seventy books, along with tapes and videos of an estimated 4,000 talks and sermons (most privately recorded), and a science and spirituality magazine translated into various languages.[2]

For others, not surprisingly, Gülen is a controversial figure. For radical Islamists, he is too "soft" on Christians and Jews and not Muslim enough because he prizes a person's moral life more highly than ritualistic prayer or fundamentalist constructs. For neo-nationalists, he is a threat to the republic's secularist nature, although Gülen insists there is no turning away from democracy in Turkey.

Gülen's social thinking supports democratization, civil liberty, and separation between secular and religious spheres. His social justice values, however, do not play well with those in the deep-rooted, pro-authoritarian establishment who resist the country's expanding pluralism, encroachment on their brand of secularism, and mobilization of the middle class.

As might be expected, Gülen had to undergo political prosecution, and he has experienced it twice. The second and most significant trial, in absentia, lasted from 2000 to 2008 amid a blistering media campaign against him. He was acquitted, and won on appeal, thanks in part to changes in Turkey's legal system, which the European Union helped bring about, as will be discussed below. The trial and appellate judges summarily rejected the myriad charges that had alleged he was undermining the republic.[3]

An advocate of nonviolence, Gülen was the first Islamic leader to publicly condemn the September 11, 2001, terrorist attacks in the United States. He took out advertisements in the *New York Times* and *Washington Post* immediately after the event and gave interviews to major newspapers.

Those who consider themselves inspired by Gülen refer to themselves as part of Hizmet, a volunteer civil society service movement. They believe in educating youth, fostering interfaith and intercultural dialogue, earning money to assist the less well-off in society, contributing to global peace, and promoting humanitarian projects. The movement draws support from all walks of life: intellectuals, political leaders and government officials from every shade of the political spectrum, academicians, working people, business entrepreneurs, writers, professionals, and even members of the military.

Hizmet followers tend to be from Turkey's aspiring middle class in the Anatolia region. Gülen reassures his compatriots that they can merge the goals of Atatürk's republic with traditional but flexible Islamic faith. Financial success is a worthy endeavor, in his view, since it allows individuals to support good causes. Gülen appeals to well-off people to assist the poor, for the benefit of all. Society, he argues, improves as people lead good lives and help others rather than just themselves. The movement springs from, and helps expand, the rising middle class, which has led to democratization and economic opportunity.

For all their emphasis on individual integrity, Hizmet participants are taught and expected to be forbearing of others and nonjudgmental. Although personally religious, they see themselves not as making up a formal religious community but rather as firm subscribers to a democratic secular society that promotes traditional civil liberties, including freedom of religion. Gülen himself famously commented that society needs more schools, not more mosques.

Hizmet followers are not revolutionaries. Rather, they put energy into seeking greater equity in society. Education is one of their main tools, and they are at home with technology, markets, multinational business, and modern communication, which they adeptly use to "spread the word."

People in Hizmet, as indicated in Tom Gage's chapter on education in this volume, have established numerous educational institutions, such as elementary and secondary schools and universities around the world, though many are in Turkey. For them, education and literacy are "levelers" in society, forming a way to bridge the rich/poor gap. These endeavors, under way since the 1960s, hold themselves out as alternatives to the more dogmatic, sometimes radical, and educationally limited madrasah schools.

Hizmet schools have been important in southern Turkey and the Kurdish region because of the shortage of educational facilities there, and they provide opportunity for less fortunate youth. Many schools have dormitories for poorer students from outlying areas. In southeast Turkey, the schools offered an alternative to the Kurdistan Workers' Party (PKK) and its violent activities. They provide an opportunity for young women where traditional culture reinforces early marriage and child-bearing duties.

These schools are nonreligious and sponsored by entrepreneurs in Turkey and the Turkish diaspora in other countries. They are expected eventually to become self-sufficient and to be supported by those whom they educate as they themselves graduate and enter business. The schools contribute to the movement's credibility and popularity.

The Hizmet aid organization *Kimse Yok Mu* ("Is Anyone There?"),[4] established with Gülen's encouragement, has helped victims of natural calamities around the world. Hospitals set up by Hizmet doctors and business people bring medical services to underserved countries.

Gülen-inspired media institutions, such as the top-selling newspaper in Turkey (*Zaman*), one of the most watched television channels (STV), and weekly magazines, try to set the example of being family-friendly and free of excessive violence, depictions of drug use, and obscenity. *Zaman* is widely respected for its breadth of coverage and promotion of civil society and democracy,[5] and it is a major player in Hizmet.

The self-supporting movement relies on volunteers, charitable donations, and financial underwriting. It is a characteristic Islamic practice to tithe, based on income, to charitable organizations. Individuals in Hizmet tend to give from 7 to 15 percent or more, depending on ability, to Hizmet charities and projects.

Because of the movement's loose-knit "nonstructure," precise statistics of its work and its financial outlay do not exist, but estimates are consistently substantial. A comprehensive study by University of Houston sociologist Helen Rose Ebaugh indicates that 20,000 Gülen-supporting businesses and other endeavors may yield as much as $1 billion annually, with some individuals contributing millions of dollars each.[6]

Gülen supporters organize around the view that humans have the potential to do better than reflected by the current state of world affairs. In sync with Sufi thought, Gülen posits greed, whether individual or collective, as the real foe of peace and harmony, not the differences in religion, ethnicity, or ideology. Greedy individuals and groups achieve their objectives by manipulating people's fear, individually and socially. Ignorance and misinformation fuel paranoia and personal and collective acts of aggression.

Thus, for Hizmet, person-to-person communication is key to social tolerance. Dialogue is not compromise, conversion, or integration. Rather, it is the coming together of people who are committed to their respective religious paths (or who have no faith but are living a good life) to better know and communicate with one another and, in due course, work together. This dynamic helps strip away false prejudices, dissipates fear and antagonism, and lays a foundation for trust, peaceful coexistence, and cooperative undertakings.

To advance these goals, Hizmet people promote conferences, symposia, seminars, luncheons and dinners, and grassroots activities. Besides dialogue for dialogue's sake, these meetings can help shape policy and civil society. They also organize and help underwrite hundreds of intercultural dialogue trips to Turkey for community leaders, political officials, and religious people around the world.

The most prominent dialogue effort inside Turkey is the Abant Platform, founded in 1994 and coordinated by the Journalists and Writers Foundation, which Gülen helped organize. The platform is a major discussion forum for scholars, writers, and leaders of all backgrounds who focus on recurring issues in Turkey, such as religion, government, ethnicity, Islam, secularism, democracy, and their interrelationship. The first Abant Platform convocation, in 1998, helped propel Gülen's political trial.

A movement with ambitions and practices like those of Hizmet, which would consider the review in this chapter to be idealistic, naturally attracts opponents. They tend to articulate four general themes, with varying degrees of logical coherence and grounding in facts. First, Hizmet seeks to take over Turkey through its economic prowess and by infiltrating the military and government and converting the country into a religious regime. Second, because the movement is atypical in not having formal organizational structures, it lacks transparency and is therefore suspect. Third, Hizmet is cult-like and "brainwashes" people. And fourth, Gülen really represents some other, disguised, power. This last point shifts, according to the audience. Sometimes he is accused of being a CIA operative, a subversive of some foreign county (usually Iran, China, or Saudi Arabia), or even a "secret cardinal" under the pope.[7]

The lack of transparency theme garners most traction. Given that Turkish prosecutors have twice made attempts to shut down all Gülen-related entities and seize their assets, as part of the political trials mentioned earlier, the wisest self-defense has seemed to be not to formalize an organizational structure. This kind of prosecution in Turkey has happened historically to organizations disfavored by the government in power. The lack of typical hierarchical organization is also a Sufi characteristic. The movement seems increasingly sensitive to the criticism and has begun to open its doors a bit, albeit slowly. Of course, there is more transparency in countries with disclosural regulations, like the United States.

As to the "infiltration" fear, what actually may be occurring sociologically is that economic and social integration is increasing and that growing numbers of people, as they become educated, seek secure and better-paying employment in the police, military, and government.

Given all that Gülen has spoken and written over many years promoting democracy and civil society, his foes have found little on which to rely when they make their accusations. Many of the charges expressed by his opponents were systematically dismantled in the 2000–2008 trial.

THE EXPANSION OF DEMOCRACY AND CIVIL
SOCIETY IN TURKEY AND HIZMET

To be sure, there are substantial problematic areas with which Turkey is wrestling, such as respecting the rights and self-identity of the Kurdish population, decentralizing state administration, strengthening local government, and depoliticizing the judicial system. There are other crucial issues, too, which are summarized below.

Hizmet's Relationship to the Government

Gülen does not involve himself directly in partisan Turkish politics, although he does interject his message on different issues in the name of civil society, which, of course, has political ramifications. He promotes addressing issues through the democratic system but not aligning with a specific parliamentary party.

Gülen has opposed political Islam, helping halt its rise in Turkey, arguing that religion is about private piety, not political ideology. He was a vocal critic of the Islamist Welfare Party, which, in the late 1990s, briefly led a coalition government with the conservative True Path Party, until the "soft coup." Even though Gülen has always supported the established order and the organs of state, many secularists do not trust him, and they see his frequent evidences of support for projects of the governing Justice and Development Party (AKP) as proof that he is a Trojan horse for political Islam.

After an initial period of tension, Gülen and the AKP leaders, who took power in 2002, came closer in their approach to common issues, although they have different social bases: AKP's is the urban poor, Gülen's the provincial middle class. Encouraged by Gülen, the AKP, with its conservative cultural background, had softened a tendency toward Qur'anic literalism and embraced the need for expanding human rights.

The movement generally supported earlier AKP reforms, though not uncritically, and sometimes spearheaded reforms that the AKP adopted under Prime Minister Erdoğan. In recent years, however, as Erdoğan has begun to show a more marked authoritarian streak, the Hizmet movement has become more critical, particularly through its newspaper, *Zaman*. Erdoğan has begun a very verbal war on Hizmet, accusing it of being a tool of the United States, manipulated by the CIA, and seeking to overthrow the government—all the usual canards used by Turkish government leaders of the past against agents of change.

Joining the European Union

Hizmet has always strongly supported Turkey's efforts to join the European Union, which had been in progress, with varying degrees of intensity, since the mid-1980s.

Although the principal motivation originally was economic, accession efforts provided a fortuitous opportunity for political and constitutional reform because the EU insisted on a series of changes that dramatically affected Turkish politics, including: abolishing state security courts (which had taken the place of military courts) that exercised jurisdiction over political dissidents; ending capital punishment; establishing civilian control over the military; enacting some standard civil liberty protections for the press, religious freedom, due process, and political speech; and halting political prosecutions (such as had happened to Gülen).[8] This brought about an astonishing democratization impetus in Turkey.

The accession process has since come to a crawl, and the AKP's interest in making changes necessary to join the EU have cooled, partly because of Erdoğan himself and partly because Turkey sees little economic gain and fears having to help financially to shore up faltering EU states, particularly its historical foe, Greece. Nor is Turkey happy with the EU's insistence on adjusting its occupation of northern Cyprus. To be sure, ample blame lies with Germany and France and the historical Islamophobia of many inside their countries.

Even though the EU's "soft power" over Turkey has dissipated, the electorate, on September 12, 2010, thirty years to the date of the 1980 bloody coup, by a 58 percent to 42 percent margin (with 74 percent of eligible voters casting ballots), adopted a series of constitutional amendments that expanded people's economic and social rights, guaranteed union collective bargaining, enhanced civil liberty and individual freedoms (such as privacy, due process, equality and affirmative action, and religious freedom), adopted judicial reforms, and opened the door to prosecuting former coup leaders. Civil society and Hizmet strongly supported this referendum.

Ultimately, a core problem is that pluralist democracy has yet to develop fully in Turkey. Although there is majority rule, there are no strong opposition parties, generally because of their own ineptness and ties to the old establishment. Turkey, though a democracy, is essentially, at this point, a one-party state. This lack of pluralism deeply troubles the EU and is cited as a major reason for the slowdown in Turkey's accession process in recent years, although, as noted, less noble reasons are also at play. Pluralism is a legitimate concern, nevertheless.

The movement and the AKP differ substantially—and are at odds—on how vigorously to push for accession. Hizmet's concern is that the further Turkey drifts from Europe, the further it will stray from democracy.

Accession talks started up again in 2013, after a three-year hiatus, having been postponed earlier because of the Gezi Park crackdown of dissenters by the military, although Erdoğan's follow-up caustic remarks are hardly helpful. They are now further imperiled by Erdoğan's crackdown on civil liberties, discussed further below.

Freedoms of Speech, Protest, and Assembly

How the government handled the 2013 Gezi Park demonstrations raised grave questions about its respect for civil liberty. The protests initially contested an urban development plan for the Istanbul Taksim park and quickly intensified over outrage at the brutal eviction of protesters doing a sit-in at the park. Subsequent solidarity protests and strikes took place across the country, protesting a wide range of concerns, such as freedoms of the press, expression, and assembly and the AKP's encroachment on Turkey's secularism.

As demonstrations spread, excessive police use of tear gas and water cannons caused thousands of injuries, some critical (like loss of sight), and some deaths. There were more than three thousand arrests.

Prime Minister Erdoğan again showed his irascible, authoritarian side in justifying the brutal crackdown, despite more conciliatory efforts by President Abdullah Gül. Erdoğan drew strong international censure for the extreme force and absence of dialogue during the protests, which he summarily and brusquely rejected. And he drew criticism from Hizmet.

A New Constitution

Turkey had been in the process of drafting a new constitution, which Hizmet strongly backed, to address many of the issues raised in this chapter and incorporate the changes the country has already adopted. However, Erdoğan and the AKP essentially stymied the endeavor, particularly over Erdoğan's unsuccessful attempt to create a strong presidency, which he intends to seek again after the June 2015 parliamentary elections, if the AKP's electoral margin is large enough.

Freedom of the Press

Turkey is also struggling with freedom of the press, especially given the media's past complicity with the military/industrial complex, as coming to light in the Ergenekon and Sledgehammer conspiracy trials. Both of these trials involved conspiracy efforts by various "Deep State" actors to derail progress toward liberal democracy. Scores of Turkish journalists are in jail; hundreds more are under prosecution or investigation; and some media outlets are claiming AKP retaliation.

It is not unlikely that some media people were actually complicit in the conspiracy activities. But Erdoğan's bombastic reactions to criticism, particularly from Europe, help cement his critics' views about a press crackdown and intimidation. These reactions have attracted extensive international criticism and contributed to Turkey's ranking as a "partly free" country in the 2012 report of the Washington-based Freedom House. This pro-democracy watchdog group evaluates countries according to the 1948 Universal Declaration on Human Rights (generally, free elections, multiparty democracy, rule of law, and equality of opportunity). Turkey has been stuck at "partly free" on the scale since 2005.

Similarly, in 2011, for the third consecutive year, the European Court of Human Rights (ECtHR) found that Turkey had the highest number of violations of the European Convention on Human Rights.[9] Turkey consistently ranks low out of 179 countries in terms of press freedom.

On a different press issue, there is considerable legitimate concern about the government's use of political power and economic leverage to structure a more compliant and less critical media. The government likewise is embroiled in Internet freedom issues and has drawn broad criticism for filtering political opposition sites and blocking those contrary to "Turkish values" (and, for a while, blocking Darwinian evolution sites). Internet freedom and civil society groups are contesting the censorship regimen in the Council of State, Turkey's highest administrative court, and also challenging a plan to require Internet users to choose one of the government's four content-filtering packages as unconstitutional and violating the right of free expression.

Civil society representatives recognize that the high profile cases under way, namely those dealing with Ergenekon, Sledgehammer, and the Internet, are of great consequence to the future of Turkey's democracy; it is thus critical that they be handled in accord with universal legal rules and human rights norms. Otherwise, the outcome will be counterproductive and lack integrity. *Zaman* has been highly outspoken on this position.

Other Issues Relating to Civil Liberty and Democracy

Erdoğan has lit other fires, as well. Right after the Gezi Park protests, he told women to have three children because "birth-control mechanisms for years . . . nearly castrated our citizens. . . . Their objective was to reduce the population of this nation and for this nation to lag behind in the competition of nations. We are disrupting this game. We have to."[10] This nationalist paternalism ignited intense disparagement about meddling in citizen's private lives.

Undeterred, Erdoğan has since moved to end mixed-gender college student houses, saying such was the duty of his "conservative" government. And, in what has set off Hizmet's alarm bells and drawn direct criticism from Gülen, the government has passed legislation that would close all privately funded preparatory schools in 2015,[11] many of which are Hizmet-operated. Educational institutions, unions, parent/teacher associations, trade advocacy groups, and opposition parties are against the plan, saying that shutting the schools would be a blow to free enterprise and the right to an education. The law also prohibits study centers that assist students prepare for high school and university examinations, another extensive Hizmet operation, which runs about 1,000 of the 4,000 such schools.[12]

Then, on December 17, 2013, a major corruption scandal broke, implicating nearly fifty people, including members of the AKP administration and, later in the month, Erdoğan's son. After that, Erdoğan began a full-scale attack on Hizmet specifically and on civil liberties generally, a scenario still playing out. For example, he has moved further to censor the Internet, punish nonconformist journalists, pack the judiciary, transfer thousands of police and officials to undercut the corruption investigations (and even charge some of them in criminal courts with very public arrests), terminate suspected Hizmet civil servants, and ally himself with the military. Despite the fact that his party won the spring 2014 local elections, chiefly because there was no credible opposition, Erdoğan, rather than seek reconciliation, promised a vendetta against his foes, even seeking to extradite Gülen from the United States.

Whether this is an effort by the AKP to diminish Hizmet's political influence and curtail its increased criticism of Erdoğan—and whether Hizmet can successfully resist this effort in a one-party democracy—will be a test well worth watching for its outcome. Will Hizmet be able to make the AKP back off, despite's Erdoğan's apparent intransigence on the matter? Will it end up in a de facto position of seeking an alliance with other political parties and thus perhaps strengthening pluralism? It is a conundrum that Hizmet surely never expected, or wanted.

CONCLUSION

Turkey's road toward full democracy has had a long and painful history, and Hizmet has been a major journey-partner in that struggle. However, there are still many, many miles to go. As Noam Chomsky noted,

> I know of no other country where leading writers, artists, journalists, academics and other intellectuals have compiled such an impressive record of bravery and integrity in condemning crimes of state, and going beyond to engage in civil disobedience to try to bring oppression and violence to an end, facing and sometimes enduring severe repression, and then returning to the task. It is an honorable record, unique to my knowledge, a record of which the country should be proud. And one that should be a model for others.[13]

The question on the table is the extent to which Hizmet and other civil society advocates can keep the government on track to honor and fulfill the dreams of those who have sacrificed to bring Turkey to where it is now, and to move forward and not change course. How much further democracy can extend in Turkey is now a very real challenge.

NOTES

1. "Secular," in the Turkish context, is different from the traditional American view of "separation of church and state," which accepts religious freedom. In Turkey, "secularism" expresses a model of the state opposing various forms of religious expression, most notably in public employment and education. The controversial head-scarf ban, which was relaxed in late 2013, is an example of this.

2. See the Fethullah Gülen website, http://fgulen.com/en/fethullah-gulens-works (English version; also available in thirty-one other languages).

3. James C. Harrington, *Wrestling with Free Speech, Religious Freedom, and Democracy in Turkey: The Political Trials and Times of Fethullah Gülen* (Lanham, Md.: University Press of America, 2011).

4. The English version of its website is http://global.kimseyokmu.org.tr /?lang = en.

5. The English version of its website, *Today's Zaman*, is http://www.todayszaman .com/home.

6. These figures are based on comments made at an April 23, 2010, discussion of her book at the University of Texas, Austin; see Helen R. Ebaugh, *The Gülen Movement: A Sociological Analysis of a Civil Movement Rooted in Moderate Islam* (New York: Springer, 2010), especially 52–59. Ebaugh's book and that of Muhammed Çetin, *The Gülen Movement: Civic Service without Borders* (New York: Blue Dome Press, 2009), are the two most comprehensive analyses of Hizmet. See also Joshua D. Hendrick, *Gülen: The Ambiguous Politics of Market Islam in Turkey and the World* (New York: NYU Press, 2013).

7. Dogan Koç, *Strategic Defamation of Fethullah Gülen: English vs. Turkish* (Lanham, Md.: University Press of America, 2012).

8. Turkey had also subscribed to the 1950 European Convention on Human Rights and subjected itself to the jurisdiction of the European Court of Human Rights, which likewise had a gradual, liberalizing effect on the country.

9. In May 2013, ECtHR made yet another finding of Turkey's being by far the worst human rights violator among the forty-seven signatory states to the European Convention on Human Rights. See "Human Rights Violations in Turkey," http:// ecohr.blogspot.com/2013/05/human-rights-violations-in-turkey.html. These numbers may decrease in the future by virtue of the 2010 constitutional amendment that gave Turkey's Constitutional Court power to adjudicate citizens' human rights complaints. Prior to the amendment, which became operative in late 2012, the only mechanism was direct appeal to ECtHR.

10. Kadri Gursel, "Turkey Pulse," *Al Monitor: The Pulse of the Middle East*, http:// www.al-monitor.com/pulse/originals/2013/06/erdogan-three-children-campaign- women.html (accessed Apr. 27, 2015).

11. See, e.g., Seda Sezer, "Feud between Turkey's Erdogan and Influential Cleric Goes Public," *Reuters*, Nov. 21, 2013.

12. Sahin Alpay, "Erdoğan Has to Respect Civil Society," *Today's Zaman*, Nov. 25, 2013.

13. Noam Chomsky, "Remembering Howard Zinn," *Resist Newsletter* (Mar./ Apr. 2010).

SUGGESTIONS FOR FURTHER READING

Arat, Zehra F. Kabasakal, ed. *Human Rights in Turkey*. Philadelphia: University of Pennsylvania Press, 2007.

Baran, Zeyno. "Turkey Divided." *Journal of Democracy* 19 (2008): 55–69.

Benhabib, Seyla. "Turkey's Constitutional Zigzags." *Dissent* 56 (2009): 25–28.

Fuller, Graham E. *The Future of Political Islam.* New York: Palgrave Macmillan, 2003.

———. *The New Turkish Republic.* Washington, D.C.: United States Institute of Peace Press, 2008.

Jenkins, Gareth H. *Political Islam in Turkey: Running West, Heading East?* New York: Palgrave Macmillan, 2008.

Kinzer, Stephen. *Crescent and Star: Turkey Between Two Worlds.* Rev. ed. New York: Farrar, Straus and Giroux, 2008.

Rabasa, Angel, and Stephen F. Larrabee. *The Rise of Political Islam in Turkey.* Santa Monica, Calif.: RAND Corporation, 2008.

Türkmen, Füsun. "The European Union and Democratization in Turkey: The Role of the Elites." *Human Rights Quarterly* 30 (2008): 146–63.

Zürcher, Erik J. *Turkey: A Modern History.* New York: I. B. Tauris, 2004).

TWELVE

Dueling Narratives

THE GÜLENISTS OF THE HIZMET MOVEMENT

R. Scott Appleby

LET US CONSIDER THE CONTESTED narratives competing to define the subject of our inquiry.

The first is sinister. Headquartered in Turkey but worldwide in reach and gaining in influence daily, the Gülen movement hides its true intentions with a decentralized, diffuse organizational structure that defies tracking, so loose are the affiliations between its media outlets, educational institutions, and (multi-million dollar) business enterprises. "Lack of transparency" is an accusation heard often from its critics. Yet the movement is also a public relations juggernaut, driven by relentless efforts on the part of local representatives and foundations to court politicians, professors, and corporate leaders, and to project itself as a modern, Western, democracy-promoting bridge between enlightened Islam and secular science. "Tolerance" is the mantra of the Gülenists, invoked with a regularity that seems rehearsed.

In truth, however, the Gülen movement wears tolerance as a mask concealing its will to power—the power to roll back hard-won Turkish

---

Every author in this volume is aware of the delicate course taken by the leaders of the Hizmet movement. We asked the authors to explain and even critique many of the movement's features, because we wanted readers to be aware of both the criticisms such movements evoke, as Hizmet certainly does, and what we might call advertisements for Gülen and ventures associated with him. R. Scott Appleby, dean of the Donald R. Keough School of Global Affairs at the University of Notre Dame, has chosen to deal with the movement through the device of listening to and portraying "dueling narratives" in a masterful and succinct work of synthesis. Appleby and I (M.E.M.) have been associates for decades, having edited a number of volumes in *The Fundamentalism Project* (University of Chicago Press), where we employed "the hermenutics of suspicion" in respect to all the authors in those books. Yet we were always eager first to let them have their own uninterrupted say, and to learn from them. So it is also in this volume, now reported on and appraised by Appleby.

secularism and to replace it with a form of Islamism more comprehensive and sustainable than less sophisticated jihadists could ever dream of achieving. Led by Fethullah Gülen, a reclusive, charismatic "mystery man" whose one mistake was allowing himself to be caught on tape urging his disciples to insinuate themselves gradually into the corridors of power without being detected, the Gülenists have succeeded in infiltrating Turkey's police force, in co-opting segments of the ruling Justice and Development Party (AKP), and in using their influence to spy on and bully their political opponents, many of whom have been arrested on flimsy charges. Indeed, Gülen shares with Recep Tayyip Erdoğan, Turkey's former prime minister, head of the AKP, and current president, a direct connection to the wave of renewal movements that shaped modern Islam in post-Ottoman Turkey. (Erdoğan's Naqshbandi background parallels Gülen's participation in Said Nursi's Nur movement.)

In 2013, Gülen and Erdoğan underwent a very public "ugly divorce," as one Turkish pundit described their falling out over the prime minister's increasingly authoritarian policies. Erdoğan rankled Gülen for, among other punitive moves, weeding out thousands of Gülenists embedded in the security services, government ministries, and judiciary of Turkey, officials who constituted, in Erdoğan's words, "a parallel state." This episode altered but did not fundamentally change the anti-Hizmet narrative; indeed, in the eyes of some Gülen detractors, it only confirmed their depiction of the movement as having been unduly and secretly influential in the affairs of state.

Further proof that the modern sheen of the movement is no more than artifice can be found in the gender segregation practiced by the Gülenists, who exclude women from the select circle of affiliates admitted for advanced study with the founder.

Hoping to spread their version of political Islam far beyond the borders of Turkey, the Gülenists have established schools across Asia, Europe, and the Americas, with a growing presence in Africa. That these schools are intended as the spearhead of a transnational cultural empire with political clout is evident in their staffing, funding, and business practices, all of which bear the distinct marks of the Turkish operation. In the United States, their charter schools and Turk-dominated faculty have come under scrutiny. In June 2012, for example, an audit of three publicly financed Gülenist schools in default in Georgia found that they had improperly granted hundreds of thousands of dollars in contracts to businesses and groups, many of them with ties to the movement.

In short, it is no wonder that one expert on the Gülen movement compares it to Opus Dei, the secretive Catholic fundamentalist-like organization that seeks worldwide political influence in order to advance its religious objectives.[1]

The second narrative tells a very different story, one that inspires hope, even excitement, in the hearts and minds of observers who are pulling for Islam to demonstrate unequivocally its capacity to generate thoroughly modern, deeply religious, and profoundly humane configurations of belief, service, and compassion. In this telling, it is inappropriate to call the movement "Gülenist," because Gülen, by his own admission and the testimony of his colleagues, is neither a cult leader nor a chief executive in charge of even one of the institutions regularly associated with his name. Rather, those millions of men and women inspired by the preacher's voluminous writings and video lectures are devoted, ultimately, not to him but to his ideas— including the idea that ideas are useless abstractions if not given life in practical, effective action. Thus, they are best described as members of the "service in action" or Hizmet movement. Some are uneasy even with the term "movement," to the extent that it connotes an explicit socio-political agenda.

In the eyes of Hizmet members and admirers, the movement is the polar opposite of an Al Qaeda–style jihadist group, and Gülen bears comparison not to Osama Bin Laden but to the Dalai Lama, the global icon of peace and tolerance. Far from targeting "the other" for annihilation, the Gülenists actively reach out to other Muslims and to other religious and secular groups, practicing dialogue as a journey of mutual discernment and self-correction designed to identify common ground and make polemics a thing of the past. Emphasizing his love of learning and deep desire for dialogue, Gülen himself has met frequently with spiritual leaders, from the pope to the Sephardic chief rabbi of Israel. He has condemned terrorism at every opportunity, proclaimed repeatedly that no true Muslim can be a terrorist, and emphasized the centrality of love, nonviolence, and unconditional compassion in the Sufi tradition that informs his practice of Islam and finds counterparts in Jewish and Christian mysticisms.

Countering the accusations of secrecy and cult-like devotion to the preacher in exile, the Gülenists point to their lack of a centralized command and coordinated organizational structure as evidence of the voluntary and independent nature of the various initiatives in education, business, and media. Hizmet people make their own decisions rather than take orders from a guru; Gülen himself, aging and beset by diabetes and heart problems, shrugs off concerns about how the movement will survive his death. And, while acknowledging the Gülenists' growing prominence in Turkey's prestigious Police Academy and their influence in the ruling AKP, supporters point to the excellent preparation for professional life provided by the Gülen schools: Hizmet members *earn* their way into the upper echelons of society, where they are not afraid to voice their own ideas and opinions, even when these offend government officials. Rumors of a rift between the AKP leadership and the Gülenists reinforce this declaration of Hizmet independence. Such rumors were substantiated in 2013, when a decisive break apparently occurred between Prime Minster Erdoğan and the Gülen movement, after Gülen himself publicly criticized Erdoğan's increasingly authoritative rule.[2]

In Turkey (this narrative of benevolence continues), Hizmet represents a much-needed middle way between the extremes of Kemalist secularism, with its hostility to Islam (or any religion) having a voice in the public sphere, and religious extremism, with its betrayal of the inner, defining core of Islam, which Gülen portrays as eternal love. Indeed, Islam, properly understood, reveals and celebrates God's purpose, which is to bring full realization of the wonders of creation through human agency. First and foremost, Hizmet serves the nation by helping Turkey to end its internal polarization between these extremes, to secularize fundamental religious questions, and to open the country to the larger world.

For those believers inspired by Gülen's preaching and lectures, secularization is the glorious end of religion, in that it extends the fundamental religious insight and commitment to all of society. This does not lead to uniformity but to plurality, anchored in God's ongoing creative purpose. Secularism in this mode is not a threat but an opportunity, an invitation to genuine unity, achieved through service. Accordingly, the emphasis falls not on religious content per se but on the scientific study of God's creation, on schools rather than mosques, and on education rather than indoctrination. "Science" (knowledge) and "Commerce" (constructive interaction) reflect the very nature of the divine presence; Hizmet members are therefore enjoined to advance these frontiers, to plunge into the divine whirlwind, in order to elicit what is best and most promising in the modern world.

Perhaps most thrilling to Hizmet members and admirers is the claim that this divinely ordained evolution of human agency and society toward greater realization of freedom and compassion is being anticipated and led by Muslims. Science, business, communication, democracy, promotion of pluralism, dialogue among peoples: *these* actions constitute Islam, and the Hizmet movement is the vanguard of the reform.[3]

THE BENEFIT OF THE DOUBT

The authors of this volume straddle these competing narratives but lean in the direction of the latter. "Something remarkable is going on in Turkey," James C. Harrington observes, in a chapter that amounts to an encomium for the "moderate Islamic reform movement" that is promoting pluralism, a softer form of secularism, and the mobilization of the middle class. The political prosecution of Gülen was to be expected, Harrington argues, given the threat that the popular preacher posed to the military's grip on state power. And he (Harrington) praises the movement's participants as forbearing of others, nonjudgmental, and steadfastly nonviolent. Notwithstanding considerable evidence to the contrary, the author concludes that the members of Hizmet "do not see themselves as making up a formal religious community, but rather as firm subscribers to a democratic secular society that promotes traditional civil liberties, including freedom of religion." Harrington notes, and rejects, the criticisms of the opposition; for example, the charge of "infiltration" is better understood, he claims, as indicative of the social and economic integration of large numbers of previously marginalized citizens, now empowered by their affiliation with the Gülenists. And, far from leveraging their influence with the AKP to punish their enemies, Gülen supporters in government civil service have themselves suffered employment discrimination. Recently, the Hizmet movement has become more critical of Erdoğan and the AKP, resulting in verbal attacks on the movement and other forms of state-sponsored discrimination.

Harrington's analysis draws on and mirrors that of the sociologist Helen Rose Ebaugh, whose 2010 study of the Gülenists is subtitled "A Sociological Analysis of a Civic Movement Rooted in Moderate Islam." Like many other U.S. academics, the present author included, Ebaugh encountered the movement as its guest on a tour of western Turkey, where she "came to admire the many service projects sponsored by the movement, including the quality schools, top-notch hospitals, a thriving relief agency and the numerous interfaith events that were a hallmark of the movement."[4]

Ebaugh devotes only a few pages of her monograph to an issue many Americans would likely not "come to admire" readily, namely, the role of women in the Gülen movement. But she reports, from her interviews, patterns of gender interaction and a diversity of perceptions and evaluations about them that are familiar to scholars such as Lynne Davidman and Shahla Haeri,[5] who have studied gender relations among other traditional religious communities (Orthodox Jews and fundamentalist Shi'ites, respectively): outsiders describe women as assuming roles "subservient" to men, while female insiders describe their situation as "liberating." What, precisely, is their situation? Within the Hizmet movement, according to chapter author Margaret J. Rausch, the wearing of head coverings by women, gender segregation, and the division of labor based on gender is typical—though supporters emphasize that such practices are elective, not obligatory. They give expression, Rausch explains, to the Islamic teaching, echoed in Roman Catholicism, Orthodox Judaism, and evangelical Christianity, that the differences between the genders are substantive, not superficial, rooted in nature and revelatory of God's will. Within the Hizmet movement, this traditional view of human nature is filtered through and amplified by a Sufi/Gülenist emphasis on the goal of self-perfection. Perfection is achieved in and through nature, and gender identity is essential to one's humanity.

Rausch, in keeping with this volume's pro-Hizmet trajectory, acknowledges but attempts to refute feminist and other "Western" criticisms. Thus she underscores the absence of official restrictions on women's participation in the public sphere and dismisses any necessary link between Hizmet gender practices and the "oppression" of women—and, indeed, Gülen and his followers consistently stress individual interpretation and expression of Islamic and movement norms. Other authorial interventions on the Gülenists' behalf are perhaps less compelling. Rausch accepts without comment, for example, the official Hizmet position discounting the possibility of social pressure or coercion, however inadvertent, and she likewise recites the party line, which holds that the exclusion of women from advanced study with Gülen is "the only practice that could be considered to be discriminatory." Such judgments seem not to reflect a mature understanding of what might be called "the dynamics of compliance" operating within a movement like Hizmet.

In similar fashion, Phyllis E. Bernard's chapter on the business practices of the movement opens by posing a question that amounts to, "Is it too good to be true?" But Bernard does not leave the reader long in suspense. "The Hizmet model of capitalism," she declares in paragraph three, "does something radical: it puts people before profits." Support for this judgment is found in studying individual examples of Hizmet commerce and trade, because the business model is "fractal," a pattern whereby the smallest unit is replicated over and over, producing eventually a global network of schools and businesses. The values inspiring Hizmet businesses derive from Islam's emphasis on provision for the poor, exemplified in the obligation of *zakat*— whereby Hizmet businessmen contribute between 10 and 30 percent of their annual income to movement institutions and activities. This charitable impulse, moreover, is wed to a modified free-market ethos that rewards relationship building and makes room for lower- and middle-class families to participate in the creation and expansion of transnational business and philanthropy networks.

Bernard lauds this approach as central to the exercise of "soft power" by Hizmet and by Turkey as a whole, accompanied as it is by unspecified but "massive" amounts of financial support for the programs of cultural exchange that bring thousands of non-Muslims, including a constant stream of Americans, to Turkey. As guests of the movement, the foreigners are treated to the finest Anatolian hospitality, and they are invited to engage in dialogue on the road to profitable longer-term cultural and economic relationships. The Hizmet brand of cultural diplomacy is remarkably effective, not least in framing the movement along lines congenial to its most passionate advocates.

Missing from this otherwise rosy picture are details—reliable data on beneficiaries, institutions, and budgets. Bernard's account raises other questions, as well. How do Hizmet businessmen navigate the world of investment and interest, given the Islamic prohibition on usury? A Western reader might be stunned by the following statement: "Cash is the preferred method for doing business. Thousands, even millions of dollars will transfer from person to person across vast distances based solely on a verbal request." Yet we are no longer trading in the bazaar: by all accounts, the Hizmet business, education, and media empire is impressively modern, efficient, and electronic. How is this marriage of personal networks, "moral management," and high-tech industry remain competitive within a global corporate milieu driven by a distinctly alien ethos?

In sum, the authors of the present volume perform the invaluable service of surveying the horizon of Hizmet and formulating the critical questions swirling around the movement. Sifting through the claims and counterclaims of the narratives dueling to define the Gülenists, however, will require a new wave of systematic and independent research.

CONTEXTS AND INTERPRETIVE LENSES

If the Hizmet movement receives a standing ovation in these pages directed to an American audience, perhaps it is because the expressions of politically relevant Islam that have preceded it (and still surround it) have left most Americans disaffected, to say the least. The Gülenists, by contrast, are a breath of fresh air and perhaps a sign of hope. In short, the appreciative murmurs uttered by the authors must be placed in social and historical context—contexts that function as interpretive lenses for those who ask: Whither modern Islam?

The most immediate context for construing the Hizmet movement is the legacy of Mustafa Kemal Atatürk, the hero of the Turkish War of Independence and founder of the Turkish republic in 1923. So central was Mustafa Kemal's leadership to the transformation of the former Ottoman Empire into a modern, westernized—and surpassingly secular—nation-state that the principles of his reforms are known as Kemalism, and he himself was granted the title *Atatürk* ("Father of the Turks") by the Turkish parliament. Atatürk abolished the caliphate, outlawed the fez and the veil, imposed Swiss civil law in the place of Shari'a, and substituted the Latin alphabet for Ottoman Arabic script. His military background and emphasis on state security established the conditions that led, after his death, to what many Turkish citizens refer to as "Deep State"—the coalition of military and financial elites that propped up successive Turkish governments and then intervened, with soft or hard coups, when the national politicians threatened the interests of the military-industrial complex, failed to repress Kurdish secessionists or Marxist-Leninist revolutionaries, and/or enabled the return of Islam to a position of influence in national politics.

Kemalism shaped modern Turkey, but it did not displace Islam entirely, nor did it undermine a hierarchy of Turkish values in which serenity, pleasure, respect, and family loyalty are at least as prominent as money or career. The journalist Stephen Kinzer's vivid analysis of the dazzling diversity and contradictions of contemporary Turkish society, *Crescent and Star,* reflects the long-standing frustration of many Turks and their friends with Turkey's inability to achieve its democratic potential. Turks, Kinzer writes, have been "taught since time immemorial that authority is something distant and irresistible, and that the role of the individual in society is submission."[6]

Yet Kinzer's account ends before the rise of Erdoğan and the AKP to power in 2003, and today, more than a decade after that fateful election,

Turkey has been transformed, at least for the time being. The most startling and unexpected development has been the AKP's seeming success in dismantling "Deep State"—and few, if any, observers deny that the followers of Gülen played a significant role in that achievement, notwithstanding the aforementioned split with Erdoğan and the AKP in late 2013. During the period of the AKP's ascendancy, Hizmet members have served in the government and promoted Turkey's efforts to join the European Union. Not least, the movement mobilized its education, business, and media networks—including one of the nation's leading daily newspapers, *Zaman*—in support of the AKP's legal and political battles to erode the power of the army's shadow government, to advance democracy, and to enhance pluralism, most notably through creating an opening to a revitalized Islamic presence in the public square. The collaboration between the Gülenists and the AKP culminated in the remarkable events of September 12, 2010, when the electorate adopted a series of constitutional amendments that, in Harrington's words, "expanded people's economic and social rights, guaranteed union collective bargaining, enhanced civil liberty and individual freedoms . . . adopted judicial reforms, and opened the door to prosecuting former coup leaders" (i.e., the operatives of Deep State). The world celebrated the referendum as a landmark in the strengthening of democracy, human rights, and civil society, and the Gülenists count it as a major victory in their quest to reform modern Turkey—and modern Islam.

Not every Turk sees things quite this way. While few mourn the undoing of Deep State, millions of Turks, not least a generation of empowered feminists, fear Islamic politics of any kind and continue to prefer the Kemalist variety of secularism. These secular liberals are among the fiercest detractors of the Gülen movement. Yet millions of Turks, constituting the majority of the electorate, continue to support the AKP and Erdoğan, despite some of the latter's high-handed policies and infringement on civil liberties and due process. One stream of support for the Hizmet movement clearly comes from this constituency, which applauds the Gülenists' rejection of Deep State's tendency to abrogate civil liberties and to regard citizens as subjects, opposition as treason, and any assertions of religious or alternate ethnic identity as threats to Turkey's territorial integrity.

A second context explaining the relative enthusiasm for the Hizmet movement is the progressive face it places on Islam, represented by the followers of Gülen as a congenial home to modern science, philosophy, intercultural dialogue, and human rights. The Gülenists' skillful self-marketing and global ambitions arrive at a time in world history when Islam, divided by a bitter and violent religious civil war raging from Pakistan and Afghanistan to Syria, Palestine, and Nigeria, is perceived as antithetical to the basic principles of democracy, just war, human rights, and peaceful coexistence. Boldly, the Hizmet movement claims that Islam, properly construed, is not merely a willing participant in the dialogue of civilizations and the progress of nations but also a potential leader. In the minds of many westerners, the priority given by Gülenists to reason informed by ethics, and to science unfettered by superstitious "medievalism," is an encouraging alternative to the spectacle of imams in Africa refusing to allow vaccinations for HIV-AIDS, or mullahs in Pakistan prohibiting life-saving organ transplants—rulings based on a scientifically illiterate reading of "Islamic law." And to peacebuilders, the Hizmet dedication to dialogue and cultural exchange with non-Muslims and nonbelievers is the essential first step on the path to the nonviolent resolution of religious and ethnic strife.

A tactical and generational shift under way worldwide among "post-fundamentalist" and "post-Islamist" Muslims provides a third and related context for receiving the Hizmet movement gladly. Rejecting the violence of the jihadists and the failures or compromises of the Islamist politicians, a new generation of transnational Muslim movements seeks economic, cultural, and social influence leading to long-term transformation of societies. Can this process of transformation properly be called Islamization? The answer is unclear, as cosmopolitan and universalist sensibilities, carried aloft through cyberspace, are recasting notions of Islamic identity and eroding the religious/secular binary that "enlightened" politicians from Thomas Jefferson to Atatürk worked so hard to construct and reify.

The French intellectual Olivier Roy argues that Muslim religiosity is being privatized in the wake of "the failures of political Islam,"[7] but other scholars refuse to equate the weakening of the appeal of Islamist political categories such as the nation or the *ummah* (global Islamic community) with the abandonment of the quest for an alternative political order. Rather, writes the international affairs scholar Peter Mandaville, "transnational Muslim solidarities represent an intermediate space of affiliation and sociopolitical mobilization that exists alongside and in an ambivalent relationship with the nation-state."[8]

In light of the 2013 repression of the Muslim Brotherhood in Egypt, the suffocating of the Arab Spring elsewhere, and the Gülenists own break with the AKP in Turkey, the push to take control of the state is hardly the only, or the most effective, way of triggering constructive social change. Mandaville argues that the coming generation's focus on individual freedom and desire to achieve prosperity according to Western standards signals neither the end of the social and public functions of religion nor the desire of younger Muslims to abandon the collective dimensions of finding social meaning in religion. "What we are seeing in the Muslim world today," he suggests, "is the rise of a number of heterogeneous networks and groups organized loosely and often flexibly around a particular discursive referent ('justice,' 'development,' 'social change through proper Islamic observance,' etc.)." [9] This array of "everyday social movements," led by new religious intellectuals, has arisen in tandem with—and often in some tension with—a new generation of Islamist political parties such as the new Muslim Brotherhood and the AKP.

Mandaville quotes the Italian sociologist Alberto Melucci to the effect that participation in these new socioreligious movements is considered an end in itself: the members' everyday practice enacts the future they envision. This practical focus on what can be achieved in the present moment is "a way of being in the world" rather than a means of advancing a particular political objective—though the way itself will inevitably affect politics and other sectors of society. A case in point is the Hizmet movement. The neoliberal practices (e.g., consumerism) and structures (e.g., global markets) adopted by the Gülenists, facilitated by their negotiation and contestation of traditional Islamic norms, signals their focus on a prize "bigger than"—more consequential than—state power. Rather than viewing the Islamization of society as entailing participation in or control over political parties separated from everyday life, the Gülenists pursue "Islamic normativity" within the pragmatic spaces of quotidian activity. Thereby "Islam is not rendered an external ideology," Mandaville concludes, "but instead is lived." [10]

WHAT'S NOT TO LIKE?

If this analysis is correct, the rise of movements like Hizmet—and Hizmet in particular—is a potentially promising development in the world of Islam and for socially relevant religion in general. How to account then, for the intense opposition of the detractors?

I have already mentioned concerns arising from the practices and procedures of the Gülenists themselves. Among the most intractable of these, the ones for which the movement itself bears some responsibility, are, first, the lingering sense outsiders have of a hidden agenda, and, second, the challenge posed to every traditional religious movement by feminist and other human rights advocates who disapprove of the way in which gender relations, and especially women's agency, are managed within the movement.

As to the first obstacle, there may be no "hidden agenda" whatsoever, and the Hizmet affiliates are certainly remarkably transparent about their values and goals. Yet they are also aggressive "proselytizers," albeit in their typically nonreligious mode, and are unapologetically eager to produce their bona fides to their progressive interlocutors and potential partners. Does that zeal lead at times to the cutting of corners and a degree of self-misrepresentation? (Seeing a Hizmet promotional brochure with my name and photo alongside a comment of endorsement I had never made, I confess, did give me pause.) And, given the mountain of suspicion the Gülenists must overcome, would it be "good business" in the long run to err on the side of full transparency with regard to budgets, resources, and the like? Similarly, the controversy surrounding gender-related practices is an opportunity for the followers of Gülen to underscore their commitment to pluralism by putting on greater display both the freedom of choice within the movement and their vision for a society in which "radical feminists," atheists, and additional potential "others" enjoy equal access to the same privileges and rights as the true believers.

Beyond the adjustments Hizmet members might make to reassure their critics, there are external factors to which there is no short-term solution. The most debilitating of these is Islamophobia, bias against Muslims rooted in stereotypes drawn from profiles of a minority of violent jihadists and theocrats who distort the meaning of Islam and its practice by more than one billion Muslims. "Guilt by association" is not a new way people discriminate against those perceived as different, nor is it restricted to the opponents of Islam. In the aftermath of September 11, 2001, however, few outgroups have taken as much abuse as Muslims. And Islamophobia certainly raises the "too good to be true" bar for the Gülenists: any group that would acknowledge its defining commitment to the fundamental principles of Islam, especially a movement that proclaims its compatibility with many of the most cherished Western values and aspirations, dare not make the kind of bureaucratic or individual mistakes—typical errors of judgment, miscommunication, and lack of discipline—to which every human enterprise is routinely subject. Indeed, there is no benefit of the doubt for the Muslim "mystery man" and his "disciples."

In this last, most difficult context, the Hizmet movement has emerged—not unscathed, perhaps, but commanding the attention and close study of those Americans who recognize that the challenges faced by humanity in this century can only be met by an alliance of religious and secular actors and institutions. It also appeals to those who perceive a promising way forward in partnering with an expression of modern Islam that opens itself to sustained and mutually transformative dialogue with anyone who is serious about advancing the spirit and practice of compassionate service.

NOTES

1. Hakan Yavuz made the comparison to Opus Dei in Brian Knowlton, "Turk Who Leads a Movement Has Advocates and Critics," *New York Times,* June 11, 2010.

2. "The Gulenists Fight Back," *The Economist,* May 18, 2013, http://www.economist.com/news/europe/21578113-muslim-cleric-america-wields-surprising-political-power-turkey-gulenists-fight-back.

3. See "Understanding Fethullah Gülen," promotional booklet of the Journalists and Writers Foundation of the Hizmet movement, at www.gyv.org.tr.

4. Helen Rose Ebaugh, *The Gulen Movement: A Sociological Analysis of a Civic Movement Rooted in Moderate Islam* (Heidelberg: Springer, 2010), xii.

5. See, e.g., Lynne Davidman, *Tradition in a Rootless World* (Berkeley: University of California Press, 1991), and Shahla Haeri, *Law of Desire: Temporary Marriage in Shi'i Iran* (Syracuse, N.Y.: Syracuse University Press, 1989).

6. Stephen Kinzer, *Crescent and Star: Turkey Between Two Worlds* (New York: Farrar, Straus and Giroux, 2002).

7. Olivier Roy, *The Failure of Political Islam* (London: I. B. Tauris, 1994).

8. Peter Mandaville, "Transnational Muslim Solidarities and Everyday Life," *Nations and Nationalism* 17, no. 1 (2011): 7.

9. Ibid., 10–11.

10. Ibid., 14.